CW01090872

Spring Term

The Sap Rises!

Nicholas Barrett

Copyright © 2018 Nicholas Barrett

All rights are reserved. No part of this book may be reproduced or transmitted in any form or by any means without written permission of the author.

This book is a work of fiction. The names, characters, places, and incidents are products of the writer's imagination or have been used fictiously and are not to be construed as real. Any resemblance to persons, living or dead, actual events, locales or organizations is entirely coincidental.

To Dolores: for constant love, support and belief.

To Mum and Auntie – for more than I could ever thank you for.

To Mike, Jackie and Patrick – my love as always...

In loving Memory of Mollie O'Farrell, an Irish Rose who made me smile every day...And always will.

And to a Brilliant writer of things Historical: Mr Peter Darman.

A true friend, and a real inspiration.

These books are also dedicated to Sir Terence David John Pratchett OBE.

And of course, "Clockpelters" everywhere.

(especially you – Mrs Challis!)

"The comedy is enhanced by the well-crafted and larger-than-life characters who bring Saint Onan's Academy to life, and that they are so vivid is down to Nick's mastery of the writing craft, a skill that many people profess to possess but in fact is the preserve of a select few. Comedy fiction is one of the hardest genres to master but Michaelmas Term proves that Nicholas Barrett has entered the first division of writers in this field, and should be ranked alongside Frances Hardinge, Michael Logan and Douglas Adams".

Peter Darman, Author of the Parthian novels,
The Ice March, Crusader Chronicles,
SAS – the world's best.

"A breath of fresh air. At last, a writer who can make me laugh loudly, and after the passing of the great Sir Terry Pratchett, this is just the sort of 'pick me up' we need. The story is easy to follow, with great characters that you instantly warm to, and the sub plots build and build. I'm looking forward to another from Nicholas Barrett. This man will be a star."

Steve Loopy Newhouse. Author of Justtin,
and LoopyWorld – the Iron Maiden Years.

"I was handed a copy of "Michaelmas Term" over lunch with a friend. I laughed from the very first page. I spilled my drink. My lunch went cold. Wonderfully inventive set pieces, instantly likeable characters, and littered with dreadful puns; Nick Barrett's books are an experience like no other. A delightful world to get lost in. Thank you, Mr Barrett – you owe me a lunch...

Dave Spearman, "Off the Page" Review.

Acknowledgements:

I wish to acknowledge the constant support of some of the wonderful individuals who have either inspired me, or urged me on during the writing of this book.

To my Family and friends – I love you all dearly.

Mr Peter Darman; for help, advice, and much valued support.

Mr Bill Peake; for re-igniting the flame of hilarity.

Mr Dave Houghton, Rock-God drummer, and all-round fine fellow.

Mr Robert Rankin; for taking the time to help a fellow author.

Mr Steve Newhouse; fellow conspirator, author, believer, and shed-dweller. This man is a constant source of trouser-threatening laughter.

Mr Benjamin Nunn, for his brilliant artwork.

Grateful thanks to Yvonne Betancourt for her skilled assistance in the process of formatting, doormatting, and other highly technical things, of which I know not...

And not least, to all of you lovely people who have bought and read, or have yet to read, or intend to read, my growing list of bizarre writings. I thank each and every one of you for your kind comments, and would remind you that cash is always an acceptable alternative...

NB

About the Author:

Nicholas Barrett was born in rural Lincolnshire. He grew up in a house which was shared by a ghost known as "Mr Goodman" who was polite and very tidy. Educated in Grantham, and then at Lincoln College of Art, Nick went on to do a variety of jobs including session musician, rock drummer, stand-up comedian, roadie and manager in a large company. He now lives in rural Essex. Having always had the urge to write, he did just that.

His first book "Michaelmas Term (or- why is that boy naked?)" was published in August 2016. Embarrassingly, most of the incidents which happen in his books did occur! He has drawn on many of his varied life experiences for the books - but has used washable crayon, so it will probably wipe off... He misses his drum kit - but the laptop takes less time to set up! He guarantees that reading his books will be the best fun that you have had whilst fully dressed…

SPRING TERM: The Sap Rises!
a novel by Nicholas Barrett.

Ahh…at long last Mother Nature had decided to tidy away the frozen white blanket of snow, and store it in the Divan drawer under the bed of Last Season.

She surreptitiously kept out a few sharp frosts for later use - just to let everyone know who was in charge here. Before the Winter had truly set in, she had set the Seasonal alarm clock, and had only pressed the "snooze" button twice. Now, the call rang loudly in the ears of every creature, and the vibrations were picked up by plants of all species. Snowdrop and Crocus thrust up proudly through the new livid green grass shoots, daring casual passers-by not to notice them. Trees pushed out the first green buds of Springtime.

This was multi-tasking at its finest, and put to shame the work of Jack Frost, who as we all know, can only do windows.

In the woodlands which surrounded the Village, sunlight streamed through the trees like laser fingers, throwing shafts of gold onto the forest floor for the mice to dance in. The urgent biological imperative was being felt by the woodland creatures of all sizes, who immediately began to spruce themselves up in order to attract a mate and, well-produce even more woodland creatures. Some famous Composer chappie had even written a wonderful piece of music about it called *The Rite of Spring*. This was somewhat unfair on those people who preferred to use their left…

Grey squirrels gazed at their fur forlornly, and had to endure the sniggers of their flashier-dressed Red cousins. They were destined to stand at the bar, looking on whilst the Red Boys got off with all of the girls. With any luck, one or two of the more fortunate ones might actually remember where their nuts had been hidden…Our little friend the Toad had awoken from his Winter torpor, and hopped over to see his Sister who lived under the bridge which crossed the local stream. Here he sat, scowling out at the young frogs from other nearby ponds - who had no respect for their elders as far as he was concerned. Behaviour like that came from reading too much Spawnography.

In keeping with the impending leap into Manhood, there were no doubt Adolescent boys out in the bushlands of Australia, who were engaged in their task to prove that they were now capable of being regarded as a Man. They followed ancient trails, they sought out food amongst the rocks and scrubby vegetation: they sang ancient tribal songs, and waved their spears in defiance. One particular boy in a small Lincolnshire village was also taking the same rigorous rituals of the transition into manhood. He however, had been told off for seeking out so much food, singing his tribal songs too loudly, and God help him if it was ever thought that he was waving his spear in public…

Chapter One:

Nicky gazed rather forlornly at the remnants of his pint, swilling the liquid around in an absent-minded sort of manner. Although far too young to be in a Public House and drinking, he had recently taken up the pleasant habit of nipping in to the "Black Pig" and sipping a beer in the company of Merry and his friend Bill from the village. They had been able to pursue their hobby unchallenged due to the fact that they had all developed the more outwardly demonstrable signs of manhood. Nicky in particular, now had longer hair, and a seemingly permanent five-o'clock shadow of beard growth. He had long since been nominated as the one most likely to be able to be served with drinks at the bar without question or comment. There was no real problem (apart from the illegality of the situation that is) as they all sat quietly at the back of the pub out of the way of the other drinkers. They all enjoyed their drinks and kept the rock jukebox well fed. Bill rolled his own cigarettes, and dispensed his Socialist wisdom to the gang of three, whilst Nicky and Merry listened, watched him set fire to his fingers, and generally took the piss as required. Nicky had never been challenged to prove that he was old enough to drink, but to be fair - he had also never been challenged to prove his real height either…

'Well…it's back to the good old Academy tomorrow, Chaps' he moaned, to no-one in particular 'I wonder what horrors the Reverend Vermin Farmer has got in store for us?'.

'Did you get the letter warning us about the Uniform inspections?' asked Bill.

'Indeed I did, and I intend to tell 'em that I haven't read it…' stated Merry.

'What possible excuse could you have for not having read the letter?' Bill queried.

'I shall tell them that my dog ate it…' said the smiling Merry.

'But the letters were all sent out addressed to our Parents!' stated Nicky.

'Then I shall tell them that my dog ate my Parents also...' said Merry, ever the forward thinker. Nicky gave his friends a despairing look:

'Well I don't know what exactly the letter said - but I know that Mum was none too pleased when she read it. She had her "Who does he think he is" face on - and that's never a good sign'.

'I think Comrades...that we should convene a Form meeting. We should take a democratic vote of all of our fellow Students, and agree a plan of action based upon a common aim. This may be the time to take up arms against the forces of oppression- and organise a revolt!!'

'They think we're already revolting as it is...' declared Comrade Merry.

'We shall stand together - shoulder to shoulder!!' said Bill, rising from his seat and raising a clenched fist.

'Don't put me next to Comrade Jackson then...' said Merry 'or I will be standing shoulder to belly button...'

'I can't see anyone rushing to arms if they have to stand next to Lordsley' said Nicky.

'Point taken Comrade Shepherd...' declared Bill: 'but I am sure that come the glorious day of Revolution - even Comrade Lordsley will renounce his evil Imperialist ways, and link arms with his Brothers in their struggle...'

'Failing that - We could link our Revolutionary boots to his arse...' Nicky suggested.

Now that Nicky found himself standing somewhat nervously in the ranks of the massed Teenager, there were some changes that could not be put off any longer. Growing out of clothing and the Academy uniform, was a non-occupational hazard which he could not avoid. There was one thing however, that had necessitated urgent change for reasons of safety. He had taken the feared satchel to a leatherworks shop in the town. It had fought him (and the odd bemused passer-by) all the way - but at great personal risk he had wrestled the leather beastie down onto the front desk of the shop. He had asked the owner to replace the satchel strap with a sturdy handle on top, thus converting it into a "briefcase" more in keeping with his image - or at least the one that he wished to portray. It would also give him a much greater degree of control over the vindictive bag, preventing strap strangulation of himself, and flesh wounds to the public, if it was in a particularly foul mood. The deed had been done - and he collected the new-look case from the scowling owner of the shop, who had a number of sticking plasters on both of his hands. The thing still looked smug though…

In moments of self-doubt (and there were plentiful supplies of these…) Nicky still felt the urge to seek the wisdom and guidance provided upon request by "The Desk". The thought that was at the forefront of his mind was that of how much more of an impact the new Headmaster would make at St Onans. He had asked the desk (via the usual mystic drawer) what he should do. The reply, equally cryptic, had come back 'Steps that are unguided may be the most dangerous…'. Well thanks for that, that really helped no end.

With the odd reply in mind, Nicky had made the classic mistake of asking Uncle Joe for his opinion. 'You want to be askin' up in the shop at the top of the village' said Joe, 'Mrs Keeble is a bit of a one for explainin' any sort of mystical philosophy'.

Armed with this sound advice from a totally reliable source, Nicky had hurried up to the village shop as directed. Mrs Keeble had listened to what he had to say most patiently, and had proved to be as much use as the Dali Lama giving instructions on DIY plumbing problems. When challenged, Joe had held up his hands in defence, and stated 'Well there's yer problem see, yer didn't ask at the right place…Mrs Keeble is a Sweetshop owner - and wouldn't have a clue about anything but strict Buddhist philosophies. You needed to go over the road to Parkers the bread shop. It's a well-known fact that all Bakers do Zen…'.

As he grudgingly boarded the morning bus to town on his way to his first day of the new term, Nicky suddenly understood all about the danger of unguided steps. There were four seats vacant on the bus, in the middle of which sat the individual responsible for the lack of adjacent passengers. Mrs Jenkins sat smiling, surrounded by empty seats. She had absolutely no idea that she was the villages very own version of the Chernobyl nuclear reactor. Herself completely anosmic from birth, she seemed to perpetually exude the aroma of a freshly-dredged canal. For some reason, she seemed to be the only person that the Charity collectors in the streets of the town never approached for money- indeed, when she went up to them and offered to donate to their cause, they all seemed to be in a hurry to get to a toilet. Nicky stood up at the front of the bus, and nodded to the cheery driver, who as usual had a face resembling a ripple on a bucket of liquid manure.

'What's up Lad?' he had grudgingly enquired. Nicky nodded discreetly in the general direction of Mrs Jenkins. 'Ah yes - I see…' said the driver, 'but she's a blessing in the Summer months'.

'How's that then?' asked Nicky.

'Well…she keeps the flies off'f me sandwiches' stated the driver.

Same bus stop, same struggle with satchel and books, same bus pulling off as he alighted from the bottom step, and the same spin and plunge into the nearby hedge. It was nice to see someone keeping the old traditions going - Nicky just wished that it didn't always have to be him. Now that he was taller, he just had further to fall.

As he passed through the massive stone portals of the entrance gates, Nicky felt a strange mixture of emotion: there seemed to be a curious blend of excitement at meeting up with his friends again, and a sort of "oh no - here we go again" sensation. He had long since got used to the fact that the Academy day was often, if not always, composed of bizarre and irrational incidents which occurred at random points. Humans within the walls of St Onans seemed to be fired around the buildings, ricocheting off any surface like pinballs in a game played by someone wearing boxing gloves. The big bang would no doubt occur when an individual decided that it would be a good idea to impose rules and rigidity upon the Academy. The new Head wanted to rule with a rod of iron, and this may or may not be the same rod that would be dug up coated in rust by enthusiastic metal-detector owners at some point in the distant future. There was a very important point here - and that was that it is not a wise thing to find yourself holding a rod of iron, unless you are absolutely certain where the next lightning strike is going to occur…

As the friends all met up in the quad, there was the immediate resumption of the inter-pupil mickey taking which typified their small group. There was much hurried discussion of who got what present for Christmas, why the dog did what he did to Uncle's leg during dinner, and whether or not Granny should be released in time for her Birthday. The usual stuff.

'It's really great to see you again Merry!' said Jackson, 'I see that despite staying with Shep up in the village - and getting all of that good, clean fresh air, you've managed to remain a Shortarse!!'

'You appear to have outgrown your wit Jackson…' said Merry, 'At least I don't have to sleep with my feet in next door's garden. Anyway, I will have you know that I am well above average height for my age…'

'Oh no you're not!!'

'Oh yes I am Matey!!'

'Look Gerry…all I am saying is that you are only boy that we know, whose Dad built him a Bonsai treehouse…' laughed Jackson.

The group broke up into fits of laughter, with Merry joining in. The comments between any of the friends never led to bad feeling. Merry didn't feel the need to have a dig at Jackson - his height was evident for all to see from a considerable distance. At the age of fifteen, he had achieved a height of six feet and five inches - and was reputed to be still growing. It was often said that if he ever fell over, he would be half way home. He was clever, well-mannered and had earned the respect of his friends. They all looked up to him, but it was true that Merry did have a bit further up to look than the others.

Apart from now occupying a space toward the rear of the hall during morning Assembly, the daily ritual had not changed since those first terrifying days when Nicky was new to St Onans. There was the usual jostling between the boys, and the same thick ears handed out by Masters who caught them behaving badly. Today however, even the Staff were feeling the atmosphere of impending doom which had settled on the assembled audience like the aroma of Mrs Jenkins in high Summer. The Masters were glancing nervously right and left from their chairs on the stage. There was a sudden bang from the back of the hall - but this proved to be merely the head of Lordsley being vigorously applied to a fire door by some new friend that he had obviously made, and so was ignored by all. Eventually, the door at the back of the stage swung open, and Reverend Vernon Farmer made his majestic (and disconcertingly silent) entrance. There was some muted hilarity when a certain section of the assembled students began to hum the Imperial Death March from the film "Star Wars" in order to herald his entrance. The Head strode angrily to the lectern and shouted -

'ENOUGH...'

And by golly, it was. The whole hall fell deathly silent.

Apart from that is, the very end of a somewhat lurid tale which Mr Newhouse was busy explaining to his fellow Tutor Hyde-Jones, who was standing beside him at the organ...

'I've still got the marks from the straps, and then she had the cheek to come flouncing into the pub - reeking of banana yoghurt...' he said.

The look from the Head was nothing short of poisonous. Newhouse urgently cut short the tale, and gave the glaring man a cheerful wave. Assuming safety in numbers, Hyde-Jones decided to wave too...

This time the silence was considerably longer, and more menacing.

'I HAVE DECIDED…' the Head began (at rather unnecessary volume) 'That the Uniform inspections will commence immediately. Any boy found to be not wearing the correct Academy uniform as laid out in the written Rules, will be sent home. Those of you that think that I will tolerate deviations from the acceptable standards, or accommodate any little "quirks" in your style of dress will find themselves to be very much mistaken. You will find me absolutely rigid - and I shall not bend!' he declared.

(A voice at the back called out 'Oooh!! - get the Madam!!' just loud enough to be heard).

The Head began to go purple in the face, a rather deep purple, with his head now looking as if it might explode into a fireball. 'We shall begin with the Fifth Formers - who I hope will be setting the correct example to the younger boys' he ranted. 'Dr Chambers will line the boys up in Forms, and Mr Thwaite will take the names of any offenders - who will then report to me in my study. Gentlemen…I will start as I mean to go on'.

The Head swept out of the hall, and as the lower year boys filed out through the double doors at the rear, the Fifth-Year pupils began to line up in their Forms. Dr Chambers looked like a man acting under protest as he began to walk up and down the rows of students, and Mr Thwaite tottered along behind him with a clipboard whilst trying to maintain his balance in impossibly high platform shoes. It had become normal practice to adorn the blazer lapels with badges which declared the wearer's allegiance to a particular football team or rock band. There was a hurried un-pinning of badges as the two Masters began to edge along the rows.

Chambers got down to William Trevill, and stared at the boy. 'What is that on your lapel, Trevill?' he demanded.

'Oi calls it a Baadge Surr' answered the boy.

'Remove it, Trevill…' said Chambers.

'No Surr - Oi won't…'tis the Heraldic Crest of Dorset- part of moi Family 'Eritage, of which oi am roightly proud…'

'It has to come off Boy…' insisted the Deputy Head.

'Well now see Surr…will you be insistin' that our good friend Singh takes orf 'is turban?' asked Trevill, innocently.

'Of course not boy - it's a symbol of his personal culture, with great significance…' answered Chambers, hesitantly.

'Quoite roight you are Surr - an' the same do apply to my little baadge 'ere…' said Trevill.

The rest of the boys began to settle in for the entertainment. No-one could debate a point in quite the same intractable manner as William Trevill, and it would be a very wise man indeed that would argue the toss with him. Mr Thwaite had already written in - and then crossed out Trevill's name three times on his report sheet. He was beginning to panic.

'Undo the badge and remove it…' demanded Chambers.

'It moight not be safe to do so Surrr…' said the boy

'What are you talking about, Trevill?'

'Well Surr…just supposin' that Oi was to try (against moi will Oi moight add…) to remove moi baadge, and that Oi was to pierce moi finger with the pin on the baack of it, causin' myself physical injury and distress of an emotional type of nature: well now - Oi would 'ave to take immediate Legal Action against the Academy and the person or persons what 'ad insisted that Oi takes it orf, in full knowledge of the danger involved…'

'The Head Master has ordered it…'

'Oi caarn't 'elp that Surr'.

'I don't believe your attitude Trevill - I mean, are you afraid of a little prick?'

'Oi don't know 'im as well as you do Surr - but Oi tell 'Ee, the baadge is stayin' put…'

Trevill smiled. Chambers fumed. Thwaite attempted to hide his embarrassment. The chests of the boys swelled with pride at the stance of their Dorset Hero. Dr Chambers walked on down the line of boys, pausing as his gaze fell upon a pair of obviously non-regulation shoes. The shoes were brown. Regulations stated that only black shoes were permissible. Chambers looked down, then looked up. He carried on looking up, as the owner of the shoes which did not conform were inhabited by the huge feet of one James Jackson. The Deputy Head left the poor unfortunate Thwaite to deal with the misdemeanour. The Master attempted to make eye contact with the towering boy, but gave up when he began to experience whiplash. Feeling himself under the watchful eye of his Superior Officer, Mr Thwaite thought that he ought to at least make some sort of token effort…

'And errm…I see that you are not wearing the correct colour of shoe, Mr Jackson'.

'Yes…sorry about that Mr T…' came the deep, rumbling reply from the massive boy.

'Is there any reason why you are wearing brown shoes?'.

'Yes Sir…'

'And what might the reason be?'

'I haven't got any black ones Sir…'

'I can see that Jackson, but why don't you have any shoes which are the correct colour?'

'It's a problem with the size Sir' said Jackson, from high above.

'Well why don't you get some in the right size then?' asked Thwaite.

'I did Sir' stated Jackson.

'You obviously did not!!' said Thwaite

'Oh yes Sir - I got these brown ones' Jackson told him proudly.

'Well they are not black, as clearly stated in the Academy rules…' Thwaite told him.

'That's right Sir, they are clearly brown. Simper and Crouch don't stock my size Sir - so they have had to send away to get me some that will fit…'

'What size do you need?' asked Thwaite.

'I need a size 16, or 16 and a half in the Winter. They told my Dad that they only had one pair in the shop that would fit me: it took them absolutely ages to go through all of their stock to find them, so he bought them for me'.

'If your Father bought you a pair, why are you not wearing them today?' said Thwaite

'I am Sir...' answered Jackson.

'You should have bought a size 10 and worn the boxes instead!!' said Merry.

Thwaite knew that there was no arguing with the huge-footed boy. It was a strange twist of genetics that had led two quite short parents to produce such mammoth offspring as Jackson. He had one elder Brother, who too had not been what we might call an over-achiever in the vertical department. Thwaite knew that James' Brother had shall we say, a somewhat chequered past. He had already spent quite a bit of his youth "At Her Majesty's Pleasure" so to speak. Brother Mark had always had a passion for athletics. Unfortunately, he had chosen to combine his natural abilities with opportunist theft. He often boasted about having done 1500 meters in a month and a half. His friends had laughed, and openly stated that they thought that this was very slow indeed. Mark had replied that the Magistrate who had sentenced him had not agreed with them...

At the Young Offenders' unit to which he was sent, he developed an interest in mechanics and cars of all types. When he was released, he indulged his passion for driving fast motors. It might have been nice if he had obtained the permission of the owners first...He was eventually apprehended performing tailspins in a local supermarket car park, and when the smoke from the screaming tyres had cleared, he was arrested again and taken back to prison. This time, he vowed to learn his lesson. He would keep his head down, do his time, and come out to a better life. A friendly and sympathetic Prison Officer Mr Murchison, had taken Mark under his wing, and allowed him a degree of trust on a daily basis. Murchison realised that Mark would be spending his 21st birthday behind bars - and so was determined to show the lad some care and concern. To this end, he provided a cake, candles and a big birthday card for the Chap. He had carried the cake with candles lit, down the corridor to Mark's cell at Recreation time, singing as he went:

'Oh…Twenty-one Today, Twenty-one Today…He's got the K-Bloody Hell, where's he gone!!!?'

As Mr Murchison heard the screech of tortured tyres from the Prison car park, and ran to the window just in time to see his new car being driven away at speed - he was forced to ask himself if it had been such a good idea to celebrate the Lad's Twenty-First Birthday by giving him the traditional Key of the Door…

Chapter Two:

Nicky had spent the previous evening with Merry, attempting to teach Dave the Chicken to play the Blues...

'I got me a little Red Rooster...'

Peck-Peck-peck-peck-peck...

'Sleeps out under the Stars...'

Peck-Peck-peck-peck-peck...

'He gonna get Sage and Onion...'

Peck-Peck-peck-peck-peck...

'Shoved right up – Ow!!! Dave, that bloody well hurt!!'

Them Boys Merry and Nicky sure got the Blues, but woah yeah! ... Dave had got the Beak. Merry had laughed until he was nearly sick, as Nicky rushed off to get a sticking plaster from the bathroom cabinet. It would be some time later that he would discover what covert act of retribution Dave had committed in one of his shoes...

There had been one of those conversations between Mum and Auntie which seem to suddenly change content, or terminate as soon as a third person enters the room. Nicky was a little worried that it might have something to do with their current perilous financial position. He was well aware that a steady stream of bills with red ink had been arriving, and that Mum and Auntie were struggling to keep up with the demands. When he got the chance, he decided to have a discreet word in the ear of Uncle Joe, to see if he knew of any little jobs that he could earn a few extra pounds from. There was a risk involved in this idea, as Nicky might well end up cleaning the brushes of the team that were engaged in painting the Forth Bridge.

It was some time before the actual reason for all of the whispering and clandestine chat was revealed. The information was more shocking than Nicky had ever expected. Mum explained (while Auntie tried very hard not to wet herself laughing) that against all odds, and common sense, come to that, Cousin Sheila had by some miraculous process managed to find herself a boyfriend. Auntie had put forward the theory that Cousin Sheila had obviously been loitering outside Mental Health facilities for some length of time - and had waited until someone that she fancied had been released. Mum had given her "A Look", and Auntie hastily retracted the statement, saying 'Yes, that might have been a little unfair…I am sure that they will make a lovely Couple - I just hope that Sheila remembers to feed his Guide Dog'. (She got another "yellow card" from Mum for saying that).

'Well that's not exactly the end of the news…' said Mum. 'I saw Sheila's Mother in the town the other day…'

'It's a wonder that you didn't end up going into orbit around her, with her being a bit on the extra-large side' laughed Auntie.

Mum continued, 'It turns out that he is called Derek, and he is the owner of a little Newsagents shop down on Wharf road. They must have been going out together for quite some time, as Sheila's Mother informed me that not only is Derek her Boyfriend - but he's apparently also her Fiancé!! It sounds like he just swept her off her feet after a candle-lit dinner for two at the local Burger King one evening…'

'He must be a bloody strong bloke to be able to sweep Sheila in any direction!' said Auntie.

'Yes - and there's more!!' said Mum: 'It sounds like the union is going to be a permanent one, as Sheila's Mother told me that they are already trying for a baby! They have seemingly been having a bit of difficulty, and there seems to be some sort of problem with Sheila…'

'Does the paper bag keep slipping off her head?' asked Auntie.

'Don't be awful…' said Mum 'the poor girl says that her "Biological Clock" is ticking, and she is very worried'.

'If Derek can hear something ticking - then I would be bloody well terrified too!!' replied Auntie. 'I remember the last boyfriend that she managed to snare - she dragged him back to her place after plying the poor soul with drink, and carried him up the stairs. I won't dwell on what took place, but suffice to say that after a little while, he apparently asked her if she would mind switching the light off, or changing places and going on top. Sheila asked him if he was "kinky"-

and he had replied "No I'm not - but I'm fed up with burning my bum on the light bulb" ...'

Nicky had to rush out and get a glass of water at this point. Even Mum just about managed to suppress a giggle.

Mum carried on regardless, and explained what the unfortunate pair were doing to assist with the production of a baby. They had chosen to attend a Fertility Clinic. There were a whole battery of tests which needed to be gone through, but firstly, what was required was a "sample" from the embarrassed Derek. He had been despatched off to a cubicle with a small clear plastic jar, and instructed to return with a sample in the pot. He had been in the tiny room for ages. Perhaps the sterile atmosphere of the Clinic had affected him, or perhaps he was overcome with the urgency of the task - either way, Derek was having trouble with providing what was required. He had tried with his right hand, until he got a cramp in his thumb. He tried with his left hand, in case that would make a difference - no good either. He had tried with both hands in an act of utter desperation, but still to no effect.

Red-faced, he had gingerly eased the door to the cubicle open, and called to the Nurse. She had joined him in the cubicle, and offered to help him. She tried with her right hand, and she tried with her left - with no result. In a moment of exasperation, she had even tried with her teeth - all to no avail...There was no way they could get the top off that little jar.

Embarrassed at getting far more detail than he could ever have wanted about Cousin Sheila and her biological struggles, Nicky let the rest of the conversation drift well over his head. It wasn't that he was completely ignorant when it came to the subject of sex, but he was still forced to deal with all of the daily hormonal horrors of a fifteen-year-old, and didn't need any more for the time being. He had long since had "The Conversation" with his Mother, and then a slightly more detailed and humorous version from his Auntie, which had hinted at some of her more adventurous exploits in times past.

He remembered with a shudder the day when aged thirteen, his voice had broken in the middle of a French class, and how his friends had all mocked his sudden vocal plummet from Treble to Baritone, as he described a trip to the local "Boulongerie". That evening he had innocently answered the telephone when his Mother had called to say that she would be late back from work, and she had heard the deep male voice on the other end of the line - and immediately called the Police, assuming that they had burglars.

His friends too, all assumed that a permanent "five o'clock shadow" of beard growth conveyed some mystical knowledge with it concerning the opposite sex. It did not. Nicky was just as much in the dark as far as the physical side of relationships was concerned as were his classmates. Biology lessons had gone quite a way to filling in some of the gaps in his romantic education, but by no means all of them. The text books were very logical and instructional, with cut-away diagrams. Nicky had often wondered just what he would say to half a girl, if he was ever approached by one. He felt as if he had seen the Blueprint for the machine - but was still not sure exactly what you were supposed to press in order to turn it on. It seemed to be the locomotion units and the upholstery that were causing him the most sleepless nights…

He would speak to Jackson and Calderman, they would help him. Jackson had a Sister, and all the rumours said that Calderman had a System. He could count on them. He hoped…

Miss Piggott made absolutely no attempt whatsoever to hide her distaste for the new Head. Ever since his indecently swift arrival at St Onans, she had viewed the man as a usurper of the throne of her former idol- the deposed and disgraced Dr Goodwill. He was at the moment better known by all and sundry as 108362, and was exiled to an open prison just the other side of Hunstanton, where he tended to the prison dahlias and ground his teeth in no particular order. Farmer had made dozens of strange and unnecessary rule changes since his arrival, and paid seemingly very little attention to the day-to-day academic running of the Academy - but seemed oddly preoccupied by image and reputation. His progress was still being closely monitored by the Venerable Board of Trustees, who met with him every so often. At these meetings (so Miss Piggott had casually observed - not that she was in any way being nosey, you understand) reports were presented, sherry drunk, future plans discussed and approved, and a good number of Masonic handshakes exchanged. There was also the rumour that if Farmer continued to elevate the Academy in the eyes of the Trustees (at least on the most superficial and cosmetic of levels), then there may well be a certain Honour which might just (allowing for their highbrow connections and contacts) involve kneeling down at some point, and having a Senior member of a certain Household who might be used to wearing, say, the odd crown - wave a sword around over the head of the recipient. For the Reverend Vernon Farmer, this had taken his already dangerously over-inflated sense of ego right to bursting point. He had now taken to issuing his edicts and instructions in the form of endless memoranda to the rest of the Staff. Getting a face-to-face meeting with the man was now only permitted if in possession of a copy of the Bible. An original copy of the Bible. An original copy of the Bible that was *signed*…

The effects upon the Masters when they received one of his numerous proclamations was predictable: Captain Brayfield read it twice, then nodded sagely and filed it, Darwin and Strangler argued over it, each claiming that it should not apply to them. Bell-Enderby made some rough pencil sketches of a well-endowed peasant girl on the back of it. Hyde-Jones stood on a chair and enunciated the contents of the memo in the style of a great Shakespearian Player, and Mr Newhouse took ages in making his copy into a rather small but fetching Peruvian hat. Madame tutted and shrugged her way through the instructions. Mrs Finucane had stood her mop bucket on it. Bannister had used it to wedge shut a troublesome desk drawer, until Elsie Noakes (patron Saintess of nosey middle-aged ladies from the Spirit World) made him at least read it once. Mr Thwaite had blushed, read the note, blushed again, and then gone into a state of panic - stuffing the memo into his handbag and rushing off to repair his mascara. Albert Brooks had torn his memo into squares, and hung it on the nail on the back of the door of the wooden privy at the back of the Groundsman's store huts.

Dr Matthews said that he didn't remember having a Niece called "Memoranda"- but he would pop out and get her a Birthday card after he had finished his lunch in the "Five Crowns" …

Whilst filing away one of the many recently-issued proclamations from King Vernon the First, Miss Piggott had unwittingly unearthed one of the many "sun and sand" beach holiday brochures that she had collected in preparation for her clandestine exit with the former Head Master. She gave the catalogue a long thoughtful look, and then filed it away with some other paperwork under "pending". She still caught a backdated chill of dread as she remembered the day that she had sold her cottage, along with most of her possessions, in readiness for her escape with Dr Goodwill. It was a completely unexpected gift of two gold bars from a mysterious benefactor simply calling himself "FSF" that had staved off the threat of homelessness. Still - better to look to the future, she thought to herself, as she began to hum a little tune to herself which in all honesty no-one else would have wanted to hear (or would have recognised, for that matter).

The telephone rang: she answered it in the upper-class tone of voice which she didn't really have, and tidying a few papers from her desk, made her way to the office of "That Person" in the study next door. She would carry on performing her job as if nothing at all was any different to a normal day - and as soon as she got home, she would carry on with the finer details of the plan which she was about to put into action…

Down in the Biology laboratory, Professor Darwin sat with his chin cradled in his hands, staring at the glass tank which held one of his favourite live specimens. At the stern instruction of the new Head, he had been forced to let a large part of the Academy's live collection of animals go free. He had coerced Strangler into using the "Vortex" to open up a doorway into a suitable habitat for each of the animals to be released - then tearfully waved them off as they hopped, crawled or ran off into the distance. He had insisted on keeping a few of his absolute favourites. He sat staring at one of them now, marvelling at the innate ability of the graceful lizard to change its colour and blend in with its surroundings at will. The creature had initially become stressed and unhappy when some of the adjacent glass tanks had been removed, and its friends set free. Darwin had brought in a small sound system from home, and had decided to try and make the lizard less fretful by means of playing music to it. He had played a variety of CDs to see what happened, and eventually came upon an album of music which had the desired effect. He may well yet write a paper on his experiment, in order to share his results.

He regularly played the little lizard a CD of the band Culture Club. You could call him weird if you wanted to - but since he had been playing the music to little George, anyone could see that he was an altogether calmer Chameleon…

Chapter Three:

'BALLROOM DANCING???' said Hyde-Jones, reading the latest directive from Commandant Herr Farmer, 'Is this idiot bloody serious??'

'Well I for one applaud the Head's attempt to instil some of the finer skills into the pupils...' said Rundell, over the top of his copy of The Times. 'It is about time that these boys were shown a little culture and style'.

'Well he needn't ask me to get involved with any of that malarkey!' declared Mr Newhouse, as he aimed a paper dart at Mr Thwaite. 'I enjoy a good half hour in the Mosh Pit as much as the next A&E patient - but take it from me Brothers- doin' the "Passage Doubly" in a pair of spangled tights, I shall not be...'

Rundell put down his newspaper: 'Well I heard the Head state quite clearly that we should all come dancing, and he said it strictly...'

'Right...well old Vermin can kiss my arse - and I mean that most sincerely...' answered Newhouse. He exchanged the customary "high-five" with Hyde-Jones.

'There eez very leetle that can ever compare with the pure animal sensuality of the Tango...' said Madame Dreadfell, her eyes slightly glazing over.

'I agree!! - Goes down a treat with a triple gin in it...' added Dr Matthews, his own eyes pretty well double-glazed.

'The Head wants the Chaps to be cultured young Gentlemen by the time they leave the Academy: this is a wonderful way of introducing them to the opposite gender don'tchernow. Reminds me of all of those Regimental gatherings in my Army days...' said Brayfield.

'Balls...' said Newhouse.

'I beg your pardon!!?' bristled the Captain.

'You held a lot of balls I expect, during your Military service?'

'Ho yes...yes indeed!' answered Brayfield, completely missing the innuendo, 'I met m' Dear Lady Wife at a Regimental excuse-me in

Poona. Whirled me around the floor like a hurricane she did: I was as stiff as a board for the next three days!!'

'I bet she was upset when it finally wore off...' said Newhouse, just before Hyde-Jones silenced him with a well-aimed cushion.

'Ballroom dancing is to a Dancer, what poetry is to a Writer...' declared Rundell, trying to re-assert his pretext of having some upper-class standing.

'If you are looking for that sort of thing - then try Market Street on a Friday night!!' said Newhouse.

'How so - may I enquire?' asked Rundell.

'Because you have to dance around the drunks, and keep an eye out for the prose...'

Hyde-Jones folded up in laughter over the arm of his chair. Captain Brayfield stamped over to the mirror and practised his most threatening Churchillian scowls. Madame tut-tutted her disapproval in general Gallic fashion. Matthews saluted the Music Tutor with another large glass of whisky, and Thwaite was desperately thumbing through a fashion catalogue to see what off-the-shoulder ball gowns were available for immediate delivery in his size. Mrs Finucane had heard the exchange from the other side of the door. She primped at her hair, and when she got to the end of the corridor, began to twirl and spin as she waltzed with her mop.

'BALLROOM DANCING???!' shouted Mum when she had read the latest in a long line of edicts that had been sent home via her Son from the Academy. 'Don't tell me we've got to find the money to start buying tuxedos and white silk bow ties now?'.

'At least it's not flower-arranging and dry stone walling, or naked blindfold dry-slope skiing' said Auntie.

'No Mum - I think that's an option for next term...' said Nicky.

'Can you just imagine your tall friend Johnny Jackson!!' said Auntie, 'He will look like a King Penguin in a room full of chickens!!'

They all took a moment to imagine the scene, including Dave, who was practicing his Moonwalking technique under the kitchen table. No-one actually spoke the words, but all of them had formed a mental image of Nicky's tall classmate as he twirled his smiling partner around the dancefloor - he in top hat and tails, and she on a wheeled scaffolding rig.

Mum carried on reading: 'It says here that Ballroom lessons will be given in partnership with the girls of St Gertrude's Academy for Young Ladies. That sounds nice - you will get to meet some of the girls from Jocelyna's school'.

'Oh, terrific Mum - thanks for that! I've seen some of them, and they're a nightmare…' said Nicky.

'Oh that really isn't fair…' said Auntie, 'Some of their beards are very smartly trimmed'.

'I happen to know that Belinda Burkenshaw-Hume from Barrowby has got a bit of a soft spot for you…' said Mum, with a cheeky grin.

'And I have a soft spot for her, Mum - it's a swamp in Borneo' declared Nicky.

He hoped that neither Auntie or Mum had noticed him flinch slightly when Auntie had made the remark about skiing a few moments ago. Another letter from the Head (which he had decided to hide at the bottom of the satchel) had stated that this term's Academy trip was to be a skiing jaunt to Switzerland. His friends had all indicated that they would be signing up for the trip, and were already planning what mayhem could be created by the injudicious use of an Alpenhorn, cow bells, various cheeses, and the precise and sustained mockery of little men on snowy hillsides wearing leather shorts. Nicky knew that such a jaunt was well out of the Family's financial reach. He had been contemplating a job of some sort at weekends or after school - just so that he could help out with a few of the bills. The only problem with that idea was that it would put a stop to his rock and roll career…He had been sort of accepted as the drummer for a band which some of his Academy mates had put together. Jackson's Dad had a collection of great musical instruments left over from his working-man's club singer days. Nicky had managed to acquire three drums and four cymbals over the past three years, and so with the addition of a few bits and pieces of kit courtesy of Jackson's Dad - he could have a full kit to play on.

The band were not bad, but poor Anthony the Bass player had dandruff to the extent that they often rehearsed with their own snow machine. He was torn between really wanting to help his Mum out, yet desperately craving the chance to get on stage with a good band and play some serious rock. How was he ever supposed to impress Jozza by wearing a lurid green apron, and shouting 'C'mon Ladies!! - Any Bowl a Pound...' at passing shoppers in the market place on a Saturday. There was no thrill to be had by performing a marrow solo - and hurling your courgettes into the crowd...

Talk of unfortunate vegetables suddenly became topical as Mum had answered the telephone. She replaced the receiver and walked slowly back into the kitchen, with a slight shaking of her head. 'What's up Mum?' asked Nicky.

'It's the latest in the legendary Saga of Cousin Sheila...' Mum explained. Auntie pulled up her chair and sat expectantly - say what you like about the weird and wacky Sheila, her exploits always gave good value for money.

'Is it the Fertility Clinic again?' asked Auntie...'Don't tell me that Cousin Sheila has insisted on an epidural for the conception?'.

'No - it's a bit worse than that' said Mum. 'Apparently one of the Doctors made a rather unwise comment about her being slightly overweight...'

'Fair enough - she does get her knickers on prescription...' said Auntie.

'Well it all kicked off in the Clinic. Suffice to say that in no particular order: The Engagement is off, Derek has had to be treated for a broken nose, a Sister was pushed out into the car park on a hospital bed, and the Doctor is as we speak having a procedure carried out to remove a pair of forceps - which I believe are proving rather difficult to extract due to the fact that they were inserted handles first. Oh, and you can throw in a charge of assaulting a Police officer while you're at it. Sheila has been taken to Court and charged. The Police were furious, but the Judge has let her out on Bail…'

'Shame really…' mused Auntie 'When she was younger, Sheila always said that it was her ambition to be one of those "It" Girls…'

'Well she's certainly "It" now, because she's been tagged!!' laughed Mum.

Uncle Joe sat bolt upright in his bed. The blood was rushing around his body like never before, and his heart hammered in his ears as he fumbled for the bedside lamp. He switched it on, causing his Wife to turn over and utter a muffled instruction which sounded a little like 'Fkurffitsonlythreenamornin'. Joe was shaking as he leapt down the steps three at a time, then remembered about his arthritic hip, and went back up and came down again a little more carefully. He took out a pen and paper from the kitchen drawer. Yes - this was the big one…This is the one that they would talk about for years to come, as they watched him drive past in his gold Rolls-Royce. 'I remember the day when he first had the idea…' they would proudly declare. Joe could see it all in his mind's eye - the vast modern factory, the shining production lines, the happy and proud workers filling the elegant boxes, and himself saying 'Yes, your Majesty - and this is where the finished products are tested, would you care to try one?' He would be the provider of so much happiness to so many people, and doing his bit to promote social cohesion and diversity for a much neglected section of the Community.

He deserved this. He had always sought to better himself and become a man of Culture. He had adopted the very highest standards of manners and etiquette. He would never pass water when he was in the bath, oh no! he would stand up and aim the stream into the lavatory. If his Wife was in the bath, and he was absolutely forced to have to pee in the sink - well, he would always make certain to remove the washing up first…

This was The Big One.

He might even be able to afford one bloody pen which would actually write....

Miss Emilia Piggott (she pronounced it "pie-got", even in her own head) was making plans of her own. Her living-room floor was covered in Ordnance Survey maps and larger scale A to Z renditions of the East Coastal region of England. Peeping out from under her coffee-table were bus and train time guides, with various entries circled in red ink. She had spent the last half an hour puzzling as to why she had circled the sleepy hamlet of Bramptonsfield Magna in purple hue. It had been some time before she had realised that the circle of great significance was in fact a stain on the map which had been caused by a carelessly-placed cup of blackberry herbal tea. It had taken all of her courage to embark upon the scheme which she was so meticulously plotting, and had involved her swallowing the greater percentage of her pride, but she had her goal in sight now - and would not be deterred.

Another figure who was now a firm fixture of St Onans was also on an unswerving mission. When the Reverend Vernon Farmer had replaced the disgraced Goodwill as Headmaster, he had brought with him a certain Dr Julius.

Dr Julius was strange by anyone's standards. His full name was still a mystery to everyone but himself - (and there was no actual proof of that, come to think of it). He said very little, never appeared to eat, and was never present at any of the Staff meetings. Before Farmer had instigated his self-imposed "segregation", he would often excuse the odd man's absence by merely stating that 'Dr Julius is undertaking a small errand...'. Mr Newhouse had openly stated that in his opinion, it was far more likely that their cadaverous colleague was 'on an errand at the Undertakers'... Hyde-Jones had further added to the man's dark reputation by christening him with the nickname of "Stiffy". This had caused the Staff to laugh, and the Matron to become rather curious...

Professor Johnathan Darwin had for some time been a House Master for the Boarders at the Academy. When the new Head had landed, he had seized the chance to remedy his homeless situation by informing Farmer that the out-going Boss had arranged for him to move in to the Boarding House. The move had been achieved without question, and Darwin was now settled in to a rather spacious flat on the premises, which he shared with Bernie - or more accurately, which Bernie shared with Darwin, due to their noticeable difference in size. It was an arrangement which worked perfectly. Bernie refrained from "nesting" with any of the soft furnishings, and Darwin agreed not to leave his pants soaking in the bathroom sink. They also took it in turns to keep a watchful eye on Dr Julius, whose behaviour even the Bigfoot thought was weird.

Julius had been summoned to the study of the Head, and tasked with ensuring that "certain occurrences" were not permitted to occur within the environs of the Boarding House. Dr Julius had accepted his orders without question or comment, and had merely bowed, before stalking silently out of Farmer's room. That very night, he had commenced the task.

Either due to rumour, gossip, or general assumption, Vernon Farmer had formed the opinion that there was altogether far too much "Night-time Manipulation" being perpetrated upon themselves by the boys of the Boarding House. In his mind, he had decided that such behaviour could only lead to moral decay, a lack of concentration, spiritual dilution, and in all probability - blindness. He had decided that such abominations must be nipped in the bud. He had once declared to a shocked Professor Darwin that 'That sort of practice is the very last thing which I would expect from an Onanist...' He had added 'This sort of thing must be stamped on'. Darwin wondered if the man was talking literally, and if so, then what the amendment in the Academy Rules would possibly read like.

Darwin had (perhaps mistakenly) shared his concerns with Hyde-Jones and Mr Newhouse. Hyde-Jones had found the whole subject hysterically funny, and when he had stopped laughing, had stated,

'I don't know what Vermin thinks he can do about that - I mean, good grief!! At an Academy the size of this - with as many Boarders as we have, and with such a wide age range, well... you're bound to get a regular squad of lads who play the odd solo on the Trouser Flute...'.

'He should get a big sign made up and nailed to the dormitory wall' said Mr Newhouse.

'What wording would you put on it exactly then, Loopy?' enquired Hyde-Jones.

Mr Newhouse adopted his best Authoritarian pose, with an admonishing finger held high in the air, as he declared,

"Romping The Maggot" is strictly forbidden - Any Boy failing to comply with this notice will be taken to the Church Tower- and tossed off'.

And so it was to this end that Dr Julius stalked the corridors of the Boarding House at night, in order to prevent any such indiscretion which might be perpetrated by adolescent hands. His watch was ever-vigilant, and woe betide the boy who was too young to smoke - and yet decided to roll his own.

In the dark, in the night, in the early hours when ghosts walk and the air sits suspended in silence, a door at the far end of the dormitory slowly creaks open. Out of the darkness at the end of the long room glides a deeper shadow, which catches odd bands of silver light from the moon as it spills its narrow beams in through the tall window. Edging slowly and silently up the central corridor between the rows of beds comes a curious figure, still only vaguely humanoid in the meagre light. Dr Julius advanced with a slow spinning gait, leaning over each bed in turn to peer down on the sleeping occupant, and extending his neck like a thirsty lizard. This bizarre figure was dressed in a full black leotard, which was augmented with corsetry, a gentleman's protector, round welding goggles and full Kabuki Theatre makeup (for Noh apparent reason). This fierce and terrifying countenance stared at each of the boys, and the cricket bat which the vision carried was made ready to administer instant justice if there was the slightest sign of self-manipulation taking place beneath the covers. Still twisting and arcing along the rows, this silent Samurai made his way to the doorway at the other end of the dormitory, pausing to adopt a Warrior stance, just before wheeling out of the door and out into the next corridor. His next stop would be the Senior dormitory - where he would inflict swift and painful punishment if there was any hint of ball-tampering…

From his vantage point under the bed of Master Peter Ashman, Professor Darwin watched the freakish figure depart, and made hurried notes by torchlight on his pad.

Chapter Four:

Strangler watched Professor Darwin as he went through one of the most ridiculous ritual dances that he had ever witnessed. The man was bright red in the face, and was turning this way and that, pulling his gown and jacket off his shoulders as he frantically hunted in every pocket for some misplaced item. Having completed a thorough search of his own upper body, Darwin then enacted the same process in his trouser regions. To Strangler, it looked like a very under-rehearsed version of the "Haka" performed by someone suffering from OCD. When the thrashing and turning-out of pockets finally abated, Strangler didn't know whether to ask what the problem was, or merely applaud. Darwin gave up, straightened his dishevelled clothing, dropped his hands to his sides, and declared:

'Well... that's me buggered - I've lost it...'

Strangler had a great feeling of foreboding, but felt equally compelled to ask his friend and colleague to explain the reason for his state of high anxiety. He did so.

'I've lost my credit card...' said Darwin, his shoulders slumping floorward.

'Well try and remember- where did you have it last?' said Strangler.

'If I had remembered where I had it last, I would have remembered that first, and I wouldn't have lost it in the first place'...

'Okay - then try and remember- what- you -were- doing- the-last -time -you- had -it' added Strangler, in that voice we use for Children and the "Differently Bright"...

'My goodness!! You're right!! I had it in my hand when I was showing it to Ein- ...errm, no I can't remember...' stuttered the Biology Master.

'You were showing it to whom?' enquired Strangler, rather casually...

The men locked eyes. Darwin was in no doubt that he would be worn down by the insistent questioning of his friend, until he confessed all. Better to get it all out in the open as soon as possible (much the same as Matron always insisted). Strangler fixed his colleague with a steely eye, and instructed him to stay exactly where he was. He disappeared for a moment, then returned with two cups of coffee. He gave a cup to Darwin, and awaited the story in full. It would appear that our man Darwin had been unable to resist the "pull" of the Vortex…He had been nipping backwards and forwards in time through the portal for "little visits".

Strangler had listened patiently, and then got his friend in a headlock quite impatiently, whilst he screamed at him about the risk to himself and others by using the Vortex as a Day-Trip device for the Hard of Thinking…He delivered the speech about actions changing history, and how could Darwin be so bloody stupid? and what if something had gone wrong? and why hadn't he been invited? - it was his bloody Vortex when all was said and done…

'Why don't we have a little trip back somewhere John?' asked Strangler, 'we're both men of Science, and we know what to do and what not to do, so it might be interesting at that!'

Strangler suddenly became quite agitated at the prospect of a trip back in time, and fished a crumpled postcard out of his own pocket. He waved it frantically at Darwin, and said 'Yes- oh Yes!! We can go back and see just how the Egyptians really constructed the pyramids - I've always wanted to know that since I was a little boy!!'

Darwin seemed strangely reluctant to take him up on the offer…

'That would not be a good idea, Dick…' he said.

'And why is that? Why do I get the distinct impression that there is more to that blunt refusal than an allergy to sand?'

'Ah…well…it's like this…' began Darwin. 'I thought exactly the same as you my friend! I thought that I would find out just how they managed to achieve all of those masterpieces of ancient construction. I went back and had a look and, to be honest, I felt very sorry for the poor buggers toiling away in the heat. I thought that it would really

29

help them if someone could do something for them which would make their task easier, and a lot less back -breaking...'

'Cut to the chase here - what exactly is it that you have done, Johnathan?' growled Strangler.

'I came up with the brainwave of helping the workers out by taking through a few DIY powertools for them to use, I thought that they would be really useful to them, and speed the job up no end. I had been talking to them you see, and it all began when they told me about the problems that they were having with the Ziggurats...'

'And you helped by?.....' said Strangler.

'I got them some poison, and loads of those little plastic trays - then I suggested that they breed loads of cats!!...I managed to hire them some better heavy-duty hydraulic lifting gear, and the Pharaoh was extremely pleased'.

'So now, we have a Hydraulic Rameses...' said Strangler.

'Well it was taking them an absolute age to get anything finished - so all I did was to help them out with a few stone cutters, angle grinders, chisels and hammers - you know, that sort of thing...'

'Did you ever stop for a moment to consider the danger in what you were doing?'

'Oh don't worry, I made sure that I gave them the full safety talk, and handed out gloves, goggles, hard hats, and plenty of hi-vis vests...'

'Which will be no doubt discovered by some future Archaeologists, and then we might have some explaining to do eh?'

'Oh no Dick, I took the stuff back when they had used it, and it was all on "sale or return" anyway'.

'Yes of course - silly old me. So how did you manage to lose your credit card, my old Engineering Supervisor friend?...'

'I needed - well, they needed more equipment, and I sort of got caught up in the heat of the moment, and I sort of... helped out', Darwin explained with a smile.

Strangler didn't smile: 'So what you are seriously expecting me to believe is that thanks to your ill-advised and stupid meddling, there is now, in Ancient Egypt, a Pharaoh with a credit account for B&Q?'

'Ah…yes, sorry'.

'Before we conclude this sorry tale of a complete pillock on his holidays - is there anything else that you might possibly wish to "confess" to?'

'Well, now that I think about it…perhaps the JCB might have been a bit of a mistake, in hindsight…'

Strangler put his head in his hands, the shock of what he was hearing almost making him drop it…

'I got them compressed air guns to help speed up the painting of the frescoes in the burial chambers. But that didn't turn out too well, the workers ended up giving each other spray -tans instead of finishing the job'.

Strangler rubbed his eyes, and said 'Look - we do need to go back and ensure that there aren't any modern artefacts left on site: just imagine the chaos and uproar that will ensue when a JCB digger gets dug up by a JCB…'

'No - I don't want to go back Dick, the last time I returned, I was mobbed by hundreds of pyramid workers all wanting fresh batteries for their drills. I had to paint over a mural on the wall of one of the tombs, because the painters had pictured their mates enjoying a flask of tea and a fag during a tea-break. Cost me a small fortune in digestive biscuits, and that was before the stonemasons discovered the delights of the cans of lager'.

Darwin continued, as his friend slumped in disbelief on the laboratory bench. He was listening to the man's tale of misguided philanthropy, but his ears were doing their best to prevent the information from reaching his brain and doing permanent damage. In a daze, he listened to how Darwin had removed the scaffolding which he had donated, after the workers began leaning over the top rail and shouting out vulgar comments at passing Temple Handmaidens…

'I must say though, they really liked my portable CD player which I loaned them. They especially liked that track by "The Bangles". I showed them the dance they do in the video - and now they won't stop copying it...I just hope that they don't decide to include that in any of the wall paintings...I got on really well with the Foremen on the job - Khufu and Imhotep, I think their names were. They really got on a treat with Bell-Enderby too!!'

'Oh, in the Name of All that is Holy!!! Please don't tell me that you took that obsessed madman with you??'

'He insisted on seeing the frescoes at first hand you see, and then he asked if he could help out with the design of the big statue which was to go in front of the Great Pyramid. Bell-Enderby really wanted to help with the design of the Sphinx. His idea was to show the more "Motherly" side of the creature. He helped to sculpt the body'.

'The front bit of the body, by any chance?'

'Why yes!! He was really enthusiastic about the work...'

'Oh I just bet that he was' said Strangler. 'So, just to clarify...you came to the conclusion, and why wouldn't you...that it was a capital idea to let a man with a well-documented mammary fixation loose upon one of the most iconic statues in history, did you?'

'Be fair Dick - he said that it was "a once-in-a-lifetime chance" and a real thrill to work on such a gigantic scale - he was quite overcome, as I remember'

'I have no doubt that he was. Well that now explains the matter in pin-sharp clarity. I now understand why the Sphinx has the headdress of the King, the body of a Lion, the head and face of the Pharaoh - and a whopping great pair of sandstone 44DD's – YOU PILLOCK!!!'

'There's no need to get so irate about it. You sound just like Galileo did when I loaned him my small telescope and told him that he would now be able to prove that the Earth revolves around the Sun...'

'YOU DID BLOODY WHAT??? HAVE YOU TAKEN LEAVE OF YOUR SENSES??' screamed Strangler. 'Well that about puts a bloody lid on the lot of it, that does…Go On - surprise me with some more lovely little incidents where you have gotten your grubby little hands on some other poor unfortunate historical figure…'

'Ah, well I might have possibly mentioned (in passing, that is) to a chap I came across called Thomas Savery, that a good old steam pump would help him no end in getting the water out of the mines a bit quicker. I seem to remember giving a pamphlet which I had on me concerning steam engines, to a fellow I met in Cornwall…'

'Let me guess…' said Strangler, 'Surname of Trevithick- by any chance?'

'Why yes indeed!!- Do you know him? What a very nice family they are - his Mum does a lovely pasty…'

'Does she really…'

'Very tasty indeed…I'm glad that I gave her Mrs Bradley's recipe now…'

'I think I'm going to throw up…' said Strangler.

'Back to Bell-Enderby…he says that he wants to go back and help Leonardo when he paints the picture of "La Gioconda", I think he said'.

'NO…NO…NO!!! We are NOT having a "Page Three" Mona Lisa…' said Strangler.

'But Matron thought that it was good idea!!' said Darwin, sounding rather hurt.

'Oh please - tell me that she hasn't had a little "Day-Trip" back in time too?'

'Indeed she has…she wanted to go and visit the Concubine Palace of the Roman Emperor Caligula- then have a word with that famous "Courtesan" Mata Hari'.

'Why - was she after picking up a few tips perhaps?'

'No…she was I believe, a Guest Lecturer at some of their Evening Classes…'

Strangler stared at the bottom of his empty coffee cup, and wished that it was full of something stronger. 'Is there maybe, anyone else that you might wish to mention? - any more of the Staff that have been tempted to treat my Great Scientific Innovation like the bloody revolving door at a theatre?'

'Let me think…ah yes, Dr Matthews did make what he referred to as a "Bijou Tripette" back to 1928 France. He wanted to pick up a bottle or two of Krug Champagne - it was a particularly legendary vintage, so he informed me'.

'I am probably going to regret asking this question…and?'

'He came home with four bottles in his pockets'.

'Oh Wonderful…I am so very Happy'.

'Yes, so was Dr Matthews - he'd already drunk another five!!!'

Chapter Five:

With the attainment of the age of fifteen, there were unavoidable imperatives that made themselves felt on a daily, if not hourly basis for a young Village boy. Nicky felt as if he were standing helpless in the middle of the road, whilst the multi-wheeled juggernaut with "Teenage Male Hormones Direct" emblazoned on the side of it hurtled toward him - and then straight over the top of him.

It was as if he had awoken from a rather strange dream, where climbing trees, flying model aircraft, and football had been the major features. The girls of the village had only had supporting roles in the script, as shrieking, chattering and hitherto annoying younger Sisters of his friends. Now, they were taller, more strangely attractive, and exuded an unexplainable allure which seemed to have an immediate and direct effect upon his speech functions…He was also aware that too much time was being spent in scanning the pages of his Mother's mail order catalogue - primarily those pages which displayed the range of Ladies' skimpy lingerie. He seemed unable to unplug the connection which linked the advertising images, and what he imagined Jozza to be wearing underneath all of the black leather and studs…

Mum emerged from the living room waving a folded piece of paper - which had the same instantaneous effect upon his libido that it would normally take a cold shower to achieve. 'This fell out of your briefcase that used to be a satchel…' stated Mum. Nicky was certain that scenes such as this were a regular occurrence in households throughout the country, where notes, messages or other hidden items would (without any hint of searching by Mum at all, you understand) suddenly leap out of the bag/pocket/hiding place where they had been so carefully secreted. In her hand, Mum was holding the letter from the Academy telling Parents all about the trip to Switzerland.

'Why did you think that you had to hide this from me?' asked Mum.

'I didn't hide it Mum: I know that we can't afford for me to go - so I just put it at the bottom of my case' said Nicky.

'Look Son...' she told him, 'we may not be well enough off that we can afford to send you off on trips all around the world at the drop of a letter, but just because we are poorer than some, it doesn't mean that you have to be ashamed and start hiding letters from me...'

'Quite right...' said Auntie, 'Now be a good boy and run along and hide the Gas Bill...'

This comment earned her a visual "Yellow Card" from Mum.

'Look Mum, it's nothing to do with the money...I don't want to go and have to slide down a mountain covered in snow on two planks with a load of toffee-nosed snobs anyway. I can't play an Alpenhorn, I never want to wear little leather shorts, I can't yodel, and I don't really like Toblerone all that much...' said Nicky.

'I bet you would soon learn to yodel if you got a Toblerone stuck up your jacksie...' Auntie helpfully supplied. (If she wasn't careful, she could very well be sent for an early bath...)

'I couldn't go anyway Mum, because it would interfere with the Band rehearsals' said Nicky.

'I've heard that tape you brought home - that singer sounds like he has already been interfered with...' said Auntie, giggling.

(Sorry Auntie - that's it...You're off!)

'And the only reason that the cows in Switzerland all have those great big bells around their necks, is because their horns don't work...' called Auntie in defiance, as she walked down the tunnel to the dressing-room.

Luckily, the conversation was interrupted by the ringing of the telephone.

It was Uncle Joe.

He wanted to come round.

He had some exciting news to tell them...

Locking the door of his study to prevent the entry of unwanted intruders, Reverend Vernon Farmer crossed over to his tall oak cabinet. He pulled at the silver chain which ran down the inside of his leg, feeding the links up measure by measure until he finally pulled the bunch of keys up into his hand. He selected the correct key. He then unlocked the pull-down drawer to his secret drinks cabinet. Having unlocked another drawer, he reached in and withdrew the Tantalus from within. This was a man who really, really liked his locks. Anything and everything which Farmer considered might possibly come into contact with anyone but himself, was secured with the appropriate exclusion devices. He swung down the silver 'handle' of the tantalus and took out the cut crystal decanter which held the sherry. Sitting down at his desk, he poured himself a small measure of the golden fluid.

Well now, it would seem that the Gods were smiling on him. He had earlier taken a clandestine telephone call from an equally secretive acquaintance, who may, or may not have been a member of the Venerable Board of Trustees. This cloak-and-dagger caller may (or may not) have been a prominent Freemason in the local Lodge: and it may (or... etc- you know the routine) have been hinted to Vernon Farmer that a "Certain Person" with possibly Royal connections, may be persuaded to pay a visit to the Academy as part of a tour of the Midlands. (Since the 'phone call was never made, and the matter never discussed, no further details were available - in fact, I have absolutely no idea what you are referring to...)

This would, as the caller may, or may not have hinted, have a very positive effect on Farmer's chances of attaining the certain Honour which he craved so badly. What was needed now was for St Onans to be featured prominently in some top-quality event, so that he could lie back and bask in the reflected glory. He would certainly not take the praise for whatever achievements were accomplished by the Academy, oh no, he would simply take the credit. It was a certainty that he would soon be welcomed into the Masonic Lodge with open arms. He was definitely ready - as he often put on the apron, the skull cap, and stood in front of the mirror on his bedroom with one trouser leg neatly rolled up. Admittedly, the copy of the Bible which he should have been holding in his right hand was substituted by a copy of *Gardener's Weekly*, and the dagger of justice in his left hand was actually the bathroom loofah - but the effect was still stunning. It might have carried just slightly more gravitas if the apron had not born the legend "Fancy a Hot Sausage Missus?" on the front.

He would beat the boys over the head with manners, culture and etiquette, until they bent to his will. The "Visitor" could not fail to be impressed with what he would see on his arrival - after which, tea at The Palace?...why, it was almost a foregone conclusion.

His plans to drag the Academy kicking and screaming into the 1950's began to take shape the very next morning. The early assembly had taken place as usual, this time with a battered toilet roll pinned to the front of the lectern. Farmer had barked his way through all of the regular announcements, including the daily list of boys who had transgressed the written laws of the Academy - and been caught breathing noisily. The Head then folded his written notes, and walked away from the lectern, striding to the edge of the stage and clasping his hands behind his back...

'Today will mark the first of many inspections I intend to put in place, to ensure that all boys of this Establishment conform to the standards which I have laid down...Hair length will be checked today - and any boy whose tonsorial range is found to be outside the required limits will be sent home forthwith. I will not permit any Pupil to display hair which is longer than the shirt collar. Masters Rundell and Thwaite will carry out the assessment'.

With that, the man turned and stormed out of the rear stage doors. Without actually understanding why he had done it, Bannister the Mathematics Tutor gave the door a quick push in order to help it shut. It closed swiftly - trapping the gown of the Head Master in it. All of the Staff heard the ripping of cloth, and the very un-reverential oaths that were uttered from behind the door. (It would later come to light that Bannister was in fact innocent, and had been acting under the implicit direction of one Mrs Elsie Noakes…).

Gideon Rundell calmly and confidently walked down the short wooden steps, and once the younger boys had left the hall, called out: 'Remain where you are, Form 5B…You will be the first group to be inspected - so form an orderly line toward the stage'.

The boys grudgingly shuffled into position. Mr Thwaite (in today's wig of a rather fetching purple) scurried up behind the Latin Master. He grinned sheepishly as he brandished the small plastic ruler which he had obtained for the purposes of hair measurement. Rundell gave the object a sneering look, as one might give to a participant who has just farted during a séance…

'What on earth do you call that, Man? - I will require something much longer…STOP THAT SNIGGERING, YOU BOYS…'

He reached into his own pocket, and produced a foot-long steel rule - smacking it into the palm of his hand in satisfaction. He handed it to Thwaite, who received the object reverentially. 'Quod Erat Demonstrandum…' said Rundell, loudly. Thwaite shrank back and made his way to the front of the queue of victims, as the fearsome finger of Rundell indicated.

Merry was the first in line, and extended his neck to its maximum, as the Geography Master attempted to estimate the hair-vs-collar differential. Under the eagle-eyed stare of Rundell, he told the boy 'Ah…sorry old Chap, I'm afraid you will have to go and stand over at the back…'

'STOP DITHERING THWAITE!!!…' bellowed Rundell, 'Just weed out the overgrown specimens and get them over in the corner'.

Weatherill was next. Thwaite approached the boy with ruler held aloft like a religious talisman. 'Excuse me...' said Thwaite, 'I really have to check your length'.

'Perhaps when we get to know each other a little better Sir? I really couldn't contemplate it on our first date!!' replied the boy.

Rundell ignored the roar of laughter that sprang up from the boys, and grabbed the ruler out of the hands of his colleague. He grabbed Weatherill, pulled down his hair, held the rule to his head, then pronounced 'Don't waste our time Weatherill - get to the back'.

With no word being spoken between them, all of the remaining boys began to slowly raise their shoulders and pull down their necks tortoise-style. The visual effect was one of a line of schoolboys who had their heads cemented directly onto their shoulders. Turning stiffly, the lads gave each other a look which stated 'If one of us goes down- then we all go down...'. Thwaite passed down the row in utter confusion, and the boys began to peel off and join their friends in a swelling throng at the back of the hall.

Kendy had caused absolute panic. He had observed Thwaite intently, and the Master was horrified to notice from some distance away, that Kendy had very long, and very purple hair. What shocked him even more was the fact that as he came up the line to face the boy himself, the hair seemed to have shrunk back to leave a "number two" crew cut - but still of a purple hue. As he turned back to Rundell for some kind of reassurance, there was a burst of loud applause from the "detainees".

More fun was had when Weatherill took it upon himself to re-join the end of the line. Jackson had to be given up as a lost cause, as Thwaite was never going to be able to reach up that far, and to have to go and fetch a chair would have been undignified. The look on the huge boy's face told the Master that asking him to bend down would not be a very good idea. Thwaite eventually came to Weatherill - who stood beaming to attention.

'Oh do come on Weatherill...I mean, I've alrea -...Oh!!' said Thwaite.

How it had been achieved, no-one knew. When he had done it, no-one was certain. What Thwaite now saw in front of him was a boy whose hair now did not reach his collar. There was no way that it could reach his collar, because it was sticking up vertically like a just-slightly-smaller version of a Grenadier Guardsman's "Bearskin". Thwaite didn't know whether to laugh, cry, panic, or award the boy points for artistic merit...

Weatherill saluted the shocked Master, and marched over to join his friends.

There was now only one boy left. That boy was Lordsley. He gave the group of boys a smug look as Rundell patted him on the back.

'One out of sixteen...that is truly appalling!!!' said Rundell.

'Well I shouldn't enter any more pub quizzes then, if I were you...' called Weatherill.

Rundell ignored the comment. The boys stood together: there was every chance that this was the start of something which would lead to trouble - but what the hell, they wouldn't be able to expel them for it. They all knew that Farmer would not want any hint of scandal, or to have bad reports in the local press. They wondered what he would do...

They found out.

'Right. You boys will report to the Head's study immediately. You will collect a report slip each from Miss Piggott, which you will sign for - and then you will leave the Academy premises. You will return when your hair has been cut to the stipulated length - and not before'.

As the boys all dutifully tramped across the quad to the Secretary's office to collect their chastisement papers, little did the Staff know that they were playing into the hands of David DeVere. He took full advantage of any chance to escape his educational Gulag, and by issuing him with official notification that he was to be sent home...well now, someone had not thought things through. With his report slip clutched tightly in his hand, he collected his belongings from the Boarding House, borrowed sufficient funds to get him to the Coast - and legged it before the mistake could be discovered.

It certainly was a very quiet ride home on the bus.

Mum had taken the news slightly less well than Nicky had hoped...She had gone into one of her rare "silent and dangerous" states. This was a time when you didn't argue with Mum. Once battle lines had been drawn, there was no way of calming her down until the field was littered with casualties. Nicky remembered with a shudder the incident last year when she had been drastically over-charged at the local Co-op. Auntie had fled for the comparative safety of the garden, where she turned the soil of the vegetable patch unconvincingly with Dave the Chicken hiding behind her. Nicky noticed that Mum seemed to have passed through the valley of Blind Rage, and had stepped out onto the sunlit uplands of Revenge…

'Right then Son…' she declared in a worryingly calm tone, 'Enjoy your afternoon off. We will be going into that School tomorrow to have a little chat with that Farmer person…'

'Had I better get my hair cut Mum?' Nicky asked.

'No you certainly will not…' answered Major-General Mother, as she lightly caressed the pistol which she was busy loading.

It was one of the most ominous and quiet evenings that Nicky could remember. Something was definitely brewing, and not just the fermentations of Auntie's lethal home-brew in the shed. Nicky began to worry that Mum's jewellery box might contain a sterling-silver set of knuckledusters…

Chapter Six:

If you had been a really, really good boy, eaten all of your vegetables, tidied your bedroom when asked, and been respectful to your Elders - then maybe, just maybe you would be fortunate enough to get a visit from the Happy and Wise God of Light Relief (as opposed to Cousin Sheila, for whom it was a relief when the light was turned off…).

Uncle Joe arrived at the door wearing his best suit. To be fair, it was already pretty worn in several places, but he had made the effort, and the family were impressed. He was ushered in and given the statutory welcome in a cup. He looked around at the gathered audience and announced 'Well people - take a good, long look at the Joe Prentiss of old, because the new business idea which I have come up with is going to make me a millionaire…' He placed a battered briefcase on the kitchen table, the overall effect being somewhat spoiled by the fact that he had to borrow a knife from the kitchen drawer in order to open one of the stubborn catches on the case. He opened the lid of the case with style, and produced a sheaf of crisp papers.

'This is it…' said Uncle, 'This is the Big One!!'

'That's not the rumour that I had heard…' said Auntie. Mum silenced her naughty remark.

Joe sat beaming like a man who had not cut his lawn for a whole year, and had just won a flock of sheep. Mum waited until she could stand the suspense no longer…

'Well come on Joe - spit it out…what's the Big Earner then?'

Joe adopted his "Speaking to the Gallery" face (only normally witnessed in Court, where he was more likely to be the Defendant rather than Witness…).

'Ahem…' He cleared his throat. 'I was just driftin' off to sleep the other night, when I began to fancy one of those sweets in the big tin that we got given at Christmas. I was wondering which ones might be left, when I suddenly had this blindin' flash of inspiration!!' he said. 'Right then…I thinks to myself: wouldn't it be nice if we could

43

do away with all the injustice in the World, and make sure that nobody got left out...'

Everyone stared at Joe.

'So here's what I thought. I realised that there are loads of sweets what get handed around at all sorts of Parties and gatherings. We've got "Celebrations" and "Quality Street" and "Heroes" and "Roses" - and certainly more chocolate selections than you could shake a mint stick at. Every Religion can dive in and enjoy these confections, and it's nice that we Christians can share these with everybody else - BUT!! It occurred to me that there is always one specific Faith that gets left out, I mean, there is no actual confectionery made exclusively for people of the Jewish Faith...UNTIL NOW!!! That's when it came to me like Moses when he came across the burning Busker - what we need is something for the Yiddish lover of chocolate!! So, I done some designs, an' I can't say that it's been easy - but I think that I have finally cracked it. Now I know what you're thinking- "has he thought it through this time?", well the answer my friends is yes! I got in touch with a Jewish friend of mine who put me in touch with the Synagogue Council: and the Chief Bloke there didn't see any reason why I shouldn't go into production straight away. I done the designs, an' me and the Wife sat up all night making the first samples of our sweets. I'm goin' into Lincoln tomorrow to get commercial sponsorship and a manufacturer all sorted out - I tell you...it's a sure-fire winner, this one is'.

Joe took a medium-sized tapered box from the case. He tipped the contents onto the kitchen table. There were a variety of coloured paper sweets. Joe was bouncing up and down excitedly:

'Go on...unwrap one and 'ave a look!!' he said.

Nicky, Mum and Auntie cautiously took a sweet each and pulled off the wrapper. Inside was a thick coin-sized round shape with a chocolate covering. Embossed on the chocolate covering was a Star of David...Joe was beside himself with pride:

44

'Yeah, look - you've got the Star of David on some, and a Menorah, and some say "Shalom" on them…. All for the benefit of our Jewish Friends!!'

Mum put one of the sweets into her mouth. She had to admit - it was surprisingly good. 'And what do you intend to call these sweets, Joe?' she casually enquired.

Joe smiled hugely… 'It may have taken me all night - but this is where the real Genius comes in…' he replied -

'I call them "MAZEL TOFFEES" …'

'Oh no…' said Mum.

'Oh Yes!!...' said Uncle 'and then me imagination really went wild! I suddenly thought of other ready-meal type products that I could supply to the Jewish Community…I 'ad another bit of a think, and I've come up with these little beauties!!'

He tipped another box out onto the table, followed by yet another "sample" of his handiwork. These appeared to be breadcrumb-coated little balls of various sizes, and were still cold from their recent spell of refrigeration.

'These boys are little balls of chopped chicken and liver - all spiced and flavoured and rolled up in a breadcrumb coating. They are the world's first microwave Kosher snack…All the Jewish Mother who wants to feed her family in a hurry has to do, is to stick these lads in the microwave for three minutes - and they're ready, my Life already!!'

'And what have you called these then?' Auntie tentatively asked him.

'Another stroke of pure inspiration...' he said, 'These are called "RABBITES" …what do you say to that?'

Mum pondered for a moment, and then said:

'Does the phrase "Lynch Mob" mean anything to you Joe?'…

Reverend Vernon Farmer put down his china tea cup and smiled benignly at the reporter from the local paper. Much against his better judgement, he had felt obliged to grant an interview to the young person from the press. It had apparently come to light that Farmer had heard about the plight of a local Pensioner who urgently needed a new hip - but found herself without the funds to pay for the operation of which she was in urgent need. Farmer had leapt to her aid and paid for the operation, making an anonymous donation. (The donor had remained anonymous up until the point that Farmer had written various letters to the local newspapers, informing them anonymously that it was he that he was the generous mystery benefactor). The young reporter scribbled her shorthand, as the Head Master explained just as humbly as he could:

'Well you see my Dear, there are some things that one simply cannot ignore in life. I have done no more and no less than any other public-spirited citizen might have done. What is important is not the amount of money that was given - but the better quality of life that the Dear Lady can now enjoy. I certainly do not seek any credit for my actions, I have merely done that which had to be done. If a small amount of thanks or vague praise is given in respect of this deed - well then, I shall regrettably have to humbly accept it. I seek no measure of recognition for myself you understand, just the knowledge that it was someone from St Onan's Academy that took that humble decision to make another person's life better...'

The Head was so humble that he only spent forty-five minutes having suitable photographs taken to accompany the article in his freshly-tidied study. My word, he thought: not only will this look good in the *Diocesan Church Echo*, but it will be bound to be seen by "certain people" who have a say in the awarding of "certain Honours".

The truth of the matter was that yes, Farmer had turned up at the hospital with a cheque, but his planned altruism was thwarted. From out of nowhere, a small local company identified only by the initials "FSF" had got there first - and not only paid in full for the lady's medical care, but a nice Mediterranean cruise where she could recuperate in style, along with enough flowers to keep several swarms of bees happy for a year. Farmer had returned the cheque to his pocket, and after determining that no-one knew the actual identity of the mystery donor, had decided that for the benefit of the local Media - it would be him…

Having concluded the interview, Farmer had called for Albert Brooks the Groundskeeper to come and have a word with him in his study. The Head had heard a whisper that Brooks had been restoring a statue of St Onan, and this had given him another idea. What a perfect opportunity to combine the twin celebrations of Founder's Day, and the unveiling of the restored statue in all its glory. This would be a perfect opportunity too, to try and persuade (via close "contacts" of course) the "Certain Person" to officiate at the Founders ceremony, and then inaugurate the statue. They were bound to be impressed, and were bound to have heard a tiny whisper of the philanthropic deeds of the humble Headmaster - especially if prompted by say, an anonymous letter…or two. He wondered how they would reward him for all of his good works? Was it his imagination, or could he already feel the ermine-trimmed cloak around his shoulders as he knelt before the throne? His reverie was interrupted by Albert Brooks, who briskly entered the study and broke wind with a dangerous degree of ferocity, especially inside the confines of a Listed Building.

'Yes -Head - what can I do for yer?' asked Brooks.

The Head Master winced at the gruff Yorkshireman's delivery, and decided not to offer him a chair. Brooks had in fact repaired the Head's chair a few weeks previously, and made a mental note to plug it in next time.

'I hear Brooks, that you are restoring the statue of St Onan for future display?' he said.

'S'right…' came the lengthy reply.

'Well look here…I need the statue to be in place for Founder's Day. I don't want any procrastination or prevarication; do you understand?'

'I didn't use them things - I used plaster of Paris, wet and dry sandpaper, and glue…' said Brooks.

'Good, well just you make sure that it is all set up urgently, because M - our reputation may well depend on it…' Farmer told him.

Brooks nodded. It would be set up all right, and that wouldn't be the only thing that was going to be set up, not by a long way, you pompous bastard…

Albert had first dreamed up a small scheme involving the statue many months ago, when he had originally intended it to play a pivotal role in the humiliation of the former Head Master, Dr Goodwill. However…this bugger would do just as well.

Imagine the slow and insistent beating of a snare drum, and a low threatening chord from the brass section as it begins to grow in volume. The drumming becomes a military marching beat, with the string section lifting a melody that troops might well whistle whilst marching to the front line…Actually, you don't have to imagine any of that stuff, because it's only Nicky's Mum putting on her own version of "Battle dress". Oh alright - you can if you really want to…

Mum picked up her Son's report slip from the table. She adjusted the ship brooch which held her neck scarf in place. With her face set in absolute determination, she closed the front door behind her and walked up the path to the front gate. Something told her that she would have no difficulty in getting a seat to herself on the bus into town this morning…

The group of "Refuseniks" had gathered in front of the notice board in the quad. Some, but by no means all, had obviously made a trip to the Barber in order to comply with the instruction given to them by the Head. There were one or two (Nicky being one of them) who hadn't bothered, as they knew that the situation vis-à-vis haircuts was due to be debated by their Parents and the man in question later today. One or two Parents had already been sighted around the small gate entrance, where they paced up and down, growling in suppressed anger. One boy however, was his normal irrepressible self. He had bounded up to his friends and greeted them with his usual joyous spirit. This was Richard Weatherill Esquire - not a boy to be downtrodden by the System in any measure. He did not have the worried and anxious look that his friends all seemed to display.

What he did have, was a foot-high bright green and blue Mohican haircut...

Nicky did not have long to wait. His Mother was ushered into the Academy by two of the Senior Prefects. She collected her offspring, and asked 'Where does this "Farmer" hide himself then?'. Nicky told her. They walked silently up to and inside the office buildings, where their progress was halted by Miss Piggott.

'Good morning - may I enquire what business you have here?' asked Miss P.

'No you may not...My business here is entirely my own - and certainly none of yours. I am here to see the Headmaster. Who are you?' said Mum.

Miss Piggott lifted as many of her chins as she could manage, and announced:

'I am Miss Piggott, the Academy Secretary, and that is pronounced "Pie-Gott"'

'Well if you do not take me to the Headmaster this instant, it will be pronounced "Next patient Please" ...' said Mum.

You didn't mess with Mum when she was in "Full Mum Attack" mode. Emilia Piggott certainly didn't. Mum turned to Nicky and told him 'You stay there - I shall deal with this Person'. He didn't argue. He sat on the long oak bench seat in the corridor, and amused himself by watching Miss Piggott's various range of reactions, as she discovered that she had managed to lock herself out of her own office. For reasons of low-level espionage, he edged himself to the end of the seat, where he could more easily hear what was being said in the Headmaster's study.

Much of the conversation was muted and indecipherable, but he clearly made out words like "Standards" "Academy Rules" "Deliberate flouting of instructions" "unwillingness to conform" and "Image of the Academy" being said by Farmer. There was a rather uncomfortable pause, and then he heard his Mother launch into the Headmaster with a vengeance. She used a variety of words, including "Out-of-touch" "Totalitarian" "Draconian" "Inconsequential" "Piffling" "Small-minded" "Mean" and "Corrupt". His argument was that young men of learning should adopt shorter hair and longer study. Mum's thrust was that the length of her Son's hair had absolutely no bearing on his ability to learn...

'Please remember that Isaac Newton himself was taught at this very site...' said Farmer.

'Just remind me - did he have a short back and sides?' asked Mum.

'Oliver Cromwell, Thomas Edison, The Wright Brothers, the Duke of Wellington...' said Farmer.

'Galileo, Voltaire, Shakespeare, Wordsworth, Brian May...' retaliated Mum.

'To ensure conformity, there must be uniformity - and the best way of ensuring that is for all of the boys to adopt short hair...'

'Like the Fascists?'.

'Ye - No!!, I mean, there are rules...'

'Yes indeed, and if you look back in history, you will find that the Great Minds often broke the rules. I have never heard anyone say about Albert Einstein or Jesus "Yes he's a really nice man and so clever - but Oooh! His hair is such a mess..." have you?

Here's what will happen. You will not persecute my Son about the length of his hair, and I in turn will not report your bullying to the Board of Trustees or the Education Authorities. If you further exclude my Son from this Academy, you are affecting his education, and trust me - that I will not tolerate'.

That was pretty much it. Mum emerged red-faced from the Head's study, grabbed her Son, and marched back out down the path to the quad.

'I shall speak to you later...' said Mum. He had no doubt whatsoever that she would.

Meanwhile, back in the corner of the quad, Keith the Raven was busy handing out business cards for his motorcycle repair shop, to any of the group of boys who looked in any way likely to buy a moped in the near future.

By the strangest twist of the laws of probability, across the County in the historic and fascinating city of Lincoln, another attempt to break into the world of trade and commerce was well under way. Actually, it had been on the verge of ending, and for once it looked like Uncle Joe may have actually begun to realise his dreams of manufacturing glory. His "pitch" to market his two products "Mazel Toffees" and "Rabbites" had gone down very well with the group of Jewish businessmen to whom he was presenting, and when the initial guffaws had subsided there had been a lot of nodding and smiles around the room. The samples had been tried by the men, who had all been pleasantly surprised at their taste and quality. There had been a lot of whispered conversations between them, and Joe felt that he was on the verge of a big breakthrough...

It was during one of these private exchanges however, that the pinball mind of the ever-inventive Uncle decided to go into overdrive. At the back of his head, a small door had been forced open, to allow out a thought which really should not have gained early release. Joe had suddenly remembered the previous failed attempt to corner the American Herbal Tea market with his NASA "Tea of Tranquillity" range. He also remembered the boxes and boxes of the bloody stuff that filled his shed and attic space – which he hadn't been able to shift for love or money. Some ill-timed mischievous idea forced its way to the front of Joe's mind. Never one to let a money-making opportunity slip past, Uncle decided to wait for a pause in the conversation, and then launch this new idea upon the meeting. Everything else had gone so well: why not throw in another great idea whilst the businessmen were all on his side?

Have you ever seen the trick performed where the Magician stands before a fully set out dinner table, complete with wine glasses – then takes hold of the edge of the tablecloth, and with a sweep and a "Whoosh!" whips away the cloth, leaving all of the items still standing? Well, just imagine that – but with the slight difference of the Magician taking hold of the table edge, and flipping the whole thing, glasses, cutlery and all, against the wall and upside down. This is metaphorically what Uncle managed to achieve with his next statement…

One of the businessmen had just finished telling Joe how impressed they were with his products, and to inject a little levity into the proceedings, casually enquired if Joe had any more brilliant new ideas up his sleeve. Joe had suddenly seen the way forward to clearing his shed and attic of the unused tea boxes, and to make even more money. The idea came to him in a blinding flash, and it might have been better all-round if Joe had decided to look away. Never a man to quit whilst he was ahead, Joe unplugged his common sense at the mains – and plunged on with his mouth in cruise-control.

'Funny that you should ask that, me old Matey!' he had declared, 'I also have the first range of Tea designed specifically for the people of the Jewish Persuasion. It's completely Kosher – and I am about to get in touch with a big tea manufacturer, to get it out on the market. I would like you all to be the very first people to hear about it…' Joe beamed.

'And what is this marvellous product?' asked one of the men.

'I call them – "PG No-Tips…The Hebrew Tea Brew" said Joe, enthusiastically- 'Just imagine the advertising slogan – "One Meshuga or Two?".

There is a certain kind of silence that occurs when someone's mobile phone goes off during a funeral. That is exactly the sound that filled the room, as the last echoes of Uncle's words died away…

Uncle turned and looked back at the exit doors which were still swinging, as he picked himself up off the pavement where he had been dumped. He brushed the dirt from his torn jacket, gathered up as many of his samples as he could find from the street, and shouted up at the open window on the first floor -

'Okay then…so I'll get my people to give your people a call then shall I? Let me know when you want the products – Saturday would be good for me, how about you?'.

Chapter Seven:

Divinity and Comparative Religion had been taught regularly and successfully in the Academy for some considerable time by the Reverend Felchingham. What he was considering at this moment was what he could do in order to look good in the eyes of the Assessor when he came to sit in on his lessons. The Headmaster had ordered Career Evaluations to be put in place, and the Rev had been first in line to face the "judging panel". He knew that any bad reports would possibly, no certainly, lead to his cosy existence at St Onans coming to a rather abrupt end. For the duration of the assessments, he would certainly have to "tone down" his constant push to get his pupils to lean over to the "Dark Side".

The other thing that was causing him great mental torment, was the new boy Jez Christo. There was absolutely nothing about the boy's behaviour that was in any way liable to cause concern or offence: far from it – he was a model student, and had very quickly become popular with every other pupil with whom he came into contact. When the Rev had delivered his lectures on "alternative" religious theories, he could feel the quiet, patient gaze of Christo burning the back of his neck as he wrote on the blackboard. The boy never got angry when the Rev put forward some of his more bizarre theories, he would simply smile his enigmatic smile, and wait patiently to ask his questions with his hand raised.

The trouble was, the more that the Rev came into contact with the boy, the more he came to question his own particular "leanings". Jez Christo didn't ever tell anyone to do anything or think anything, you just got the feeling that after you had spoken to him – you got a sudden sense that you really ought to try to be a better person, and that you should start now. Drip by drip, like the annoying action of a neglected tap, he could feel himself wanting to reject evil in all its forms, and buy a denim shirt and beads. Even his previous tormentors seemed to have noticed a change in the Rev's demeanour, as Stan hadn't left any chalk-written abusive messages on his blackboard for quite a while, and even Abolochyn the demon had not made an appearance to deliver another of his severe and lisping admonishments from the realms of "below". It was truly dreadful – the Rev was (although he hated to admit it) beginning to feel quite cheerful, if not happy. You know, when the Assessor turned up in his lesson to examine the standard and content of his teaching…he might just smile.

At Nicky's house, there had been no smiles as Mum discussed the subject of the forthcoming Academy trip to Switzerland. He knew that money was extremely thin on the ground, and with the costs of replacing the clothing that he was either growing out of, or destroying on a regular basis, he also realised that any trip abroad was out of the question. Mum had sat him down at the kitchen table, and explained the situation to him. What had driven a nail into his heart was the look on his Mother's face as she said that she was sorry- but he might have to miss out on the trip this time around. It was as if Mum felt that she should have to apologise for not being rich. He had explained to Mum that he couldn't care less about going to Switzerland with the "Posh Boys", and anyway, he was far too busy with his band practice to take time off. He made sure that he told her that as far as he was concerned – he had everything that he could possibly ever want right here in this room, in this house, and in this little village. These were things that didn't cost any money, but to him were absolutely priceless. Mum had smiled, then turned away and looked out of the kitchen window. Nicky sneaked up behind her and gave her a squeeze.

He knew that she didn't believe him for a second…

Today at St Onans, there had been much discussion amongst the boys as to who was planning to go on the trip, and who wasn't. There was no mention of those individuals who were too poor to afford the exorbitant cost of the jaunt, but the faces of various boys betrayed the fact that this year's school trip was way beyond the financial capabilities of their parents. There were various off-hand excuses given for why certain boys didn't wish to go on the visit. Calderman had stated that he didn't like the cold, and in any case, he refused point blank to be forced to dress like what he had termed "a fur-lined train spotter in an anorak", just for the pleasure of sliding down a snow-covered hill backwards. Davis had informed the gang that he couldn't travel by aircraft on account of the fact that it was an enclosed space, and "he suffered from panic attacks". Jackson had pointed out that he had medical evidence which pointed to the fact that what Davis actually suffered from was "pancake attacks", which had caused a good-natured tussle between the two friends. Nicky had joined in, telling his friends that he needed to concentrate on his Rock Career. Merry wished him well in his future job of producing long sugary sticks at the seaside, to the amusement of the lads. Nicky countered by insisting that it would be unwise for Merry to go on the Swiss trip – in case his diminutive size got him mistaken for a novelty souvenir key fob. There was much mickey-taking, and some quite astute suggestions as to where and how the keys should be attached. The general consensus was that they hoped that the rich kids had a lovely time. Why, the word "avalanche" had hardly been mentioned.

The morning had also seen the next round of checks on the boys' uniform standards. It would appear that Vernon Farmer had now issued a stern instruction concerning the Academy tie. The Masters who carried out the inspections had been issued with three sheets of paper, outlining what was, and more importantly, what was not acceptable, tolerable, and ultimately punishable. Farmer had very definite ideas as to just how long a boy's tie was permitted to be. Lord help anyone who thought that they would possibly be able to get away with a "stubby", or a "loose knot". The Headmaster's edict that 'At this Academy we act like Gentlemen – and will dress correctly, like Gentlemen' had angered the boys, and enraged Mr Thwaite the Geography Teacher (currently wishing to be known as "Geraldine"). The draconian attitude toward hair length had been bad enough, but there was also the uproar caused when Farmer had insisted that boys' shoelaces should be ironed flat. Now there was all of this unnecessary rubbish about the length of ties.

Within the ranks of imposed uniformity, there are always certain individuals whose personality and rebellious nature will always come to the fore. Mr Thwaite had been left speechless during the uniform inspection, when he was presented with the vision of one Richard Weatherill, who had chosen to present himself wearing a boot-lace tie. Not only that – the string accessory was augmented by a "Teddy Boy" drape jacket, drainpipe trousers, and crepe-soled shoes. The whole ensemble was elegantly topped off with a full Rockabilly hairstyle, which in itself was a work of art. Thwaite was at a complete loss as to how he should deal with the boy. He stared at the bootlace tie, as Weatherill grinned at him…

'A bit on the thin side, Mr Weatherill, don't you think?' stated Thwaite.

'Yes Sir!' the boy answered, 'but I have been working out…'

As a body – the pupils had decided (at least the ones who were old enough to dare to mount a challenge to Authority) that enough was enough. Meetings were held, and votes had been taken. Comrade Bill had addressed a great gathering of St Onans students from a soapbox in the quad, urging them all to 'Rise up and overthrow the oppressive shackles of repression by the so-called ruling classes, and if possible, could we please move to a vote Comrades: as I have to finish some Chemistry revision in the library, before first period…' There had been a clamour of excitement, which as everyone knows, is rather like glamour, but slightly more clammy. As Comrade Bill vacated the soapbox, his place was swiftly taken by Merry, who raised a clenched fist and declared 'We shall fight, Brothers!!'.

Now that's fighting talk…

Meanwhile, back in the Bat cave…Well, there was a noticeable lack of anything which could be remotely described as a bat. Tell the truth, it wasn't actually a cave either. This was the prissy and fussy front room of Emelia Piggott ("Pie-Gott", if you don't mind), who was surrounded by the various paraphernalia which she had accumulated for her master plan. Her ornate Welsh dresser was loaded up with various tools, pliers, wire cutters, bolt cropping devices and the like. You could hardly see the Dresden shepherdesses for all of the equipment piled high on the furniture. The coffee-table with the wobbly leg had fared no better, and it groaned under the accumulated weight of maps, rail and bus timetables, gaffer tape, and a baffling variety of male disguises. There was also a box containing a rather sweet device for removal of hair from ladies' persons, but over that, we shall draw a veil.

Sipping her Earl Grey tea through pursed lips, she cast her eye over the various things, and checked off a long list of items in lilac ink. It would work, she knew that it would work. She had done several "dry-runs" in order to ensure that it would work. If her Finishing School had taught her anything – it was that perfect planning was the secret to success. All that remained for her to do now, was to hire a suitable vehicle with enough room in the back to transport a ladder, and wait for the Visiting Order to arrive through the post.

Across the quad, now duly re-installed in his own freezing study, Dr Chambers was puzzling over the actions of the new Headmaster. Apart from an obsession with dress standards and etiquette, the man seemed to have another all-consuming area of focus. On the rarer occasions when he had been actually permitted to enter the "inner sanctum" of Farmer's study, he had noted that the desk, cupboards, and an ever-increasing area of floor space was being taken up with books on the subject of Heraldry. There was a vast amount of pamphlets and brochures containing designs of coronets, ermine robes, and other regalia pertaining to those of a "titled" persuasion. Above the fireplace, there was now a large and expensively-framed photograph of the Queen conducting a Knighthood ceremony. Her Majesty was pictured resplendent in a designer dress and crown. What had disturbed Chambers was the fact that someone had stuck a cut-out face of the new Headmaster onto the body of the man who was kneeling in front of the Queen, in the act of receiving his Honour. There was also a noticeable space on the wall, amongst the usual framed certificates and group photographs from Farmer's past, in the middle of which had been stuck a gummed note reading "Place crest here". On the Head's desk was a rather important-looking sheet of paper headed "Etiquette pertaining to a visit by Royal Persons". The only Royal that sprang to Chambers' mind was Jim Royal – who drove the van which delivered the potatoes to the Academy kitchens. What on earth was Farmer up to now? More to the point, if there was any kind of "special event" in the pipeline, then why the hell had he not been informed?

He gazed out of his study window, and noted with a degree of pride that some concerned students had taken it upon themselves to try and coax young Ashman down from his perch on the Old Block roof. He allowed his mind to drift back to times past…

For some inexplicable reason, he was suddenly transported back to the time when he had stood in that room, as the tears coursed freely down his face. As he had looked down, he had not known what he should feel, or what he should do. All he could bring himself to utter, in a voice so completely and utterly choked with emotion, had been the phrase 'It's a Boy! - It's a Boy!'.

He had vowed then and there, never to visit Thailand again…

The Assessors had arrived as promised for the lesson of Reverend Felchingham. There was a tall man who looked as if he had been drawn hurriedly by an artist on too much prescribed medication, and a shorter woman who it has to be said, looked more of a man than the other gent would ever be. They both carried leather-bound notepads, and the Female Assessor appeared to have a matching leather-bound face. They introduced themselves to the Rev stating 'Please carry on with your normal lesson – we will sit at the back and observe'. The boys entered the classroom, the house lights were dimmed, and the Felchingham show began.

The title of today's lesson as planned by the Rev, should have been "The Good Samaritan – should we really assume the right to interfere in every case?". The Rev had begun his speech, telling the students how in his opinion, it was harmful in the extreme to get yourself involved in any situation which you might come across in the street – and moreover, why was it assumed that it had to always be the "good" Samaritan who stepped in to offer assistance? Could help have just as easily have been provided by one who did not apply such strict standards of altruism? Had there been any attempt to find out if the good works actually carried on after the initial deed was done? Had the Samaritan merely performed some little act of kindness in order to salve his own conscience?

It hadn't turned out to be anything like that at all. The Rev had begun his speech quite briskly, and had waved a Bible aloft in preparation for presenting an alternative opinion, but then…He had become aware that the quiet, measured gaze of Christo had fixed upon him. He began to stammer and stutter. Glancing in panic at the two Assessors at the back of the classroom, he ran his finger under his dog-collar, which all of a sudden seemed to have become terribly tight. Beads of sweat began to run down his forehead, and he felt unable to break away from the kindly stare of the boy in the third row of desks. Like a ventriloquist's dummy in a cassock, the Rev suddenly felt that someone else was in control of his mouth. He listened to himself as he heard himself telling the boys – 'Look Chaps…let's get to the real point here. It doesn't matter what we might call ourselves, or how good we think that we might be. If we see someone in trouble, then we as Human Beings have a duty to our fellow man to get stuck in and help them in any way that we can. Don't do something nice just because you think that it might look good – do it because you want to. Just think what a great world we could have, if everyone looked out for everyone else, and gave a little help when needed…' The Assessors had dropped their pens, and sat open-mouthed as the Rev continued…

'Just be Excellent to each other – that's all it takes!' he declared.

He put the Bible down on the desk. Wild applause broke out from the boys, and at the back, the two Assessors joined in enthusiastically.

Here endeth the Lesson that the Rev hadn't actually intended. The boys filed out of the room happily, Jez Christo giving the Master a knowing smile, and the "inspectors" actually shook the hand of the startled Rev on their way out of the room. Just before the last of his class had departed, the Rev tapped Merry on the shoulder. 'Can I ask you something, Merry?' asked the Rev.

'What do you want to know, Sir?' said Merry.

'That new boy Christo – just what is it with him?'

Merry shrugged, 'God knows, Sir…' he said.

Chapter Eight:

Now that Nicky and his friends were older, they were able to form a more personal and socially interactive bond with some of the Masters, at least the ones that didn't gibber or dribble quite as much as the rest. He had discovered that selected sections of the Staff were just as involved in the day-to-day conflicts with the Senior Team, as were the rest of the boys. There were very clear divisions of "Us" and "Them"- and also very firm opinions about which Master belonged on which side. A couple of the Staff were viewed by the boys as not belonging to either camp. In the case of Bannister and Matthews – it was touch and go as to just how they could be viewed, perhaps from behind toughened glass maybe, purely in the interests of safety…

It had been during a Physics class (where Strangler seemed to be having an oddly "normal" day for once), that Nicky had mentioned to the Professor that he regretted not being able to go on the trip to Switzerland. Strangler had listened to the boy, nodded and frowned in all the right places (i.e. on his face), and then adopted a somewhat conspiratorial look and said 'There may be more than one way to get there, that might be very much cheaper'. The Master had tapped the side of his nose in a secretive fashion, and Nicky began to wonder how the man might possibly achieve the feat of foreign travel by means of nasal hair. The reality had proved to be far stranger than either Nicky or his friends could ever have imagined…

Strangler had obviously kept his ear to the ground (or at least someone's ear – the actual donor could never be found). As well as his finely-tuned scientific mind (tuned slightly off-station) and his rapier wit (slightly blunted), the Professor had always had a dislike of injustice in all its forms. He thought it "damned bad form" that some of his "Chaps" couldn't afford to go on the holiday. Whilst in the bath one evening, he had suddenly had a blinding flash of pure inspiration! Yes! – just think how much cleaner he could get himself, if he actually put some water in. It was after that revelation that he had the thought about using the Vortex and a picture postcard of the intended destination abroad, to enable those boys who were missing out to be able to have their holiday after all.

The next morning, he had assembled the group of Nicky's friends together, and excitedly told them about his plans to help them get to Switzerland. The boys were both ecstatic and terrified in equal measure, as they were all well aware that the Professor's experiments were apt to go so far awry, that you wouldn't be able to see them with the Hubble space telescope. The Physics Master assured them that the "teleportation" function was quite safe for people to use, and that it had been done before – with no ill-effects at all. To this end, he quickly dashed out and got hold of his friend Darwin, and asked him to verify to the boys that the Vortex could be used in complete safety. Darwin had to admit that he had used the Vortex for the odd trip here and there before, and that he had suffered no side-effects. With smiles all round, the boys were finally persuaded. It was agreed that both Strangler and Darwin would lead a small party of the boys through the "doorway" – arriving in the same location as the boys who had paid the exorbitant fees for the Academy trip. Strangler was also at great pains to point out the great advantage of travel by Vortex: namely, that they would depart, enjoy, and return without any time seemingly to have passed. Calderman had asked if that were the case, then was there any chance of him meeting himself, and asking himself if he had enjoyed his trip? Strangler had laughed. Darwin had laughed, but not quite so heartily as his colleague, because he was aware of a slight problem with inter-dimensional travel.

When Darwin had returned through the Vortex, (escaping the hordes of Egyptian builders who were harassing him for steel-capped sandals) he had thought that all was nice and normal. When he awoke on the following Saturday morning, he had gone to the bathroom and turned on the shower. In the clouds of steam, he had sung as many West End musical numbers as he could remember, enjoying the deluge of hot water. He had turned off the shower, stepped out of the cubicle, and begun to towel himself dry in front of his full-length bathroom mirror. It was when he used the edge of the towel to wipe the steam from the mirror that he realised that something was not quite as it should be. The mirror was not reflecting as a mirror is obliged to do. He looked again. When his brain confirmed what his eyes were telling him, he dropped the towel in shock. It was not surprise at what he saw that caused him to drop the towel, it was rather what he did not see.

What he did not see was a reflection looking back at him – he was invisible...

He had made a frantic telephone call to Strangler, who had assured him that the effect was only going to be temporary, and was a result of "mis-alignment in the stability harmonic at the point of reverse dimensional flow" (whatever that meant). Darwin had screamed down the phone – demanding to know how long it would last. Strangler had said that now would be the perfect time to quickly go into town, and look up Ladies' skirts.

'Oh great – and what if it wears off as I am doing it? I will be a) stark bollock naked in the high street, and b) arrested seconds later...' he answered.

Strangler eventually managed to calm down his irate friend. When he had ended the phone call, Darwin decided to just pour himself a very large drink, and sit it out until normal visibility was resumed. Suddenly, he had a horrible thought...What if whilst marking the homework, he came across a particularly poor piece of work which required a very low mark...How the hell could he write "See Me" at the bottom of the page?

He must have fallen asleep. When he awoke, he felt an immense wave of relief sweep over him, as he was back in the land of the visible. Okay, so his colleague must have been correct, the effect didn't last that long. When he had gone out shopping later in the day, the passers-by thought how vain the man must be, who kept checking his own reflection in every shop window that he passed.

Despite his reservations, Darwin insisted that he accompany Strangler and the group of boys on their trip through the Vortex. On the day of their "departure", instructions had been given, and safety procedures set out. Dr Matthews (who had been hovering unsteadily just outside the Physics lab) had been gently ushered further up the corridor, out of harm's way. As the group of travellers stood before the "doorway", Strangler told the boys 'Whatever happens chaps – do try to stay together'.

'Does that apply if we get accidentally vaporised?' asked Nicky.

'Mind the Gap!' said Weatherill.

There was much pushing and shoving, as well as attempts by all of the boys and Staff to get to the back of the group, in truly heroic fashion. Although the scene laid out before them looked idyllic, no-one seemed to want to be the first one onto the sand, just in case…

The spirit of the intrepid explorer within Professor Darwin suddenly shouldered its way through the thronging doubts, and the man stepped purposefully through the doorway, and out onto the silvery sand beyond. When no hideous scaled monstrosity emerged out of nowhere and bit the head off the Professor, his colleague and (slightly more timid) friend Strangler followed him out onto the beach. The boys began to slowly step through the doorway, glancing nervously about themselves all the time.

Gathered in a tight huddle, the group looked at their surroundings. The immaculate sandy beach stretched away on both sides for miles, with a gentle tide lapping at the edge. It was a scene straight from any of the beautiful tiny islands of the South Seas, although what sea they were looking at, and how far south they might be, was a complete mystery to everyone. Twenty or so yards back from the water's edge, tall curving palm trees bent their heads in supplication out of a thick border of what looked like mangrove bushes. Above their heads, large and familiar-looking seabirds wheeled and spun, riding the breeze which blew in from the new sea. Apart from the fact that the plumage of the birds was mostly a rather lovely pale blue, they could have been looking out at a harbour scene from any tropical paradise.

When the initial surprise of the beach had worn off slightly, the boys turned to look back at the doorway from which they had recently emerged – mostly out of fear that it may have disappeared behind them. The door was still visible and solid-looking, with a faint iridescent blue glow outlining it. Ever the pessimist, Jackson had laid a heavy chair down in the doorway, to hopefully prevent the door closing behind them…

'Now you can call me "Mr Picky" if you wish – but I notice the distinct absence of err…snow', said Weatherill.

'Is no-one going to say it?' asked Calderman.

'Oh yes – do excuse me…Where are we?' said Darwin.

Strangler was busy bending down and letting the pristine sand run through his fingers. He brushed off the last of the sand and stood up.

'As far as I can estimate…' he began, 'the Vortex has opened up a doorway through to a parallel dimensional location, commensurate with the reactive constant provided by a random source or imperative…'

'And the first prize of a large box of luxury chocolates and a bonus prize of a brand new brain, goes to anyone who even slightly understood what the Professor just said…' announced Weatherill.

Strangler blushed ever so slightly, and said 'Yes, erm…what I meant was that the Vortex has opened up a doorway into a place which it has selected from some object or stimulus which it has assumed is what we requested – and where it assumed we were trying to get to. I have studied the physical surroundings, and I have come to the conclusion that we have arrived on a beach location…'

There was a rather long and uncomfortable pause.

'How long did you study at University, exactly?' asked Darwin.

'Sorry – I mean to say that although we would appear to have walked onto a beach, it may not be the kind of beach that we are all familiar with. It may not be like any beach which we have ever encountered before: it may well prove to be an alien landscape which contains none of the usual forms which we would normally associate with sea and sand…'

'You could be right...' said Darwin, 'I haven't seen a single ice-cream stall, there is no Punch and Judy show taking place, I haven't spotted any sand castles – and there seems to be rather a noticeable gap in the donkey department, now you come to mention it'.

As the boys turned back to see the response from Strangler, they noticed that against all odds, their friend Weatherill was now wearing a wide-brimmed straw hat with the legend "Kiss me Quick" on it, as well as a very loud Hawaiian shirt, surfing shorts, and flip-flops. More baffling, he had somehow managed to acquire an ice-cream cornet of epic proportions, which he was licking with unmitigated glee. Davis took immediate action, and entered determined negotiations with him for possession of the chocolate flake which protruded from the cone.

'I think it might be me who got us here...' said Strangler, in an apologetic tone.

'What makes you say that?' asked Darwin.

'Well...I received a postcard from my Niece this morning. She is on holiday in Barbados with her husband. I must have stuck the postcard in my pocket and forgotten about it – and I think that the Vortex must have picked up on it, and opened up a door to this place. You know how careful you have to be around it. I was once holding a piece of gingerbread – and I ended up in Grantham...'

'Well that's not the end of the world, is it?'

'No – but you can see it from there...'

There was a sudden hoot of delight from the water's edge, and the group quickly turned to check where the unexpected sound had come from. They all watched in disbelief as Dr Matthews came running through the breaking wavelets, minus shoes and socks, and with a white handkerchief knotted at all four corners placed upon his head.

'What the hell are you doing, Matthews!!' shouted Darwin.

'It's what we call "Paddling" Johnathan...' answered Matthews, 'come on in – the water's lovely, and see if you can get me some more ice for my G and T, there's a good Chap!'.

Darwin ignored the History Tutor's plea. The boys began to relax, and look around their very private beach area. Merry picked up a curiously-spiralled sea shell, and held it to his ear. 'Wow!!' he declared, 'You really can hear the sea in these things...'

Nicky laughed: 'Merry, you idiot, the sea is three feet behind you – you could hear it in an old bike frame!'

Merry grinned, Calderman went off to scout around, Weatherill was busy applying suntan lotion, and Davis set off to search for anything vaguely edible. Nicky and Kendy stayed with the two Masters. Darwin was closely examining some of the lush vegetation which grew almost down to the sea, and Strangler was muttering and cursing at his pocket compass and his mobile phone alternately. His concentration was broken by a cry for help.

Merry approached the Biology Tutor with his head bent, and the unusual shell held in both of his hands.

'I need your help Sir...' he told him.

'What – to determine the type and species of shell?' asked Darwin.

'No Sir – to ged dis bloody hermit crab to let go ob by dose Sir...'

With some difficulty, the angry crustacean was finally persuaded to release Merry. Just then, the boys who had walked off up the beach returned in rather a hurry. They looked from one to the other. It was Calderman who spoke up:

'Sir...we're not, that is to say, I think...I don't think that we're alone here Sir'.

'Have you found something, Calderman?' asked Darwin.

'No Sir, but I saw...well, tracks or grooves left in the sand up the beach a little way – the tracks go up into the bushes!'

Strangler took charge: 'Right then chaps – no need to panic, we will be perfectly safe. Just let's stay together, and we'll have a look shall we?'

With every head turning around to check for any approaching danger, the group walked carefully up the beach a little way. There were indeed tracks or grooves in the sand, not deep, but quite clearly showing where someone or something had dragged some object up the sand toward the bushes. They were all mightily relieved to see that apart from their own, there were no footprints. From behind them came an angry hiss…They all spun around to face the direction from which the sound had come. They were treated to the comforting vision of Dr Matthews, who was now sitting at the water's edge having opened the first can of six-pack of lager. He gave them a happy wave, as the gentle and happy waves rolled in and over his feet. Surrounding the man were several expertly-made sandcastles, all of which were proudly flying a little Union Jack flag on a wooden stick. No-one had a single clue where the deck chair had come from…

'Matthews…what the hell are you doing?' yelled Strangler.

'Balls!' replied the happy holidaymaker in the deck chair.

'I beg your pardon?' said Strangler, somewhat affronted by the response.

'Balls, Richard!!' Matthews repeated.

'Look old chap – there's no need at all for language like that in front of the b -'

'No…Balls! – look behind you Man!'

Seven heads spun around to look behind them. Just in front of the bushes which met the edge of the sand were a line of pale off-white spheres, which had appeared out of the foliage.

One of the globes rolled forward toward the group, and they all saw what had been responsible for creating the strange tracks in the sand. The ball edged a little closer to the tight cluster of spectators, somehow managing to radiate a degree of spherical menace as it did so. Strangler began to hurriedly search his jacket pockets. 'It's okay Lads...' he declared, 'I shall defend us if necessary!'. He removed various odd objects from his pockets, culminating in a small clear rubber ball, which fell onto the sand with a "thunk". The sphere that had rolled forward suddenly decided to roll slowly backwards, as if startled by the appearance of the rubber object. Strangler stared down at the ball at his feet, and gave Darwin a look of horror…

'Oh Crikey! - you don't think - it couldn't possibly, I mean…I haven't, have I?' he stammered.

'Out with it, Dick!' urged Darwin, 'What are you, I mean, what have you done now?'

'I confiscated this ball from some First Year bugs that were playing football with it in the quad, I'd forgotten that I had it in my pocket…I've got a horrible suspicion that the Vortex has picked it up as the "key" to where we were trying to get to, and has directed us to this place…'

'What has that ball got to do with those balls over there then?'

'Well, if you have a closer look at them, don't you think that they look more than a little "organic"?'.

Kendy stepped forward and spoke up for the temporarily confused Master – 'What I think Professor Strangler is saying, is that the Vortex has opened a door for us to a place where those spheres are the natural indigenous life form. If you think about it, it makes sense – as the sphere is a shape that occurs throughout nature automatically, from drops of rain up to the size of planets, so why would a higher life form not adopt the same shape?'

'How do you know all that, Kendy?' asked Nicky.

Kendy whispered to his friend – 'Because I've seen them before. My Father and I got chased by some of them when we were on holiday in the Andromeda system last year. They are highly intelligent, and have senses just as acute as our own. You have to watch out for them as they can be aggressive if provoked, and are masters of camouflage – providing what they want to disguise themselves as is ball-shaped, that is…They are quite common throughout the galaxy: Father referred to them as "Go: nnads", if I remember correctly'.

The "leader" of the ball brigade edged closer again, as Strangler tossed the rubber ball up in the air and caught it. It looked to the Physics Master as if the ball was turning an angry shade of red, and was slightly pulsating in the strong sunlight.

The Physics Master stood and gazed into the clear blue sky, and his lips moved as he silently calculated some urgent theorem.

'Okay you chaps…' he began, 'I think that I have come up with an equation which will ultimately come to our assistance in this present situation'.

(oh no…thought Nicky – here we are with our lives at risk on a strange beach, in a strange place, and he's about to start calculating how many men it will take to dig a hole weighing three tons on a Wednesday without trousers...).

'I see our situation in terms of $8+N$ $(2x-n)$ $+y$: Eight being the number of persons present, X being the unknown quantity, and N being the current number of Balls, or ball-like objects so far encountered…' said Strangler.

'Please Sir…you forgot about "Y", didn't you?' asked Calderman.

'No indeed I have not – the "Y" represents "*Why* the bloody hell are we not running away"?

Darwin frowned at his colleague, 'We have been handed the unique opportunity to study a hitherto unknown species at first hand, as men of Science, we can't just turn our backs and walk away, surely?' he said.

'I don't intend to walk Johnathan – I intend to run like buggery!' answered Strangler.

'Oh come on…just what kind of Scientist would that make you, if you ran away from the chance to study these creatures?' asked Darwin.

'A live one Mate…!' declared Strangler.

'That sphere looks like it's getting ready to attack!' said Merry.

'I think it wants the ball, Dick…' said Darwin.

Acting as if the ball had suddenly become red hot, Strangler threw the rubber ball onto the patch of sand just in front of the leading sphere, which then rolled over it as if to protect it.

'What do we do now?', asked Calderman, as behind them, Dr Matthews drifted gently by on an inflated li-lo, clutching a tall drink with a small umbrella poking out of it…

The question was answered almost immediately, as the sphere expelled the ball at lightning speed, at head height, and in Strangler's direction. Darwin stared open-mouthed as his erstwhile colleague was felled by the rubber projectile, landing in an untidy and completely unrehearsed heap on the sand. The boys moved closer together for protection, all except for Kendy, who stood alone and declared:

'I think the creature assumed that the Professor was threatening one of their own kind. Now it has discovered the truth – it might be a good time to consider slowly and very carefully backing away from here, and going back through the "doorway" before they decide to investigate us any further…'

The suggestion was never likely to meet with any resistance, and the group began to edge their way back toward the safety and security of the open doorway. Darwin shook himself, gathered what remained of his shredded wits, and said 'Boys…head slowly back to the door – no running until I tell you, or unless you see me run past you'. Nicky was despatched to collect the sun-lounging Dr Matthews, who had drifted back into view. The good Doctor was most put out by the order that his holiday should be cut short – 'But I've got tickets for the "End of the Pier Show" later on…' he moaned.

Nicky informed him of what they had witnessed on the beach, and the absolute necessity to return to the Academy with all haste, in the name of safety. Grumbling angrily, Matthews shuffled out of the water, clutching his li-lo under one arm, and his tall drink in the other hand. Still muttering, he cast an irate glance at Darwin, then gathered up his shoes and socks in his beach towel. He wouldn't be able to see the show now – dammit! if there was one thing he really hated, it was being forced to give in to pier pressure…

The poor and unconscious Strangler was dragged up the beach to the door without ceremony, as the boys kept a watchful eye on the spheres which were slowly shadowing their progress up the sandy incline.

'Get through the door two at a time…' instructed a nervy Darwin, 'and we'll haul Dick in between us. Davis – make sure that we haven't left anything on the beach, I don't want any of those balloon-buggers getting hold of any of our property and following us back through the Vortex. Matthews… what in the name of God are you doing now?'

'Just writing a couple of postcards to send home, Johnathan…' said Matthews.

'Look – to hell with that…get through that door, before any of those damned things decide to come with us. Right…get ready: one…two…three…NOW!'

With a sudden rush of panic, the two Masters still standing and the group of pupils shot through the doorway like a cork from a bottle of Champagne. Strangler regained consciousness enough to leap over and shut down the power to the Vortex main unit.

Matthews stood grinning, glass in hand. He declared 'Well I don't know about any of you chaps – but I'm certainly thinking of booking there again for next year!'.

Darwin counted the heads, and was relieved to see that all were present. 'I think that it might be an idea to keep this little incident between ourselves?' he declared. Every head nodded in total agreement.

Davis put the litter that he had collected from the beach into a nearby bin. He had even been careful to collect the ball which had fallen from Strangler's pocket. Now he thought about it, the ball seemed to be a slightly different colour, and a bit heavier than its size would appear to indicate, but he had retrieved it as instructed, so no harm done…

Chapter Nine:

So at last it was working. Finally, the Rev seemed to have made that elusive "break-through" with the boys that he had been desperately looking for. He seemed to have achieved the elevation in status that he had worked so hard for all of these years to attain. Just this morning, his pigeon chest had swollen in pride, when he had overheard Morris of the Fourth Form refer to him as "a cult"…

For a number of years, the Academy had proudly produced its very own glossy brochure within the pages of which were tales of the goings-on with the school, its various achievements, and everything pertaining to academic life within the confines of the Academy. A Headmaster from times past had considered it a good idea to name the publication "Superbum" ("Proudly"). To subsequent generations of St Onans boys, it merely gave the impression of a disturbingly anally-fixated Comic Book Hero. Inside the covers of the quarterly-produced paper, there were endless articles written by Masters and pupils who would extol the virtues of the Academy, in a deluge of pseudo-Dickensian prose. There were photographs too – and curious as it may seem, every picture which featured Dr Matthews showed him with glass in hand (apart from the rather unfortunate Founders Day cricket team photograph – where his legs could be clearly seen protruding from under the long table…). Many educational establishments produce similar papers, and aim within the content for a degree of style, elegance, and a certain gravitas.

The publication created at St Onans was vastly different to any other School newspaper – as it came with its own Wine List at the back…

In retaliation for the imposition of the new draconian uniform laws imposed by the Headmaster, a small task force of conspirators had met in a darkened room. They had then decided that perhaps the room was a little too dark to plot Resistance properly, and so they put on a couple more lights. Comrades Calderman and Jackson had come up with the idea of producing an "alternative" version of the

Academy newspaper – this time featuring the opinions and editorial content of the boys themselves. This paper, it had been decided, would tell it like it really is: and would be a "warts and all" version of life within St Onans (although you did have to collect tokens from the paper in order to get your free warts – collectors' album extra of course). There had been much shouting, and banging on walls and doors. Eventually, they had taken a vote and decided to let Merry come into the meeting.

This Pupil-produced paper would be known as "The Truth", as it told the facts about day-to-day Academy life. It had been edited and printed by the more technologically savvy members of the group, and soon became a much sought-after part of School life (at least by the other pupils). The Headmaster had been furious when a copy had been brought to his attention, and immediately vowed to root out the contributors. Dr Chambers had quite liked it. Mr Newhouse and Hyde-Jones had placed a regular order, and it even received the seal of approval from Mr Thwaite (although he insisted that it should have a "fashion section" featured in it somewhere).

"B" and "Agent J-Cloth" were regular contributors to the paper, on behalf of the ODD. They both regularly supplied photographs which featured members of Staff a) committing some strange or dangerous act, b) in the act of doing something which they would later vigorously deny, or c) in the case of Dr Matthews – not being as vertical as ought to have been the case. The boys now had a way of letting off steam in print, and some of the Masters had begun to submit articles for inclusion. Despite his best efforts, Farmer was unable to prevent the paper from reaching a wide audience. His attempts to suppress the printing of the paper were doomed to failure.

Too late Vernon – "The Truth" is already out there…

The protests against the decrees issued by the Headmaster were also taking other forms. Under the leadership of Comrade Bill, protest placards had been produced in the art class. At chosen points during the morning and afternoon breaks, these were handed out hurriedly to boys who would then parade up and down in the quad, handily outside the Staffroom windows. The first round of slogans were concerning the imposed rules about the length of pupils' hair. At morning break, a line of boys had marched up and down displaying placards which declared in large letters "WE DEMAND IT LONGER". The Staff that were looking out of the window were somewhat surprised to see the Matron marching at the back of the column, with a placard stating, "SO DO I…".

When the placards concerning the wearing of Academy ties had been unveiled declaring "THICKER IS BETTER", no-one was particularly shocked to again see Matron at the back, with a banner which said "I AGREE". Really, there was no way of keeping a good woman down – (unless you were paying the full "executive" hourly rate, that is).

Calderman the astute businessman had suggested offsetting some of the costs of production by selling advertising space in the paper. This had caused a row with Comrade Bill, who had loudly declared that he would never, under any circumstance, allow the downtrodden masses to give in to Commercial Capitalist pressure. The matter had been settled when he had eventually been forced to give in to the pressure of a headlock imposed upon him by the mighty Jackson.

Nicky's Uncle Joe had been one of the first business people to place an advert in the Academy paper. He had finally (after numerous telephone calls and repeated letters) received a response from the Businessmen with whom he had met concerning his plan to market edible Kosher delicacies. Their written reply had contained various quite specific advice as to what he could do with his products – the least offensive of which was the inclusion of the Yiddish term "chutzpah". Joe had immediately seen his opportunity. Completely misinterpreting both the word and its context, he had headed urgently for his shed, finally emerging some hours later with a complete set of designs for a Jewish Sauna…

Merry's Mother (now having decided to live a semi-nomadic existence in a yurt at the bottom of the garden for part of the week) had wanted to advertise her Yoga classes. Due to what was assumed to have been a printer's error, the unfortunate woman soon found herself inundated with requests for bulk supplies of yoghurt.

Comrade Bill had wanted to urge the People to rise up and move toward a Revolution, and so had advertised that there would be a Rally on the Town Hall green at noon on the following Saturday. His political action had been thwarted by the Police, who had held him personally responsible for the fact that seventeen numbered and mud-splattered cars had turned up – jamming up the high street for well over an hour.

It was by no means all bad news though. Some witty chap had placed an advert in the back of the paper which stated "Free to good home – one Henry Albert Lordsley: almost house-trained – can deliver". So far, there had been eight genuine replies.

Dr Johnathan Darwin was still suffering the after-effects of the recent trip through the Vortex. He was complaining bitterly to his colleague Professor Strangler.

'I am still suffering from a lack of sleep' he moaned, 'I keep on having this recurrent nightmare, where I am being chased down the beach by this huge pink pulsating wobbling balloon – which wants to get hold of me…'

'Why on earth would you be having dreams about Mrs Bradley the Cook?' Strangler innocently enquired.

'When I feel strong enough, it is my sworn intention to do you some lasting harm for that remark…' said Darwin.

The Physics Master paid no attention to the remark, as he was pondering another problem of his own at the moment. On the return of the group from wherever it was that the Vortex had sent them, Strangler had noted that some boy had seemingly left a blue football under the table in the laboratory annexe. He had gone over and opened the single glazed door to the lawn area outside, with a view to throwing the ball out onto the grass. When he had bent down under the table to retrieve the ball – it had disappeared. He had noticed it again at the back of the main lab when he had gone to collect some of his notes. It had rolled away from his grasp, and taken up station at the side of the old radiator. When he had taken his first class of the afternoon, he had been surprised to see an extra globe (similar to those which covered the classroom lights) sitting on the side of his bench. The ceiling light globes were a discoloured white. Oddly, he noted that none of the globes were broken – and so there was no need for any of them to be replaced as yet. The "extra" glass ball did not seem to be quite the same as the rest, as it was a pale blue colour. What really caused him concern was the fact that by the end of the lesson, it had disappeared again.

It would appear that the Rev had come through his "assessment" with flying colours. He had received glowing testimonials from the two people who had observed his progress during the recent lesson. They had apparently been most impressed with his relaxed teaching style, and his friendly and engaging attitude toward spreading the Christian Ethic in his class. This had thrown the Rev into a complete state of confusion. He had pledged himself to be bad, and he saw that as good. The trouble was, that he had now started to enjoy being good, which he knew that he ought to see as bad. The bad thing was now that he quite liked to be good, and that would necessitate a rejection of all of his old ways…too bad. He had a horrible inkling that this Rev had suddenly had a Revelation. What if the combined forces from the "Dark Side" had noticed? There were bound to be repercussions. They tended to frown upon that sort of thing. To be honest, with some of the more bizarre combinations of tooth, fang and scales on the faces of the demons – they tended to frown upon everything, all of the time. He tried to remember if he had actually sold his Soul to hell. As far as he knew, there was no actual paperwork that would support this theory. He worried that he may have entered into some ad-hoc "HHP" (Hades Hire Purchase) agreement with the Dark Forces without realising it, and moreover, hadn't bothered to read all of the very small print. Was a verbal contract just as legally binding as a written one? It would certainly be very difficult to be verbal with a torn-out tongue, and he daren't speculate about the exact nature of any "bindings" which might be involved. When their Lawyers had finished with him, he wouldn't have a leg to stand on – they would personally see to that, and probably take photographs whilst they did it, to amuse their children over dinner.

Other forms of non-aggressive resistance had begun to be undertaken by the boys, in opposition to the laws imposed upon them by the Evil Lord Farmer. A plan had been agreed that should any boy from their Form year be asked or nominated to help out at any Academy event, then the response would be to make themselves unavailable by means of going sick. The regular diet of Bradley-cooked food and healthy exposure to the elements during games periods, meant that most of the boys had developed an iron constitution. On swimming days for instance, it was unheard of to see a boy hand in a note from Mother, pleading to excuse their progeny from immersion in the icy waters of the St Onans pool (as far as we know, the only note written by any Mother was one from the parent of Lordsley – and that one was to apologise profusely for having given birth to him…). All of a sudden, pupils became unavailable for various duties due to being afflicted by a host of sudden and mysterious ailments. Nicky's Form and year were for some inexplicable reason being laid low with sore throats, tonsillitis, tinsellitis (anticipating next Christmas), influenza, migraines of varying intensity, back pains, muscle spasms, chicken pox, and mumps. Before you begin to panic dear Reader – this was not one boy who suffered from everything on the list…

"Monitor" duties were thrown into chaos, and heaven forbid – Masters had to carry out their own mundane fetching and carrying. Even the massive human structure that was known as Jackson had telephoned the office of Miss Piggott, to inform her that he could not attend classes due to vertigo.

Now as the excuses began to become more regular, and the Staff started to get a little wiser, the boys had to become ever more inventive with the reasons for their absence from school. Calderman had called in sick with a broken lunchbox. Davis had telephoned the Academy and told them that he was unable to attend due a vicious attack of dandruff. The legend that was Richard Weatherill had ever-so-slightly overplayed his hand, when he called in on a Friday to say that he had broken both legs in a paragliding accident – but would be back at school on the following Monday.

Nicky himself had made the excuse that he was suffering from "Mump". When questioned about his illness, Nicky pointed out that yes, Mumps was normally referred to in the plural – but he, being the child of a poor village family, could only afford one...

Dr Chambers had gone through the list of boys who had telephoned in sick for the day, with the assistance of Roy Hyde-Jones. The English Tutor had to suppress the urge to laugh when he had happened upon the note of apology handed in by William Trevill, for a previous absence last week. The note had stated 'My Son William Trevill will not be attending school on Doctor's advice – as he is suffering from an acute case of Dyer – Dierr – Daier – Dyarr – (all of which had been vigorously crossed out), the Shits...' What had amused Hyde-Jones even more, was the fact that the beautifully written note was carefully signed "My Dad".

Jonef Kendy had apparently gone down with an unexpected case of Scurvy. Gerald Merry had opted for the more bizarre and exotic version of illnesses, and had opted for Dengue fever. Peter Ashman's excuse had been an impassioned plea concerning his being diagnosed with acute syndrome CBA (the syndrome in question being more correctly described as "can't be arsed").

Phillip Ardley had taken the boldest choice of all – and had gone all-out, claiming demonic possession as the cause of his non-attendance.

There were still other unused excuses to be considered, such as "total bodily rejection", "symptomatic split personality" (where neither of the personalities could be bothered to attend school), and Davis was toying with the idea of faking monosodium glutamate poisoning, or claiming to have overdosed on After Eight mints.

One poor individual had excused their absence by claiming that they were suffering from an acute chalk allergy. That had been Dr Matthews…

But there were of course, other byways that led off "Sabotage Street" …

Disruption could of course also be caused if a Master could be tricked into stepping away from the comparative safety of their lesson plan, by casually slipping into the conversation some reference to one of their "pet" subjects. The boys had long since discovered that the Staff (minus the odd favoured couple here and there) all had a few little chinks in their educational armour – and could easily be encouraged to veer off into the world of their own favoured topics, or violent dislikes – if you could just find the right lever. Since most of the Masters teetered over the precipice of sanity on a daily basis, such "triggers" were not hard to engineer. On a good day, the venerable Captain Brayfield could be persuaded to go from a standing start – to foaming at the mouth, at the mere mention of the French or the European Union as a concept. Whilst the angry man began to turn purple in the face and shout, boys would have the chance to enjoy a packed lunch, including a piece of fruit and yoghurt for dessert. The Captain would also react quite badly if faced with any behaviour which tended toward "the vulgar" in his opinion.

There had been a simply perfect example of this earlier on in the year. During Chemistry, Brayfield had asked the class the question 'What is the closest thing to Silver?'

It had been Trevill who had set the man off on a forty-minute rant, when he had innocently answered … 'The Lone Ranger's buttocks, Sir?'

Amongst the ranks of pupils who had sworn allegiance to the God of non-compliance was one individual who had taken matters to a whole new level. David DeVere showed his contempt for his incarceration at St Onans by seeking to remove himself from the Academy on a daily basis, whenever the opportunity presented itself, and by any means at his disposal. Repeated bids for freedom had been thwarted, but this did nothing at all to lessen the resolve of the boy to remove himself from the premises.

The cross-country run had been a good vehicle for his vanishing tricks. When the Sports Masters Burke and Hair had finished arguing between themselves as was usually the case, they would bark at the boys to form up in a group in preparation for a run along the outer edges of the games field, then through the wire fence and up the side of the railway line and out into the countryside. The reluctant runners would take a left turn through an old Victorian tunnel arch, and then set a course toward the church in Nicky's village. For a boy set on absconding, the run would present a variety of opportunities to change into normal clothes (suitable hidden under running kit) and leap onto one of the many buses which stopped along the route through the village. Of course there would be Masters at the halfway point, checking off the boys as they passed, but Burke was always concentrating on screaming abuse at boys whom he considered not to be putting in the required effort – and Carter ("Hair") was constantly engaged in a titanic struggle to keep his unruly toupee in place. Overall, there were dozens of places where an inventive escapologist might choose to slip away, and DeVere had done so on occasions too numerous to mention. Burke had once demanded that he be fitted with a radio tracking device, so that the boy's progress could be constantly monitored throughout the run, and any attempted "break-out" instantly spotted. When the radio "target" had seemed to be taking rather a strange route through the woods, a hasty search party had been sent out. This time, DeVere had got as far away as Nottingham again, and the radio tag had been located high up in an oak tree – attached to an extremely angry squirrel.

Having reached the age of fifteen, the Staff of the Academy formed the opinion that DeVere would grow out of his Houdini habits soon, and adopt a more grown-up attitude where he would accept his place in the school – and knuckle down to the business of education. They seemed to have missed the point that as he had got older, DeVere had honed his skills into a fine art. Oh yes – he did concentrate all right: in Metalwork and Craft lessons, he designed and created wonderful and efficient "skeleton keys" which would open every lock in the Academy. In Art classes, he perfected his design skills to the extent that he was now quite capable of forging copies of Airline tickets for any of the leading flight companies, which even fooled the airlines themselves.

The old saying is "You can't keep a good man down". This was certainly true in the case of David DeVere. He was also a member of the Academy RAF Cadets, and this was about to present him with an opportunity to maximise the potential of "up" …

Chapter Ten:

Nicky had been very eager indeed to get into the Academy RAF Cadet Force. Being a part of the contingent gave him the chance to indulge himself in his passion for all things airborne. Ever since he had grown big enough to climb onto the tall wooden fence of their side garden, and leap off – landing with a "parachute roll" on the lawn, he had wanted to be a pilot (not that the role of a qualified pilot was to climb the side garden fence and leap off, but no doubt Mum would happily supply the RAF with tea and biscuits if they did...). There was also another major consideration (or rather, Squadron Leader consideration) to consider. The uniform that the RAF Cadets wore was far superior to that handed out to the mere Army Cadets. Nicky had followed the expert advice of Brother Mike, and used the old "hot spoon" technique on his boots. Next came an intensive session of spit-and-polish. The result was boots that shone – and toe-caps that gleamed like wet paint. True, Mum had washed his beret for him when new, and it had shrunk enough to cause severe migraines until it had been stretched back into a wearable state. All in all, with a good brush down before inspection, Nicky could present himself as one of the best turned-out Cadets at the Academy.

The uniform was also more than a little useful to a fifteen-year-old boy for attracting the attentions of the young female members of the species...

Members of the Cadet Force were excused lessons on a Wednesday afternoon. The boys would gather in ranks, according to their particular chosen "branch of the Service". Having breezed through the lectures on the theory and control of a basic aircraft the week before, Nicky and his fellow would-be aviators were all up at the games field today. As Albert Brooks supervised, out of the "long hut" came what the eager boys were waiting for. This was the glider, which the RAF Cadets would use to gain actual experience of free-flight. The body of the glider resembled a giant wooden ice skate, with a seat at the front of the "skeleton", and a long metal-reinforced runner underneath the structure. Large wings and tail sections were brought out of the huts, and bolted on to the main body of the glider. When "fully assembled", the glider looked just like a model which some giant boy might have become bored with – and never quite got around to finishing. However, it had all of the control surfaces necessary to achieve flight, a fact that had not escaped the notice of one Cadet DeVere.

The glider would be towed to the very far end of the games field by an eager set of volunteers. The boy flying the glider would be firmly strapped into the control seat, and would make the required pre-flight checks to flaps, rudder, and ailerons. When signalled that all was well by the pilot, twenty or so boys would stretch out a long, thick bungee rope, with ten of them on each side. The rope would be hooked under the front of the glider. The boys then paced away up the field, with the glider pegged firmly to the ground, pulling the rope tighter as they walked. When the rope tension was at its limit, the boys would fan out slightly (as much as the cord under tension would allow) and take up the very last bit of slack out of the rope. With muscles straining, and much juddering as they attempted to hold the rope at its maximum tension, the sign would be given to release the glider by the Master.

Like using a rubber band to launch a balsa toy aeroplane, the glider would lurch forward as the tension of the rope propelled it up the field. Now it was time for the Cadet pilot to use the joystick and rudder pedals to achieve take-off into the wind – and send the glider skywards in a long and graceful arc, perhaps turning a little to port or starboard before making a controlled and gentle landing on its central skid at the other end of the games field. The glider was then dragged back to the starting place, and the next happy test-pilot installed in the seat. Although such flights were all too brief, they did give the boys true experience of the air. Windy days were a real treat, and there were always contests between Cadets to see who could remain airborne for the longest time. The current record holder was Weatherill, who had completed his epic circuit of the field complete with leather flying helmet and "Mae West" life jacket. When he had finally landed, he had casually ambled back up the field, smoking a pipe and declaring 'Damn bad show – had to put the old Girl down: only managed to get two of the Blighters, and then Gerry came at me right out of the sun…see you all for drinkie-poohs in the Mess'.

Davis should have been the next flyer to take to the skies, but there had been rather an unnecessary fracas when he had demanded an in-flight meal. He had been banished to the back of the line by Pilot Officer Thwaite (resplendent in WRAF uniform with tight skirt and sensible flat shoes). Never before in the history of Cadet Training, has so much been eaten by so few, on so many occasions…

DeVere was next to take his place in the pilot's seat.

The bungee cord was pulled tight to its fullest extent. PO Thwaite knelt under the wing of the glider, ready to release the retaining hook and send it aloft. DeVere released himself from the harness straps and dashed away to pick up a rucksack. He climbed back aboard and strapped himself back in.

'What are you doing DeVere?' asked Thwaite, 'Are you ready for take-off?'.

'Just getting some ballast sorted Sir – I'm ready to go' answered DeVere.

Unseen by the crouching Thwaite, and too far away to be noticed by the boys holding the now humming bungee cord, DeVere had quickly made an "addition" to the glider. Out of his rucksack he had pulled a small yet highly-efficient engine unit, and had fixed a propeller onto it. He turned and fastened the rucksack and motor onto the back of the pilot's seat. He yanked off his beret and called 'Let her go Sir!'.

Let her go they did. The glider lunged forward and began its acceleration along the short grass. DeVere gently eased the stick back, and the glider rose up and up. The watching Cadets then heard the sound of a petrol engine start up, but could see nothing around them which could have caused the noise. DeVere grinned to himself, and opened the throttle as he climbed up and over the tall poplar trees at the perimeter of the games field. He took out a compass and studied it as the glider rose steadily. His preferred target was the East Coast, where there would be plenty of grass or sand to land on once his fuel supply had run out. But first – he was determined to have a little fun.

WRAF Officer Thwaite stood and stared at the top of the distant trees, with the boys in silence all around him.

'Oh my word!' he exclaimed, 'What on earth could have happened?'.

Nicky answered 'DeVere may have caught a really good thermal, Sir'.

'Yeah – either that, or our man Davey has just buggered in the direction of Off...' laughed Weatherill, still with pipe in hand.

From his RAF blue matching handbag, Thwaite pulled out a small pair of binoculars, and began scanning the horizon...

'My Dad's got some like that Sir, he uses them to observe the Blue Tits in our garden' said Davis.

'Never mind your Blue Tits...' said Thwaite, without turning around, 'If I don't get that boy to come back – I'll look a Complete Tit...'.

They all noticed a dot in the sky, just above the poplars. The dot grew bigger, and they could hear the sound like an angry wasp trapped in a matchbox getting ever closer. They saw DeVere dip below the line of trees, and then rise up again as he came in low over the games field. Thwaite screamed out to the boys 'Look out Chaps – I think he's coming in!'. The Master didn't have time to call out any more helpful instructions, as the entire group were forced to throw themselves flat to the ground, as DeVere made a low pass over them – upside down.

As DeVere's maniacal laughter and the sound of the little engine faded into the distance, the boys slowly hauled themselves up from the grass. Merry however, was still lying flat out on the ground.

'Do get up Merry, he's gone now – there's no need to panic' said Thwaite.

'Too late Sir', answered Merry, 'I think I've already panicked myself...'.

As the glider soared away out into the wild, free yonder, two figures stood on top of the Groundskeeper's hut roof and cheered wildly. When their cheering had subsided, Albert Brooks and Agent J-Cloth both gave a smart salute in the direction of the disappearing boy.

Nicky began to wonder just how much of the practical side of flight theory could be taught when all you had left was a twenty-five-foot elastic band. Thwaite began to wonder just how long he would keep his job, once he relayed the news to the Headmaster that one of his charges had made a bid for freedom in the Cadet Force's only glider.

The news of the escape had been passed on via Dr Chambers, who to be honest, had not seemed that surprised by the revelation that DeVere had tried his luck again. He had interrupted the Head with the news, and had received an icy reception, as the man was in his study with a cushion placed on the floor in front of him – apparently practising kneeling down, for some odd reason. The Headmaster had immediately instructed Miss Piggott to contact the local RAF base, and alert them that there was a boy aloft in the Academy glider, which might possibly present a hazard for any other local air traffic. This had caused further problems. The excitable Miss P had finally got through to a very young-sounding Airman at the nearby RAF station. She should have given a low-key warning about a boy and a missing glider, but oh no, not our Miss P. She had seen far too many action films featuring many a pilot at the controls of a fast jet aircraft, and she tried to remember exactly how the Air Traffic Controllers in those films had spoken...

'You have unidentified Foreign Traffic in your airspace – destination unknown' she had declared.

This was just enough to send a young Officer into panic mode, which to be fair, he did extremely well. Radar screens were immediately scanned for "Blips", and two Happy Meals were swiftly cancelled. Having recently dealt with an incursion into English airspace by a Russian bomber, the Commanding Officer was not about to take any chances. The call to "Scramble" was immediately put out, and very soon, three Typhoon Eurofighters were airborne and heading for the map reference which they had been given.

As the fighters screamed out over the fenlands, DeVere was munching on a packet of crisps. He had a full tank of fuel, the weather was good, he had U2 playing in his headphones, and he was wearing sunglasses. Life was good at a cruising height of three hundred feet, and a top speed of five miles an hour.

With a cruising speed of 1142 Miles per hour, the fighters were soon in the vicinity of the "foreign blip" on their radar. The control tower at the base was calling…

'Blue Leader Two-Five… Blue Leader Two-Five – are you receiving me, over…'

'Tower One-Zero…we receive you' answered the fighter leader.

'Do you have target in visual: repeat – do you have target in visual?'.

'Confirmed…Target in visual, Tower One-Zero'.

'Please confirm target, Blue leader – repeat, please confirm target'.

'Tower One-Zero – confirm: target is boy in RAF Cadet uniform - in an old glider with some sort of crude engine attached'.

'What the hell is the target doing, Blue leader?'

'Eating crisps Sir –' answered the pilot.

'Did you say the target is - a glider?' asked the Commander.

'That is affirmative Sir…' said Blue leader.

'What type, Blue leader – repeat: what type?'

'Unable to identify flavour at current time Sir…' answered the pilot.

'NOT THE CRISPS YOU BLOODY FOOL – I MEAN THE AIRCRAFT!' screamed the Commander.

'Ah…Yes, sorry Paul – I mean Comm– I mean Tower One-Zero…' the pilot answered hurriedly.

'Blue leader...make radio contact with pilot urgently' said the Commander.

'Negative Tower One-Zero, I am unable to make radio contact with target...' said the pilot.

'What is target doing, Blue leader?' asked the Commander.

'Tower One-Zero- He's playing air guitar at the moment...I don't think he's seen us yet'

'Right Blue leader – get yourself noticed, and force the bugger to land' said the Commander.

'But he's just a kid in a glider Sir!' wailed the pilot.

'He's a bloody kid in a glider in Commercial airspace – get him down on the ground NOW' instructed the Commander. 'Get in front of him and slow him down'.

'No can do Sir – we can't go that slow, otherwise we'll stall and drop into the fens, I'm having to circle around as it is – if I get in front of him, my jet wash will tear his aircraft apart!'

Another voice cut in over the airwaves...

'Tower One-Zero, Tower One-Zero – this is Blue Two- One. Do I have authority to arm rockets?'

'NO YOU BLOODY WELL DO NOT!! Just make sure that he stays below Civil Traffic height, he will probably land soon anyway...'

'I suppose that a quick burst of cannon fire would be out of the question?' said Blue Two-One.

'Only if you fancy a quick burst of Court Marshall...' replied the Commander.

There was radio silence as the would-be defender of the airspace had a good old sulk.

In the fifth-floor tower block studio of the local broadcaster known across the airwaves as "Fen Raydee-o", the afternoon DJ was chatting away in his usual banal fashion, 'And this is a little tune for Marjory and all of her lovely Girls at the flower-arranging group out at South Kyme, who have written in with a request to play something to help them get on with their busy afternoon's work: well here at Fen Raydee-o we always like to do our best to keep the young ladies happy

– if you know what I mean…So Marjory, here is a bit of music just for you and all the laydees…Why not have a nice cup of tea, sit back, and relax to the sounds of Motorhead and "*Ace of Spades*", whilst I- WHAT THE BLOODY HELL???'

The DJ was startled as a skeleton glider with a boy in the pilot's seat gently banked around the building, as the boy waved to him with a free hand. There was a sudden roar as three Typhoon aircraft passed overhead, causing the professional DJ to drop his cup of coffee onto the radio console. Just before the shower of blue sparks, there had just been enough time for the professional DJ to be able to broadcast a very unprofessional word indeed. It was a word that had special magical powers… It certainly had the magical power to transform him from a daily afternoon radio show host, into an unemployment statistic.

As the Radio Station Boss came flying out of his luxury office, and stormed down the corridor clutching the DJ's P45: high above his soon-to-be sacked employees' head, the radio call went out:

'This is Tower One-Zero…Aircraft return to base; I repeat – all aircraft return to base. Let the silly little sod get on with it. If he gets as far as the coast and runs out of fuel, then the bloody Coastguard can handle the problem…'

With his eyes tightly shut and his headphones cranked up to maximum, the boy had assumed that the thunderous noise above him was…well, thunder. As the sun broke through the clouds, the engine carried on putt-putting its way out toward the coast.

DeVere was thinking about treating himself to some nice fish and chips…

Chapter Eleven:

It had arrived. To disguise the true nature of its contents, it had conspired to secrete itself amongst others of its kind, in the vague hope that its formal and elegant appearance might be hidden, and pass unnoticed. This might well have been the case, but for the eagle-eye (and hawk nose) of one Miss Emilia Piggott. She had spotted its distinctive style, and had separated it immediately from its travelling companions. There had been one or two immediate clues – such as the embossed crest, and the legend which bore the words "Buckingham Palace". Unless the Electricity Company were getting ideas above their station, and were issuing final demands with an "up-market" style, this was something out of the ordinary...

It had been reverentially received by the hand of the Reverend Vernon Farmer, and had been placed in front of the antique clock on his study mantelpiece. He really had done his best to ignore it. He had busied himself with the day-to-day minutiae of Academy life on paper, but however hard he might try, the buff envelope on the mantel continued to draw his eye like a badly-hung picture. He put down his pen, with which he was enjoyably signing punishment slips for various miscreants, and stared at the letter. With his heart hammering in his chest, he arose from his seat, with a noise that he continued to blame on the polished leather. Carefully, as if the envelope were likely to explode or burst into flame, he lifted the letter from its resting place. He sat down again in the chair. Opening the slim drawer of his desk, he selected a bone-handled letter opener. He pulled the opener out of its carved and inlaid wooden scabbard like a Knight preparing to do battle: how appropriate, he thought to himself.

Farmer slit open the top of the letter, and withdrew the contents as he held his breath...

For a couple of seconds, and before he put on his reading spectacles, the page swam before his eyes. So this was it. He held in his hand the most significant item of his own personal history to date.

His dream had finally come to fruition, and his hand shook as he read the wording of the letter.

'On behalf of Her Majesty the Queen, it is my pleasant duty to inform you that a serving member of your Academy of St Onans has been duly noted and recommended to be conferred Knight Order of the Garter: for due diligence and service to both the Academy, and to the general public at large. The Honour will be presented by Her Majesty at the Palace, on a date and at a time that will be notified to you in due course'.

Farmer allowed himself a slight grin of satisfaction…At last!! All of those expensive dinners at expensive dinners with his Freemason friends had paid off. The time that it had taken to write all of those hundreds of recommendation letters in disguised handwriting to the Palace had been well worth it! He re-read the letter. In fact, he spent the next half an hour re-reading the letter. When his brain had absorbed as much of the wording as it was possible to soak up, he continued reading the last paragraph of the note:

'Her Majesty has requested that the details of this letter, and the name of the recipient, be withheld until such time as the full details of the Honours listing is made public. The receipt of this letter, and the information contained herein, should not be made known to any persons or agents of the Press Media, and must be treated as confidential. Her Majesty requests your absolute compliance with this instruction, as any disclosure will be liable to forfeiture of declaration, and will hence disqualify the proposed recipient from the Honour. You will be notified in due course of the full details. Yours Faithfully, Sir Bernard Cranleigh-Home KGC DSO and Bar, Secretary of Honours to Her Majesty Queen Elizabeth II…'

(In Farmer's opinion, Sir Bernard had a very common signature).

The Headmaster placed the letter on the desk. He stood up, and saluted it. He then lifted the telephone receiver, and pressed the button which would allow him to contact Miss Piggott.

'A cup of tea please, if you would be so kind Miss Piggott ("Pie-Gott", she corrected), and be so good as to use the Earl Grey if you will…'

It was not long before the Secretary scuttled into his study, bearing the tray with the required array of items huddled together upon it. The Head treated her to an ingratiating smile, and asked her – 'Will you be so kind as to do the HONOURS Miss Piggott?' The Secretary poured the tea into the delicate china cup, baffled by the unnecessary emphasis that he had placed on the word. There was an odd squeaking sound…

'The chair always makes that noise when I get out of it' Farmer explained quickly,

'But you are already standing up, Headmaster…' Miss P replied.

'Would you care to join me?' asked Farmer, indicating the tea tray.

'Why thank you yes, that would be nice' she answered.

Farmer gave an unaccustomed giggle, 'a bit of an HONOUR, would you say?'

Miss Piggott gave him another confused look, similar to a Ring-tailed Lemur who had just been asked to supply a quotation for completely re-wiring a house.

'Is everything alright Headmaster?' she enquired.

'Oh indeed it is, My Dear Miss Piggott. I am having a really good day – and I predict that it will also be a very good KNIGHT…'

The two sat together in the study, the Head with a self-satisfied look firmly cemented onto his face, and she with a look of utter bafflement, on which the cement was not yet dry. Miss P leaned over and selected a biscuit, keeping her eyes firmly glued to the grinning face of the Headmaster. She brushed some crumbs away that had fallen onto her knee.

'Having trouble Miss Piggott?' asked Farmer, 'I do hope that it isn't a problem with your GARTER…'

The Secretary had started to become very uncomfortable in the presence of the Head. There was obviously something odd about the man today. She made an excuse about having to deal with a mountain of paperwork, and exited his study as swiftly as she could. Gerald would never have gone insane like that – he was a Gentleman who knew how to treat a dedicated Secretary. She hurried over to her own desk, and hunted out a silver-framed photograph of the former Headmaster and herself, laughing in the sun at a cricket match on the Academy sports field some years ago. She lovingly placed a kiss upon Gerald Goodwill's image, hastily polished up the frame on the sleeve of her cardigan, and replaced it underneath the pile of papers in her drawer. Not long to wait now Gerald… not long now.

Farmer strode across the floor in a regal fashion and stared out of the window in a self-congratulatory manner. He was supremely happy that all of his mixing with "the right sort of people" had paid dividends at last, and that all of the credit that he had taken for other people's hard work had been finally noticed and rewarded. He sat back down in his chair (there was that noise again...) and suddenly realised – but he couldn't tell anyone, could he! How was he ever supposed to keep news like this to himself? It could be ages before The Palace sent him permission to share the news, and there were so many people that needed to know, and so many newspapers to let slip the details to. Perhaps he could make a telephone call to the local Radio station and give them the news – if he was able disguise his voice? No, perhaps not, at least not from the Academy premises, where that damned nosey Piggott woman was bound to be listening in on the extension.

Right then – if he could not release details to his circle of friends, well, some of his friends, well, his one friend at least, then he could at least get some idea of prices for some of the things that he would be required to have. Once the title had been conferred upon him, there were certain standards to be maintained. Grabbing the telephone directory from his bookshelf, he began to search for local Companies who could quote him a price for the purchase of a white charger, ermine-trimmed robes, decorative heraldic shields, and of course – a sword.

His eye caught sight of an odd object which was sitting under the chair in which Miss Piggott had been sitting. It must have fallen from her pocket, or perhaps from her capacious sleeves, wherein dwelt enough tissues to have caused the depletion of twenty square miles of Rain Forest. It was a curious pale blue marble. He would pick that up and- no, he wouldn't. That stupid Irish Cleaner could pick it up when she came in to hoover his study later on. He was certainly above having to pick up his own rubbish, now that he was about to enter the ranks of nobility.

He sniggered as he thought of just how much one member of his Staff would hate the idea of having a "titled" Headmaster. It would certainly get right up the toffee-nose of that Latin Master Gideon Rundell. He made a mental note to ensure that he put a memo with the details into the Master's pigeon-hole, just as soon as he got permission to let the secret out…

Gideon Rundell himself was not having anything approaching the best day that he had ever had. Not by a long way.

The man's innate vanity had led him to start believing that it was about time that he did something to reverse the ravages of time – more accurately, the ravages that he saw upon his face every time that he looked at himself in the mirror (which believe it or not, was quite often). He saw himself as a young Latin God with swept-back hair, and an air of unspoken breeding and intelligence. He was well aware that the mirror had a completely differing opinion…

He had sought the advice of his friend, colleague and confidante Madame Dreadfell, as she had (how to put it tactfully?) "some previous, albeit remote, experience with the process of cosmetic surgery". She had been flattered that he had approached her for advice, and had given him details of a well-respected cosmetic practitioner who plied his trade in the Home Counties. With personal vanity outvoting the cheque book, Rundell had booked in to the clinic for treatment which he hoped would turn back the clock for his face. He hoped that the boys, when they saw the results, would not call him "clock face".

He had opted for "Botox" treatment to begin with. The clinic had been friendly, very modern, and impeccably clean. He had been greeted by a nursing assistant who looked about eighteen years of age – yet who had insisted that she was in fact fifty-seven. That was all the vain Rundell needed by means of persuasion. He had filled in the required forms, and been shown into the treatment room by yet more friendly nurses. The Doctor had introduced himself, and told Rundell all about what he could expect when the procedure was completed. Rundell was thrilled. He opted to be given a general anaesthetic, to overcome his innate fear if needles, and was assured that he would very soon be looking at a brand new Gideon.

Oh indeed he was…

He had awoken to find that his face had been wrapped in bandages. This had terrified him, and he had called for the Nurse immediately. The Doctor who had carried out the procedure was summoned, and had returned smiling to Rundell's bedside.

'Whummpphh thummgh blurggmm ellph appemmph?' Said Rundell, his voice muffled by the bandages.

'Ah Mr Rundell – nothing to worry about, you just had a mild reaction to the injections. We have carried out everything that you requested on your form, and I'm certain that you will be more than happy with the end results!' said the Doctor.

'Cnngh Yurgghh tnnk urrfgh thhgh bnndggs?' said Rundell.

'What's the magic word Sir?' giggled the Nurse.

'Pllmmffhh…' said Rundell.

Like the ceremonial unwrapping of the mummy of an ancient Pharaoh, the bandages were slowly and carefully unwound from the head of Gideon Rundell. The Doctor stood back and beamed in satisfaction at his handiwork.

'There we are Mr Rundell – all done. Once the redness and swelling has gone down a little, I'm sure that you will be happy with what we have done for you.' Said the Doctor.

Rundell felt the cool air on his hot cheeks. He beckoned for a mirror, which the teenager/pensioner Nurse handed to him with a fixed and surgically-created smile. With a great degree of trepidation, he held up the mirror to get a glimpse of his new face. He stared and he stared – unable to find any form of words which would allow his tongue to express what his eyes were reporting to him…

His face had an enormous swollen bulge on either side of his aquiline nose, and resembled a deep fissure in an unripe plum.

'The initial swelling will go down in a day or so…' said the Doctor.

'What the bloody hell have you done to me…you…you…silly bastard!' screamed Rundell.

'Now there's no need for that kind of language Sir…' said the Doctor, 'I have done exactly as you requested on your written form'.

'Give me that bloody form here now!!' shouted Rundell, as the Doctor cowered behind his clipboard. Rundell scrutinised his written instructions, and then hurled the form back into the face of the Doctor…

'I stated that I wanted Botox – ruddy *Botox*, for God's sake Man!'

'Ah…Yes, I see where there might just have been a teensy misunderstanding' said the Doctor.

'You'd better believe there has – you have made my face look like someone's backside!!' screamed the angry Rundell.

'Well Sir, it's a genuine mistake that anyone might have made – you see, I must have mis-read your handwriting. I thought that it said "Buttocks", not "Botox". You must admit though, it has done wonders for your frown lines Sir…'

'Yes it bloody well has! – the weight of these bum cheeks has pulled them all downwards under the weight, you pillock!' said Rundell.

'Well, if Sir is not completely satisf-'

'No I am not bloody satisfied – completely or otherwise: I've paid you a small fortune to look younger, and this is what I've ended up with. You are going to put this balls-up right. You are not going to charge me a penny for the work, and when it is completed, and when I am absolutely happy with it – then, and only then, will I be obtaining the services of the most expensive Barrister that I can find, and suing you for everything that you have got…' declared Rundell.

The Doctor went white, then a deep shade of red, and then nipped over to the wall and helped himself to a quick blast from a handy oxygen cylinder.

'As you say Sir…' he said meekly, 'please do excuse me for a moment whilst I make the necessary arrangements'.

The Doctor staggered into the reception area, where colleagues and nursing staff surrounded the man, who was gasping for breath as he gripped the counter of the front desk for support.

'Better get the Rundell bloke prepped and taken back in to Theatre One a bit sharpish…' he said.

'He was the "facelift" chap, wasn't he?' asked a fellow Surgeon.

'Yes – he was supposed to be' answered the Doctor.

'Is there some sort of problem?' enquired his shocked colleague.

'It's his face, Bryan…' said the Doctor.

'What about it?'

'I've made a complete arse of it…'

Chapter Twelve:

Out in the vast blackness of space, beyond the farthest planets of our Solar System, and surrounding the sun at a mind-boggling distance of 20000 to 100000 Astronomical Units, is the phenomenon which is known as the Oort Cloud. It is from this gathering of cold material left over from the formation of the galaxy, that a lone comet will detach itself from its near companions, and begin its long sweep in to fly by our sun. Within this frigid "bowling alley", there are regular collisions between the icy bodies – a kind of cosmic game of snooker in which comets and asteroids collide with titanic force.

These impacts are minute, when compared to the impact of puberty upon the libido of a fifteen-year-old schoolboy.

There was a time when Nicky's near neighbour Jozza had been nothing more than a precocious and annoying village girl. There was no way of avoiding the fact that the girl who had once been nothing more than an occasional target for snowballs, had now become a target for adolescent lust…

With her sudden transformation from snobbish little madam to Goth Rock Queen, Nicky had no choice but to obey the male teenage hormonal imperative, and begin to take notice of her. There was a seemingly endless list of things that demanded to be taken notice of. This week, her hair was cut shorter, and stood up in spiky defiance of convention, highlighted at the ends with electric blue. The biker's jacket (which she wore with enviable style) covered her latest tee-shirt, which was inevitably torn to perfection. Nicky often had sketchy thoughts about Jozza, and what could almost be seen through the gaps in her torn tee-shirt certainly filled in the details. The most mentally disturbing part of the girl were, well… her legs. She had developed the habit of wearing the shortest patent leather micro-skirt that Nicky had ever seen, imagined, or encountered. The biker boots which she wore should have acted to play down her femininity, being an inherently masculine item by design. Alas, all they achieved was to make her shapely legs look the same length as the A1 – and to cause immediate droop to the bottom jaw for one certain observing critic.

It was not that there was a shortage of very pretty teenage girls in the village – quite the opposite, but to Nicky none of them exuded the same raw attraction and irresistible magnetism that his local Goth Queen seemed to be able to achieve. He had worked so very hard in trying to capture her attention recently. Nicky would place his record deck speakers on the window cill in the front room. He would put on a rock album of his choice, and wait…

By leaning right over into the right hand side of the window, he could get a clear view up the footpath in the direction that she would appear from. When he saw Jozza slinking down the pavement in his direction, he would immediately crank up the volume and open the top window. With the sound booming out, he would perhaps casually twirl a drumstick or two as he mimed along to the music. As Jozza looked over to see where the loud sound was coming from, he would casually notice her, turning down the volume and calling out 'Hey – how's it going?' as he opened the larger window. Being too hasty with his plan had been a bit of a mistake. Knocking one of the speakers off the window cill and into the front garden had been another mistake. Perhaps his biggest mistake had been to make a grab for the speaker as it had fallen: and falling out of the open window after it had been the biggest mistake of all. Nicky quickly got to his feet, but the image was ruined. Jozza gave him a puzzled look as she took in the sight of a teenage boy tangled up in speaker wire, bleeding from contact with rose bushes, and with a face half-covered in damp soil…

Damn! She had laughed at him. And what happened next was another dagger to his heart. As the giggling Jozza turned away, a red sports car had pulled into the bus stop. She had waved back at the compost covered would-be suitor, and climbed into the car. The driver of the car was some bloke with a pony-tail and dark glasses. Just before the two roared away in the car, he turned and kissed Jozza – actually kissed! Kissed his Jozza! With his actual face! This was poor Nicky's first sighting of "Rodney", or "Rod" as she called him.

Nicky sagged. Now he knew that he had competition. What he needed was some means of getting the lovely Jozza away from Red Car Guy. What he needed was to show her that he was a much better person than that pony-tailed pillock. What he needed was a plan.

But what he really, really needed at this moment in time, was some sticking plasters...

It was around this time that Nicky and his group of friends became embroiled in one of the most legendary scandals ever to strike St Onans Academy. This particular incident was destined to pass into the realms of history, and would be spoken about in hushed tones in dark corners for many years to come. It had all been caused by a game of Rugby...

Dave Kilby was a stocky, mild-mannered boy who had joined the Academy late on in the term. He had quickly been adopted by Nicky's gang of friends, not least for the fact that he was a fellow rebel against the injustices perpetrated upon them by the Farmer regime. He was a very likeable chap, and excelled at all academic subjects. He was particularly brilliant at Rugby. When you had hold of the ball, you just knew that Kilby was about to hurtle into you and steal possession. When he had the ball, you might as well get changed and go home – as there was no way that you were going to be able to get that ball back from him until he was over that touchline. Even "Hair" the Games Master openly raved about the boy's abilities, and he swiftly put him in to the first team. He had what for him was an average first game – and only scored five tries. It seemed obvious to everyone, that it was only a matter of time before his talents came to the attention of the County Selectors.

News went around that there was to be a "Sevens" rugby trial for the County. This involved teams of seven boys playing short games against each other in a "league". It also threw up any players who were considered good enough to try for full County selection. Dave had been automatically selected to play in "the sevens", and the twin wide-boys Burke and Hair had engineered it so that the trials were held on the Academy sports fields. Nicky and the rest of the gang were very proud of their new friend, and looking forward to shouting their support and encouragement from the touchline. There was absolutely no way that their new mate would not be selected to play for the County side. Calderman had already offered his services as his personal manager, for an appropriate and significant fee, of course. Matron had offered him a relaxing post-match massage "to help with any stiffness". Weatherill had offered him a reinforced jockstrap, and a warning about any "personal services" that were offered by the Matron.

The day of the trials had arrived, and all of the boys were looking forward excitedly to the afternoon games. Kilby was seemingly unconcerned, and was not at all nervous at the prospect of being watched by County "scouts". No-one's mind would be particularly focussed on lessons, until their friend had proved to be victorious. The last lesson of the morning had been Chemistry. Today however, there would be one difference which would prove to have major implications...

Their normal (if that word could ever be deemed to be appropriate in any context) was ill. He had, according to rumour, managed to contract Measles. Despite his fevered state, the Captain had loudly declared that these were decent, honest, hardworking, traditional ENGLISH measles – and certainly not the German variation, which he described as 'nothing more than a pale imitation of our own much superior illness'. Ever the stickler for tradition, the Captain had made clear the fact that our own measles would always knock the spots off the competition.

His place had been taken by the henchman of the new Headmaster – Dr Julius. As the boys filed into the class and took up their seats at their benches, the strange man sat hunched over the front desk like some be-robed vulture, awaiting the final death throes of his prey. When the boys had settled, he unfolded himself vertically, and without saying a single word, began to write on the blackboard behind him. It would appear that today's lesson would be about the chemical processes involved in the production of steel.

There was no attempt by the Master to call the register. Julius spun around to face the class and declared, 'Let us consider the beauty and purity of...sssteel'. Everything about the man was unsettling, from the way he seemed to almost slither from one position to the next, down to his actual speech – which sounded reptilian and odd to the ear.

'I will begin by describing the workings of the Bessssemer Converter. You will all sssee how it enabled the conversion of sssteel from mol-ten pig iron. The processs involves the remo-val of impuritiesss within the iron by meanssss of blowing air through the mol-ten contentsss of the furnace...'

There was none of the normal "question and answer" of their usual lessons, indeed the man had adopted the attitude that his job was to dispense the knowledge to his class, and their task was to absorb the information. Julius did not pause, but went straight on with his hissing description of the chemical processes that take place within a blast furnace. Another odd thing about the man, was the fact that he made absolutely no attempt at eye contact with any boy in the classroom. Whilst delivering his detailed list of facts, he seemed to be speaking to a point which he had selected at the back of the room, above the heads of the boys. It was some considerable time before the torrent of information began to slow down a little, and Julius began to bombard the ears of the boys with details of the waste products from the steel-making process. Turning swiftly back to the blackboard, he snatched up a piece of chalk, regarded critically with a steely eye, and wrote "Calcium Silicate" on the board in large letters.

'Calcium Carbonate is added to the furnace...and this sitsss on top in liquid form and isss easily removed. What is the chemical formula of Calcium Carbonate? – You Boy!' (he pointed at Kendy).

'$CaCO_3$ Sir...' replied Kendy, seamlessly.

Julius eyed him with suspicion, 'And what isss the chemical formula for Calcium Silicate?' he hissed. There was a pause as his reptile eyes scanned the room for a suitable victim…He suddenly pointed at Dave Kilby – 'You Boy!'.

'CaSiO3 I think, Sir…' answered the shocked boy.

Julius stared at Kilby. There were a few uncomfortable seconds as the Master continued to fix him with eyes that refused to blink. The expression on the face of the Master left no doubt that for some reason, he had taken a dislike to the boy. Julius moved forward slightly, giving the impression of a Cobra that had just cornered a mouse…

'What isss another name which isss given to Calcium Silicate, Boy?' he demanded.

'*Slag*…' answered Kilby, with perhaps more emphasis than he should have.

There was another rather nasty silence. Julius continued to stare at the boy, who now stared back at him. Julius smiled his reptilian smile:

'You think that it isss funny to insssult your Massster?' he said.

'I was merely answering the question Sir!' declared Kilby, confused.

'You and I shall dissscusss thisss at four o'clock today – when you will report to me for detention…' hissed Julius.

'But I can't Sir – I've got the rugby trials up on the sports field!' said Kilby.

'I have given you an insssstruction Boy! – and it will be obeyed…' said Julius.

'But please Sir, this might be my only chance of getting into the County Side!' said Kilby in desperation…

'Oh dear me…' said Julius, 'I am ssso sssad that you will now be misssing that chance…'

Kilby rose to his feet angrily, sweeping his books and equipment from the bench if front of him – 'You can't do this – you bastard!!' he shouted, 'I've trained hard for this!'.

Julius continued to stare at the boy impassively, 'And now you feel that it isss appropriate to add insssult to injury...isss that the cassse?' he said.

Kilby stood clenching and unclenching his fists, he tried one last time to get the man to change his mind...

'But Sir...please Sir – I can't miss the trials, I just can't'.

'Lisssten Boy: I can sssee the future, and yesss, you will indeed misss your preciousss trialsss'. Said Dr Julius. 'You will report to me at four o'clock today. Not a minute before, and not one minute after. Furthermore, you will now leave my classsroom – you are dismisssed...'

Kilby gathered up his books and walked quietly from the room. The door closing behind him sounded like the boom of a jail cell door as it sealed in a prisoner. The rest of the lesson was one of the most unpleasant experiences which Nicky had ever had at St Onans. Dr Julius made no attempt to speak to the class – who would certainly not have answered him if he had. There was a toxic silence as the man completed his lecture. No notes were taken by the boys, and when the bell sounded the end of the lesson, they all left the chemistry laboratory in single file, like silent Monks.

Dave Kilby had gone immediately to see Dr Chambers, and had tried to plead his case with the Deputy Head. Chambers had listened to the boy, but had backed up Dr Julius in the interests of maintaining a united front amongst the Staff. That was it then...Dave would miss his beloved rugby trials. When Hyde-Jones, Newhouse, Bannister, Darwin and Thwaite had heard about what Dr Julius had done, there was a furious row. What Mr Newhouse suggested should be done to the man was both specific and very descriptive, not to say quite biologically inventive. The boys tried to rally round and give their friend as much support as they could, but the poor boy was inconsolable. He had instructed them to go and watch the trials anyway – and just to leave him alone. This was a problem that even the likes of Trevill, Weatherill or Jez Christo couldn't fix...

The angry group of boys left their friend reluctantly, and gathered in the quad in front of the Art block. They had to leap out of the way, as a van belonging to the workmen who were installing the new heating and filtration system for the Academy swimming pool rattled past them and around the corner toward the pool area. The group were forced to scatter again when having collected their tools and tidied up for the day, (and being paid overtime rates in order to knock-off early) the van clattered past them again, and made its way out of the quad gates.

Trevill seemed to be preoccupied...

'Hang on a minute, Moi Luvvers...' he declared, 'Oi've got me a great idea...'

Chapter Thirteen:

The vehicle of choice for Dr Julius was a rather ancient and weather-beaten Hillman Imp from 1967. This was a small car with the engine in the rear, and looked rather like a version of its competitor the Mini, but made for people who didn't like rounded edges. It was a squat, square little car, with a large amount of glass all the way around. When other road users passed Julius on the highway, the car and its driver gave the distinct impression of a lizard which was peering through the sides of its vivarium tank. He had the habit of parking it in the quad so that it could cast an unblinking eye out over the whole of the Academy. Despite its size, the pale green beast always seemed to exude a certain degree of menace, and other Masters were somewhat reluctant to park their own cars too near to it. Today, it sat scowling out at all and sundry from a position in front of the Science Block.

There was little human activity for the car to observe, as the Academy as a body had all gone up to the games fields to watch the rugby trials. Up near the changing rooms, there were a number of large and smaller coaches, which had brought in boys from other schools and colleges for the event. Off to one side were parked a number of large and expensive cars, these belonging to the County rugby selectors. Already crowding around the bottom two pitches were an exited throng of Staff and boys – awaiting the start of the games. The crowd had been swollen greatly by the number of Groundling supporters, who had come out in their masses to lend their support to the St Onans boys, and enjoy any entertaining dislocations which might occur. The Elder Jedekiah in particular, had really gone to town to show his unbending support for the Academy – with shirt, hat, scarf, flags, and a forest of badges, all in the proud colours of St Onans.

The chanting had already begun in earnest – but the vocal encouragements of the visiting supporters were drowned out by

Jedekiah and the Groundlings, as they sang out at the top of their voices:

'THOU ART EFFLUVIA! – AND THOU KNOWEST THAT THOU ART…'

'THOU SHALT SUFFER NON-LIFE THREATENING CRANIAL INJURIES!...'

'PLAY UP – PLAY UP ST ONANS…OUR BALLS ARE AN ODD SHAPE…'

'CANST THOU DISCERN THE SINGING OF THE OPPOSING SUPPORTERS? – NOT TO ANY APPRECIABLE DEGREE!!'

Suddenly, the word that the Academy's star player would not be appearing on the field spread like wildfire amongst the Home Crowd. There were looks of astonishment and anger on the faces of the crowd – especially the Groundling squad, who immediately took up a loud chant of:

'ONE DAVEY KILBY…YEAH VERILY - THERE IS ONLY ONE DAVEY KILBY…'

Indeed, there was but one Davey Kilby, and that particular jewel in the rugby crown of St Onans was at this moment in detention, incarcerated in a silent room being watched over by a smirking Dr Julius…

At the far end of the touchline, just outside the beer tent which had been mysteriously set up in haste by Dr Matthews, Roy Hyde-Jones was nervously talking to Mr Newhouse.

'Well Loopy…' asked the English Master, 'What do you think our chances are?'.

'Well Roy, we seem to get on together rather well, so if we carry on going out together on a regular basis, then-'

'Not *us*, you twit – I mean Us, I mean our Mob out there'.

'Ah yes, all becomes crystal, Royston…' said Newhouse, 'We're in with a fighting chance of doing well…I mean, look, they've brought in Mark Davis to replace Kilby'.

'Is he any good?'

'Any good? – I hear that he's twice the player that Kilby is' said Newhouse.

'Honestly?' said Hyde-Jones, somewhat surprised.

'Ah no…now I think of it, I heard that he's twice the *weight* that Kilby is…'

Newhouse stood and grinned at his dear friend, as beer fountained out of the English Master's nose…

'APPROACH AND TAKE DUE PART - IF THOU DOST CONSIDER THYSELF TO BE SUFFICIENTLY UNYIELDING!!'

Thus sang out the Groundlings, as they performed a particularly well-rehearsed and executed Cheerleader routine. Ezekielvis was catapulted high into the air, spinning deftly before landing atop the pyramid of boys who had formed up beneath him. There was loud applause as he landed, and even more raucous cheering when the pyramid collapsed – burying Mr Thwaite the Geography Master under the heap of bodies. Being Mr Thwaite, it was highly unlikely that he would ever find his way out again without outside assistance…

St Onans first opponents were Hugo College of Stamford. They had fielded a squad of epic size, each massive individual casting huge and threatening shadows across the pristine turf of the pitch. After they had been playing for a little over fifteen minutes, it soon became apparent that their monstrous stature might have belied the fun-sized brain that was supposed to be in control of the body. When the big boys got possession of the ball they would work their way up to a lumbering run, but having to think about the complexities of changing direction caused them an immediate problem. The result was that there were a lot of pile-ups, as St Onans players collided with the "living statues" of the Hugo boys, as they suffered from genetic navigational complications. Mark Davis, having been a surprise and late addition to the Academy side, had worked out exactly what the strategy should be in order to overcome the juggernauts in shorts. To the great surprise of the supporters, and not least to himself, he was playing the game of his life – and to his complete shock, was enjoying it! Not what we might term "the most elfin in stature" himself, Davis was running, feinting and jinking his way around the much bigger boys. He made as if to throw the ball to his left – then twisted and ran to the right, leaving the Hugo boy veering off in the wrong direction. If he had a fault, it was that as he sold the opposing players a "dummy", he felt obliged by means of good manners to shout 'Excuse me', 'Pardon I', 'Coming through!' and other assorted niceties as he sped past the static opponents. Before he knew it, he had reached the touchline, and was assisted by a push from a fellow forward to get him over the line for his first ever try.

After a brief celebration, Davis stepped up to take the conversion kick. The ball sailed high and proud over the goalposts, and there were yet more celebrations amongst the St Onans team. The Hugo College boys were furious, and the ball was kicked back onto the field by one of their irate forwards – where it bounced erratically, and struck Gideon Rundell the recently surgically-enhanced Latin Master full in the face. Rugby is supposed to be a game played by Gentlemen, so there was no need at all for him to have used language like that…

It was half time. The two teams gathered in groups within their own halves of the pitch (well that is, the St Onans boys gathered, and the lumbering hulks of Hugo's thudded their way across the grass to form a rough circle – rather resembling a sweaty Stonehenge. One boy had to be retrieved from the bushes, having completely misjudged a turn).

Mrs Betty Bradley the Academy kitchen guru had been horrified by the thought of half an orange being the only sustenance available to the boys at half time. She was having none of it – and had descended with her full retinue of staff, bearing silver trays groaning with all manner of tasty goodies for the delight of hungry rugby playing boys. Burke and Hair the Sports Masters gazed at the trays – the empty trays, and wondered just how Davis could possibly have managed to get so much food packed away in so short a period of time. Davis wiped away a stray crumb with a napkin, and asked 'Are there any of those oranges left?'

The Groundling supporters were determined that there would be no let-up in their vocal support for the Academy:

'HUGO'S – THOU ART PLAYING AS WOULD A GROUP OF UNSEEMLY WENCHES!' they called out.

In the middle of their half of the pitch, the St Onans team were called into a huddle, to receive their instructions for the second half.

Down at the Academy, another team were huddled together, and they too were receiving their instructions before commencing their task.

'HANG ON - WE'RE GOING TO DO WHAT?!!' shouted Merry.

He was 'sshh'd' into silence by team leader Trevill. He dragged the shocked Merry back into the huddle by his lapels, and began to explain in detail what the plan was. When he had finished, the boys all shook hands. Calderman and Nicky sped off to obtain the items which they had been told to fetch. They returned with two long scaffolding boards, fully eight feet long, with metal capped ends. It was only a short walk up the slight incline of the path, and then the group were standing in front of a small sickly-green Hillman Imp car.

'Roight Jackson – just 'ee keep a sharp lookout!' said Trevill.

Keith and the rest of the Ravens were the only observers, as the boys slipped the long planks under the car at each side. Apart from Dr Julius and his detained captive Kilby, (who were in a classroom on the very far side of the Old Block), the group of furtive boys were the only people left on Academy soil – the rest being up at the sports field.

The boys formed up into two teams of three, with Jackson at the back acting as "spotter". On Trevill's command, they grabbed a hold on the planks, and lifted the car up. On the next signal, they began to carry the car back down the path and around the corner of the gym toward the swimming pool. Jackson went ahead at this point, and when he gave the signal that all was clear, the boys walked as quickly as they could down to the pool entrance with their stolen booty.

At the bottom end of the swimming pool (which was only about a third of the size of a normal one), the firm of builders had dug a large rectangular hole in which the new filtration and heater units were to be fitted. There was a convenient slope down to the deep trench, and one which would greatly assist the boys with what they planned to do. As they got to the top of the incline, Trevill stopped the crew and gave them their next instructions:

'Nice one Laads…' he declared, 'Now we'em goin' to slip them boards out from under the car, lift the back end where 'eem keeps 'is engine – and roll it down the slope into the trench'.

This they did, and the car was slowly manoeuvred down into the hollow at the bottom of the slope.

'Now we needs to dig out a bit for Ee' said Trevill.

Ashman, Nicky and Calderman began to dig out the right hand side of the trench, with shovels conveniently left by the builders. When they had gone down about three feet, the earth was cleared out of the enlarged hole, and the little car rolled back into it. It was a good fit – the car sat in the hole almost up to its windows.

'Loverly job Mateys!' said Trevill, inspecting the trench from all angles, 'Now all we'em needs to do is fill 'im in, all noice an' neat loike…'

Ashman, Kendy (who for some reason couldn't stop laughing), Weatherill and Trevill gathered up some of the huge plastic sheets from the workmen's supplies, as well as a couple of tarpaulin covers. The car was firstly sheeted over with the plastic, ensuring that there was a good soil-tight fit all around. When two of these sheets had been placed over the vehicle and weighted down with "spare" bricks, it was covered over with one of the big tarpaulins.

'And now, Moi luvvers – I would loike to say a few words…' said Trevill.

'What are you buggering about at?' asked Jackson.

'Please do have a little respect' said Christo, 'after all - it is a burial…'

Trevill clasped his hands together in front of him, and some of the boys bowed their heads. Trevill put on his most caring and sympathetic look, and declared:

'In the name of the Father, and of the Son – and Into the Hole he goes!!'

There was a short burst of respectful applause from the boys.

The car was duly covered over with the loose soil, and all of the excavated material which the boys themselves had dug out. When they had put all of the soil back into the rectangle, they began to stamp it down flat, until it matched the level of the rest of the trench. Having done a perfect job, the lads walked up the slope to the shallow end of the pool area. They turned back to look down at their handiwork, when suddenly, a loud shout caused them all to jump in panic:

'AND JUST WHAT DO YE LITTLE FECKERS TINK YE ARE DOIN'?'.

They spun around to see the figure of their friend and Cleaner Mrs Finucane, who was holding onto the wall, while she fought for breath as she laughed at the looks of horror on their faces.

'Jaysus – ye should ever see the puss on the lot o'yez...' she laughed. 'What in the name of Saint Pat do ye tink ye are up to?'.

They told her. She was impressed.

'Just ye wait 'til Oi tells yer man Brooks about dis caper... Oi swear he'll pi- he'll wet his trousers with the laughter!' she said. 'Now let's get dis place cleaned up all nice and proper so dat no-one tinks dat dere was ever anyone here at all...'

Agent J-Cloth set about helping the boys remove any traces of human interference. Something about the highly efficient way that the woman worked seemed to tell the boys that she just may have done this sort of thing before. When they had completed the task to her satisfaction, she put a Motherly arm around a couple of the boys and said 'Now ye bugger off up to the field, and catch what's left of yer rugby game, and if any nosey bastard should ask ye – well, ye haven't seen me...roight?'.

114

The boys filed away, and Mrs F ruffled their hair as they passed. She saved a quick clip round the ear for Trevill, because he was one of her favourites.

They ran up to the games field, arriving breathless and hot as they mingled in with the crowds. No-one paid them much attention as they joined the throng of spectators. There was something much more interesting which was happening on the pitch. It would appear that Davis had just scored another try – but it had been disallowed by the Referee. The Groundling Elder Jedekiah had sprinted onto the grass, and was at this moment nose-to-nose with the ref (a sports Master from Hugo's College), and was explaining to the shocked man that there were certain circumstances which cast doubts upon the validity of his Parent's marriage… Burke was desperately trying to restrain Jedekiah from physically damaging the referee, and Carter was writhing on the ground, desperately trying to restrain his feisty hairpiece.

Eventually, the referee saw sense (rather than seeing the swift approach of Jedekiah's fist, HoBi or no HoBi), and accepted defeat. The try was given. The irate Elder was led from the pitch, still uttering threats of eternal damnation against the ref.

The final whistle was blown, more in relief than anything else, and a great cheer went up from the St Onans players and their dedicated supporters. The players went to lift Davis up in order to carry him chair-like from the pitch on their shoulders. It wasn't long before they realised that with Davis being…a little more "robust" than they had previously accounted for, it might be a good idea to get some bigger muscle in on the job. Davis was therefore carried shoulder-high by the biggest players from the Hugo College side – who hadn't actually realised that they had in fact lost the game.

St Benedict's School were awarded the "best sportsman" trophy. St Onans picked up an award for "best new player" in the shape of Mark Davis. Dr Bergman's Academy took home a cup for "best team performance", and Dame Hilda Tonk's Ladies Hockey Squad wondered just what the hell they were doing there in the first place.

Meanwhile, the Sumo-like boys of Hugo's College were bouncing off the side of their coach, all eager to try and find the door. There was one trophy left to be awarded. It had gone to a boy called Aubrey MacLeish, from the Van Dell College for Troubled Young Men. Aubrey was an habitual arsonist, but nevertheless, was awarded "Man of the Match" ...

Dr Julius unlocked the classroom door and released his "captive". Kilby said nothing to the man as he left. There were no adequate words which could possibly express the cold hatred that the boy felt toward his tormentor.

Julius looked out into the quad with satisfaction.

Wait a moment...hadn't he parked his car over in the corner next to the Science Block? He was certain that he had – and yet there was now an empty space where a Hillman Imp should have been standing. If not where he remembered parking it, then he had no earthly idea where it might be. It was beginning to look as if it might rain...he wished that he had put the car somewhere safely under cover.

If only...

Chapter Fourteen:

Far beneath the Boarding House of St Onans, if you knew just where the secret panel that gave you access to the long corridor was located, you would be able to merrily stroll along the immaculately clean passageway, and up to the new metal ladder at the end. If you carefully descended the ladder (hold on properly now, and don't scuff your new shoes on the sides), you would come to an expertly-varnished folding door. This was the door to the lift. The lift took passengers down to the very lowest levels of the Groundling domain, where some quite complex and skilled building works were being carried out.

It had been a long time since Jedekiah and the Elders had finally been persuaded to open up a rock club on their premises, and a restaurant called "The Vault", which served beautifully cooked food to all customers. No-one ever left the restaurant feeling hungry, and not one customer ever left unamazed at the décor – not to mention the polite and welcoming attitude of the serving staff. It had been Jedekiah's idea to use the facilities to provide free food and regular lodgings for the homeless people of the surrounding town. The underground network of rooms had greatly expanded, and now included a hairdressing salon, bespoke tailor's shop, shoe repair station, and a very well-stocked library. In the upper levels on alternate Tuesdays, Mrs Bradley the Academy Cook and her team gave cookery classes to anyone who might feel like turning up. Ever inventive in their building expertise, the Groundlings had established a network of tunnels and passageways which led to nearly every classroom in the school – and so a wide range of facilities could be partaken and enjoyed by visitors, even if their visits had to be shall we say, somewhat clandestine in nature.

At the moment, Samuel, Lemuel and Obadiehard (he loved the films- don't ask…) were drilling down to tap into the freshwater spring that ran beneath the Academy. This would, when fully connected and tweaked, provide unlimited water supply for the new shower units which they had installed especially for the homeless visitors. The work was going nicely – in fact (sorry- I'm going to say it…) it was going well.

Obadiehard raised his safety goggles, scratched his chin, and announced:

'Sorry to worry thee Samuel, but dids't thee hear that just then? I tell thee – it sounded as if the drill had broken through into altogether softer rock…'

'If thou hast bust that drill again Chummy – it will verily be stopped out of thy wages this time!' answered Samuel.

'Thou might have just gone off course with thy drilling, Obadiehard' said Lemuel, 'Thou must admit that every time thou gettest anywhere near expensive equipment, then HoBi dost smite thee with fingers which are mightily buttered…'

'Thou art a fine one to talk!' said Obadiehard – 'that wall that thee replastered for me last Lammastide…verily the job was rubbish!'

'I swear by the Grace of HoBi - The finish on that wall was nothing short of perfection!' said Lemuel, rather hurt. 'Anyway, thou cannot talk, any tool that thee gets thy hands on – thou loses it in about a minute! Remember how thee lost that brand new spirit level?'

'And dost thou remember how I found it again when all of the plaster dropped off that wall? – because thou hadst plastered over the bloody thing!...' answered Obadiehard.

'Look, will thee both stop arguing…' said Samuel, 'We must verily get this well sorted, because Jedekiah is getting very worried about the cost of water which we must pay. If we cannot get our own water supply, then we shall not be able to help all of the needy people who require our services. It is a well-known fact that we are skint Brothers: and if thee dost not get on with it, then I tell thee verily: the boot of the Brother Elder Jedekiah shall smite our sorry arses mightily…'

The argument ceased. It was decided that the gang would go and fetch some fresh drill sections, and return to finish tapping into the spring. They walked off up the corridor, and climbed the ladder up to the upper level workshop.

Behind them, quietly and completely unnoticed, water had begun to seep up and out of the drilling hole. There had been a very good reason as to why the sound of their drill had suddenly and subtly changed its tone. Out of the hole, the fluid was now seeping faster from the aperture, and was pooling in quantity on the cellar floor. Their work had been more accurate than they had realised.

The liquid that now bubbled out of the drill hole was not the pure, fresh and clear water from the underground spring. This water was slow moving, viscous, and inky-black – and was currently selling at a price of sixty-three American dollars a barrel…

Encased in her tweedy carapace, miss Emilia Piggott was now reaching the final stages of planning for her big venture. All she needed to do now, was to settle on an exact date for her action. She scowled in mild distaste at the calendar on the wall, torn between fixing a specific day in her mind, and admiring the photograph of a ridiculously fluffy kitten poking its head out of a flowerpot. Of course – Easter! This would be the ideal time, and since the Academy would be on a week's holiday, there should be enough time to do what must be done, and fit in a suitable amount of chocolate consumption.

She was still struggling to finalise the Guest Speaker for the afternoon of Founder's Day. It had always been the tradition at St Onans that a suitably inspiring guest be invited to address the boys. The purpose was to try and motivate the boys, and drive them on to greater achievements. Miss P hoped that there would not be a repeat of last year's debacle, when their guest had been the Chairman of the British Union of Trawler men – who had only agreed to come and speak at the Academy because he had mis-read the written request that had been sent to him, and thought that the invitation had said "Flounders Day".

Dr Chambers had been asked to assist with procuring the services of an interesting speaker for the occasion, but had not been very successful so far in gaining access to the hallowed ground of the Headmaster's study. He had stood patiently in the draughty corridor, and been amazed by the voice that he could hear coming from the other side of the door. It sounded as if the Head were talking to himself. Chambers could only hear one half of a conversation, which baffled him:

'Yes, of Course Your Majesty...Well indeed – one does try to exhibit the very highest standards...No Your Majesty, I have never considered it a burden...You are very kind, Your Majesty...Shall I bend down a little?...Why Yes Your Majesty! – I would be honoured to have any future Princes as members of this Academy...Naturally Your Majesty, I seek no Honours for myself, but hope that I may be able to help Charitable Causes by using this award...Why yes, Your Majesty, how kind of you to notice – it is in fact a specialist surgical device which I have to wear due to an old bingo-calling accident...'

Had the man gone stark raving mad? This was strange to say the least, as it normally took at least three years at St Onans, for the symptoms of insanity to begin showing outwardly. Chambers knocked again on the study door- this time with more ferocity. From within, there was the sound of someone being surprised mid-sentence, and knocking objects off a desk. The door was opened by Farmer, who was in an agitated state.

'What do you want? – I was busy' he declared.

'We need to sort out a speaker for the Founders Day lecture Headmaster' said Chambers.

Dr Matthews had followed Chambers into the Head's room, and stood grinning amiably just behind him, smelling noticeably of expensive cognac...

'I need to get an invitation sent out now Headmaster, because we don't want any repeats of the disasters which we have had in previous years' stated Chambers.

120

'Have we not always had good forthright, motivational and interesting speakers?' asked Farmer.

Dr Chambers looked at the carpet, as Matthews tittered behind him. 'It has not always been the success for which we had hoped...' said Chambers, 'In the past, we invited Sir Michael Whipp to address the boys. He set up his own hair-gel business in the North of Scotland, but he let us down at the last moment – citing a sudden illness as the cause for his absence'.

'Oh yes...Slick Mick from Wick, went sick...' said Matthews.

'And then we sought the services of William Cropper – the manufacturer of bathroom fittings. He turned up most elegantly dressed, but rather disgraced himself by not making adequate use of the zip on his trousers..' explained Chambers.

'Ah yes – we all remember Cropper, who made stoppers, turned up in his Topper, and we all saw his ch-'

'-I am well aware of what we all saw Dr Matthews...' said Chambers, swiftly. 'There was also the incident involving Cranston Spooley. He claimed that he could deliver a great motivational speech, based upon his own life experiences. We treated him to a slap-up dinner in the dining hall, including a selection of fine wines - after which he proceeded to make remarks of a lewd nature to the Matron, remove all of his clothing, and had to be escorted from the premises by the Police...'

'Spooley...' said Matthews, 'Attested, digested, suggested, divested – and arrested...'

Chambers glared at his giggling colleague, and carried on – 'At very short notice, we were able to obtain the services of Sir Donald Mulgate, who had for many years acted as the Attaché to Saudi Arabia. He came down all the way from the North specially to help us out. The visit was ruined by some boy who had vandalised the quad entrance, and then insulted the man by attempting to blacken his reputation!'

'Indeed – Mulgate, our Surrogate from Harrogate, who worked for the Potentate of a Foreign State, was jammed in the narrow gate by some Reprobate, who then proceeded to Denigrate…'

Chambers and the Headmaster stared at Matthews…

'Well I am certain that this year, the Founders Day service will have a guest of an altogether more Noble bearing – not that I am able to divulge any more information at this point in time' said Farmer, smiling benignly, yet still casting odd glances at Matthews. 'Suffice to say that matters are – in hand'. A *white-gloved* hand, he failed to add…

That seemed to be the end of the conversation. Chambers and Matthews found themselves ushered swiftly out of the study door and back into the corridor. Dr Chambers looked mystified, whereas Matthews was smiling broadly at his colleague.

'Sorry – what was it that you wanted Dr Matthews?' asked Chambers.

'Oh yes, nearly forgot! I wanted to give you this…' said Matthews. He produced a brown paper bag out of his jacket pocket, and handed it to the Deputy Head. The bag was heavy, and out of it Chambers pulled a large Shire Horseshoe.

'Oh, err…thank you very much' he said.

'Please tell me that you don't already have one?' said Matthews.

'No…no indeed I don't' said Chambers.

'It's really lucky!' said the delighted History Master.

'How thoughtful – thank you again…' said Chambers.

As Matthews staggered off down the corridor, Chambers heard him mutter – 'Bloody lucky for me anyway… thought that I'd never get rid of the damn thing…'

The local Town Police were baffled. There seemed to have been a spate of recent offences which the Force had never encountered in all its years of masterly inactivity. Desk Sergeant Dickens scratched his head – greatly increasing the risk of splinters, and thumbed through a large legal tome that he had liberated from the tiny Police "library", at the back of the old filing cabinets in the back office, near the wicker dog-basket, next to the as-yet-unclaimed artificial leg in the corner. Despite bringing to bear all of his accumulated Policing skills from his years in the force, he was unable to find any legal precedent which might be able to apply to this string of outrages.

''Ere, Constable Swallow – you're a legal expert aren't yer?' asked the Sergeant.

'Not really Sarge…' he answered.

'But I thought that you said that when it came to crime, you had (and I quote) "the whole package" sorted out.

'Yes Sarge, but I was referring to the fact that I have got the complete box sets of *Midsomer Murders* and *Inspector Morse* DVDs in Mum's sideboard cabinet…' said Swallow. 'I just can't see what, assuming that we ever catch them, that we could possibly charge them with!'.

Figg, Swall and Bert "Bendy" Fletcher had been at it again. Under the direction of Gregor Duggan, they had set about finding impoverished Pensioners within the community, and waiting around the corner until they left their property unattended. Once they had gone out – in went the FSF team, and once they had gained entry, they would fit complete new kitchens, and re-decorate. The owners of the property returned to find a home make-over, and a vase of fresh flowers on the kitchen table. If the house had looked a little under-nourished in the cash department to the men, then there was usually a nice wad of notes left on the side of the sink. The local Police had been inundated with reports from bemused Senior Citizens, who didn't want to make a complaint as such – but did want to find out who to thank for their generosity. Thus far, Granchester's Finest had drawn a complete blank…

Constable Swallow put down the legal casebook which the Sergeant had forced upon him. 'It's no good Sarge…' he declared, 'there's just no legal precedent for taking action against someone who is intent on doing good deeds – I mean, what the hell could we ever charge them with?'

'Malicious Improvement?' said the Sergeant.

'Breaking and Decorating, perhaps?' added Swallow.

'Going equipped to commit Wallpapering?', Dickens mused.

'Committing Grievous Bodily Artex?' said Constable Mills, stirring his tea.

'There's nothing that we can get 'em on lads...' said the Sergeant, gloomily – 'They've even done work on the gardens at some houses...'

'Right – then we've got 'em there!' said Dickens.

'How's that then Sarge?' asked Swallow.

'We charge 'em with Fencing!!' said the happy Sergeant.

In the gymnasium at St Onans, there was a similar amount of confusion which had just occurred. There was a basketball game taking place between members of the Fourth Form. The action raced from end to end, as each side attempted to score a basket, only to have the attempt blocked – at which point the opposing side would take possession of the ball and hurtle down to the other end of the court. An infringement in the "key area" had led to the Sports Master Hair blowing his whistle enthusiastically, and dislodging his errant toupee in the process. As the Master fought to restore the ginger beast to its proper location atop his bonce, the boy lined up with the ball at the edge of the shooting area for the throw.

The boys stood in lines around the edges of the key zone, waiting to pounce on the ball, should the boy's shot rebound off the hoop. The player grasped the ball, one hand under, and one toward the back, in preparation for launching the ball toward its goal. Mr Carter blew his whistle, and the other boys tensed, ready for action. There was a sudden shout of pain from the boy taking the penalty shot.

'What the hell's the matter with you, Allenby?' asked Carter.

The boy answered with his eyes wide in fear:

'The ball Sir...it just bit me!!'...

Chapter Fifteen:

It should by all normal standards have been a lesson all about our Climate, the Weather, and various ways in which the Meteorological Intelligencia seek to predict our share of daily rainfall. It was anything but. Today was the day that Mr Thwaite the Geography Master (or as you will by now be aware – Miss Geraldine Thwaite, the Geography *Mistress*…) received his (or her) visit from the Assessors.

Thwaite was extremely nervous about their presence, and vowed to be on "top form" during the lesson, enough to impress the adjudicators in the room, and deflect any possible threat to his future career prospects. It had all gone quite swimmingly, until Thwaite had allowed himself to be side-tracked during a question from the class concerning rainfall over the French Alps. For some inexplicable reason (let's call it…Weatherill, for instance) the conversation had drifted off into the realms of the French Revolution, and the exquisite dress sense of one M Antoinette. As the boys sat back and relaxed, basking in the satisfaction of a goalpost well and truly moved – Thwaite went into full flow, gushing expansively about wonderful silks, wigs, shoes and lace. When he got to describing some of the more elaborate jewellery which was worn, well now, he really changed up into top gear.

It was the steely interruption of the Assessor, whose voice had fallen like the blade of the guillotine, that had finally shocked Thwaite back into reality.

'And that Boys…is why however grand we may think ourselves to have become, we are always at the mercy of the weather…' said Thwaite, hoping that he might crow-bar the lesson back on track with a seamless link. He hurriedly lurched into a description of the workings and uses of an Aneroid Barometer, hid himself in one of the evacuated chambers at the back, and hoped that no-one would notice.

Indeed they had noticed. As the lesson ended, the Assessors felt silently out of the room. The last man out tore a sheet of yellow paper from his clip board, and placed it on Thwaite's desk, face down. The poor Geography Master was almost too terrified to turn over the paper, but what he saw when he did so, was most unexpected. The Assessor appeared to have written down his telephone number.

Whether it was some sort of "efficiency drive" that was taking place, or perhaps some "Assess One, get One Free" offer, the Review Body had decided to make the Music room their next chosen port of call on their luxury cruise around the Academy. Their brief sortie onto land, away from the SS Criticism, would not include the purchase of over-sized straw hats, stuffed donkeys, badly-painted castanets, or bullfight posters bearing the name of "El Torro – Alf Clegg". Little did they realise that they were just about to encounter one of the most powerful educational forces ever to tread the creaking wooden floors of St Onans. Mr Newhouse was the name of that force, and despite the fact that he displayed an air of rebellion, and a marked distaste for anything that even vaguely resembled rules, he cared passionately about his music. When giving his classes "music appreciation", he would play recordings of the great classical pieces at a volume that would rattle the windows, and cause the mice behind the walls to put on their ear defenders. 'It's gotta be loud!!' he would shout – 'Orchestras are not quiet things…Holst and Wagner should blow the pants off the audience!'. He is right about that in every respect…

The Assessors sat at the back of the class, and prepared to take notes. Newhouse noted their self-righteous and snooty expressions – and prepared to take the piss. The lesson was structured to show just how themes and harmony are used to give a sense of power, and included an eclectic mix of Gustav Holst, Gary Moore, Mussorgsky, Metallica, Dvorak and Dave Lee Roth. Newhouse was his usual animated self throughout the lesson, playing "air guitar" with aggression and style, and at one stage, playing drums on the head of Mark Davis. Nicky and his friends loved it – the class of Newhouse was just as much about performance as it was the actual music. He didn't just play it…he really lived it. It was considered an honour and a rare privilege indeed to have witnessed a Newhouse guitar lesson –

and then see him destroy the unfortunate instrument against the wall at the end of the lesson. On days when he felt rather less inclined toward demolition, he would merely set fire to the piano.

As the strains of *A Little ain't Enough* by Dave Lee Roth faded out, Newhouse noticed that one boy was sitting with a look of boredom and disinterest on his face…

'Rock, Roll, and Rachmaninov…yer can't lick it!' said Newhouse. 'Right Lordsley – you've got a face like a well-smacked arse…what's the problem, eh?'

'Well Sir…' began the boy (in the full knowledge that he had the ear of the Assessors),'I don't see why I need to learn Music'.

'Music is life…' answered Newhouse.

(scribble, scribble, scribble, went the Assessors at the back…)

'It's not going to be my life Sir' answered Lordsley.

'And why is that – poor delusional boy?' asked Newhouse.

(scribble, scribble…)

'I intend to become a Banker…' said Lordsley.

'You already are' said Newhouse.

'Sorry Sir..?.'

'My apologies – I must have misheard you' said Newhouse.

(scribble, scribble…)

'I simply do not see the need to learn music…' Lordsley stated, with a glance behind him.

Newhouse gave a long sigh, and climbed up to sit on the edge of the piano.

'Music gives us everything, whether it is the life-giving beat within our chest, or the earliest Stone-Age man banging out a rhythm on a hollow log. Music is Mathematical – the notes are laid out on the staves with numerical precision, and we count in order to keep time to the beat of a metronome. We measure the bars until we come in with our power chords, and feel the tempo of the piece. Music gives us exercise – mental and physical, if we are putting all of ourselves into it that is: just observe the drummer in any rock band, and see how much energy he or she puts into their performance. Playing a musical instrument teaches us manual dexterity'.

(scribble, scribble…)

'Music sings to us the songs of History, as we play the works of the great Composers from long ago. Most of you will know songs from the time of King Henry VIII and perhaps even earlier…Music is food for the Soul, it can be intensely spiritual – it can raise us to the heights of joy, and calm us when we are anxious. It can give us healing and peace in times of trouble'

(scribble, scribble…)

Newhouse stood up on top of the piano:

'We also communicate through music – whether it is playing to other people, or taking part as a member of a group or orchestra. Even the busker on the street corner is "speaking" to the passers-by. If you have ever been in the audience at a rock gig, then you will see exactly what I mean. The crowd are like the fans at a big football match – but everyone is on the same team. When your favourite band plays your favourite song, it's better than winning the FA cup! People across the planet who do not speak each other's language can be bonded together in music – it is the Universal language of harmony for all mankind. We have even sent our world's music out into space, where it may one day be enjoyed by other beings who live far outside our galaxy. Most of all perhaps…music is Art. Music can paint a picture in our mind, with just as much depth and colour as was ever achieved by Leonardo. There is art in the simplest melody sung to a baby as a lullaby, and just as much in the slide-guitar playing of the old man in the swamps of Louisiana. He may not be able to read or write – but he can sing to your soul like Tchaikovsky, if you just listen….

Music Gentlemen…Music is Life itself.'

Newhouse punched the air, as the boys leapt to their feet and cheered. There was a clatter of falling clipboards as the Assessors joined in with the applause. They picked up their equipment, waited whilst Newhouse leapt down from atop the piano, and heartily shook the hand of the Music Master on their way out of the classroom. Newhouse let the door close behind them. He turned back to the class of smiling boys.

'I hope you all paid attention to that, Lads…' he said.

'But honestly, just so you know – "Dance music" and "Boy Bands" are shite!!'.

'WE ARE ANGRY!' shouted the graffiti that had magically begun to appear on any spare wall or vacant space on noticeboards throughout the Academy. The Resistance movement that had sprung up against the newly-imposed iron laws of the new Head, were now intent on making their shadowy presence felt. This campaign of "announcing with menaces" was the latest in a string of measures designed to rebel against the new system. The message had been sprayed in large letters on the wall of the Physics laboratory which faced into the quad. (The Revolutionary tone of the slogan had been slightly spoiled by Mark Davis, who in a moment of supreme dietary weakness, had amended the last word of the phrase to "Hungry").

Comrade Bill had convened a number of meetings with the boys of St Onans, and it had been unanimously agreed (by Comrade Bill) that the best and most effective way forward would be to organise a mass protest (led by Comrade Bill). To back up this collective action, there would be a strike (led by Comrade Bill) of all Academy students. There would be a rally in the quad, and a guest speaker would address the striking masses (Comrade Bill). Bill had planned to produce placards and posters to support their protest, which should have been ready and distributed by now, but there had been a slight delay in the production pipeline – as Bill's Mum needed their front room for her knitting circle ladies on a Wednesday night…

Dr Matthews had heard all about the boys' protest on the ever-active St Onans grapevine. He had instantly recalled the wonderful days of his own Student Protests whilst at University. He had decided there and then to lend his wholehearted support to their cause. He immediately organised his own personal "sit-in" in solidarity with his students. He would continue his protests until the forces of oppression were well and truly ground into the dust, and truth, justice and equality had once again triumphed. He decided to have his sit-in protest over the road at the "Five Crowns" ...

The younger members of the Groundlings had pledged their support for the would-be strikers, and had suggested that they act as a kind of "Underground Resistance Movement".

On a day-to-day basis, the boys had agreed to take any and all possible opportunity to confuse and disrupt the enemy. Whilst non-compliance with a given instruction was out of the question, as it would lead to immediate disciplinary action, they found that adopting a policy of strict *compliance* would do just as nicely. When a boy was told to 'fill the sink' in a Chemistry lesson for instance, it was hardly the fault of the boy if no order had subsequently been issued to turn off the taps. There was a "no running" policy in relation to the bottom corridor of the Old Block. Quite right too, in the interests of safety. Miles Bannister had found out to his utter frustration however, that there was no Academy rule that made any mention of hopping...

Even that doyenne of decency, that paragon of propriety, the master of morality that was William Trevill had staged his own small rebellion during a Divinity lesson. He had immediately been taken out of the class by the Reverend Felchingham, and escorted to the study of Dr Chambers the Deputy Head. Whilst Trevill stood impassively just outside the open door, the Rev was stating his case loudly to the bemused Chambers.

'I really am not prepared to put up with this!' the Rev had declared.

'And what is it exactly, that you are prepared not to be prepared to put up ...er...with?' Chambers asked.

'I want his boy disciplined!' demanded Felchingham.

'And what has he done?' enquired the Deputy Head.

'He has used the "F" word during my lesson...' said the Rev.

Chambers frowned, and called Trevill into his study. The boy stood impassively before the desk. Chambers reached into his drawer, and withdrew a discipline slip. He paused, with his pen hovering just above the paper.

'Is what I am told by the Reverend true, Trevill?' said Chambers.

'Yes Surrr, Oi did indeed say the worrrd' he answered.

'And for the sake of my records, will you please repeat the "F" word which you used?'

'Yes Surrr – it wurr "Floccinaucinihilipilification" ...'

'Pardon?...' said Chambers, aghast.

The Deputy Head stared at the Reverend. They both turned and stared at Trevill. Trevill grinned back at them. There was an uncomfortable silence...

'Why have you considered it necessary to bring this boy to my study, Reverend?' said Chambers, calmly.

'Well Charles – it's just that...it's just...I have absolutely no idea what the word means!' squeaked the Rev.

'It do mean "contemptuously dismissing something as worthless", according to moi Dad' Trevill helpfully informed the Masters.

Chambers continued to stare at Trevill, open-mouthed.

'Please return this boy to his class...' instructed Chambers.

'But Charles – he, I mean, I don't...' stuttered the Rev.

'Look Gerald...I am very busy at the moment, so why don't - '

'But I cannot have-'

'GERALD! ... WILL YOU JUST B- just buy yourself a decent dictionary, there's a good fellow' said Chambers.

Dorset 1...Establishment 0.

Chapter Sixteen:

Nicky was fifteen and three months old. Having grown up in a rural community with woodlands and fields on all sides, the various species that he encountered on a regular basis held no terrors for him. He wasn't afraid of heights, he would spend hours outside with his telescope in the pitch dark, and he made a point of capturing visiting spiders, and giving them their liberty. It was a little strange then, that the very thought of Ballroom Dancing absolutely petrified him…

Farmer had instructed that a weekly portion of the boys' drama classes be given over to dance lessons involving the girls from the local St Gertrude's Academy. This was supposed to equip the young men of St Onans with the skills that they needed for the future. Nicky pictured the day that he turned up for a job interview for the position of Assistant Nuclear Scientist, only to be turned down by the interview panel because his Foxtrot was considered to be rather below par. He had sought the advice of Mum and Auntie –

'But I don't even know which bits I am allowed to get hold of!' he had wailed.

'It might be a case of "Trial and Error" then…' said Auntie.

'What do you mean?' he asked.

'Well, if you make the error of grabbing the wrong bits – you will probably end up on Trial!' said Auntie, giggling.

'You might make some new friends, with all of those nice young ladies about' Mum said.

'Oh yes Mum – I can really see that happening. Those girls from St Gertrude's have their noses so far in the air, that when you look them in the face, you can see behind them!'.

What had made things worse were the disturbing dreams that he had been having recently. He was standing on the polished dancefloor in elegant evening dress, with a sea of admiring faces which lined the floor on all sides. Through the crowd of fellow dancers had emerged a vision in black silk. Jozza had made her way toward him with an enigmatic smile on her face, as she lovingly took his hand. He had placed his hand delicately around her waist, and had smiled in acknowledgement of a secret shared only by themselves. He glanced down, noting the silver laces in her biker boots, and breathing in the soft and enticing promise of her delicate perfume. The music had begun, and they spun and twirled away, lost in their own private reverie as the envious onlookers gazed at them. The beams of the spotlights glinted off her deaths-head earrings, and reflected the myriad hues of her Apache Indian necklace. As his head swum, his eyes fell to check the dream-like motion of his own feet, encased in their highly-polished shoes, and realised that he was not wearing any trousers…

He had mentioned the dream to Auntie. She had listened to the boy without any hint of mockery. When he had finished, she had gently taken his hand and explained –

'That's why your choice of trousers is so important when it comes to dancing' she said.

'Really?' asked Nicky.

'Oh yes! You see, it is important to make sure that you've got enough ballroom…'

Auntie folded over with laughter, Mum suddenly found the washing-up in the sink very interesting, and Nicky went an impressive shade of red…

Tapping on the inside of his head though, was a tiny but insistent thought that was doing its best to attract his attention. What if…what if he did actually learn to dance – as a means of luring the lovely Jozza to some posh venue, and then impressing her with his nimble footwork? Would she possibly go for it? It had to be worth a try, and he had to find some means of luring the object of his desires away from that pillock who he had christened "Red Car Rod". That idiot had legs like cocktail sticks, that didn't look capable of supporting his upper body, never mind perform the sort of elegant dancing that Jozza so richly deserved.

Like the fabled Knight Errant, who rides battle-weary into the ravaged settlement and gives aid to the cowering inhabitants, Uncle

Joe knocked at the back door. Had he been such a famous man of legend, he would have tethered his faithful horse outside. It was far more plausible to imagine that Uncle would have already sold the horse – or at very least rented it out at an exorbitant hourly rate. Joe was ushered into the kitchen, plied with tea and the last of the decent biscuits, and told all about the dancing scenario. He had immediately vowed to go straight back up to his house, and return with an evening dress suit which would "suit the boy down to the ground". Just how long was the jacket?

As good as his word, Joe had leapt up from the table, and sprinted to his car. He screeched off towards the top of the village in a cloud of exhaust smoke – forcing the local Postman off the road and into the thorny hedge.

He returned half an hour later with something black which was wrapped in brown paper, and smelled very strongly of mothballs. Mum refused to let Joe open the parcel on their table, and so the mysterious treasure was revealed on the kitchen floor. Much to the surprise of everyone in the room, the dress suit was in first-class condition.

'How's about that then Lad?' declared Uncle, 'I haven't worn it since they sent me to meet Mahatma Gandhi on Nottingham railway station – look, I've still got his comb in the pocket'.

'But Gandhi was bald, Joe…' said Mum.

'I didn't say that the suit was *new*, did I…' said Joe. 'Get the Lad to try it on'.

'He's not trying it on until we've done something about the smell!' said Mum.

'Well maybe if he has a bath, it won't get into the suit?' said Auntie.

Mum gave her "a look", and Auntie buried her head back in the Racing Section of the newspaper.

'We'll hang the suit outside for a while, and let some fresh air blow through it' said Mum, 'That should get rid of the smell of mothballs. Is there anything else in any of the pockets that we need to be aware of?' she asked Uncle Joe.

'Yeah – I think I've still got Elvis Presley's Swiss Army knife in the inside pocket' he answered.

'Has it got one of those little tools for extracting bullshit?' asked Auntie.

Joe gave her a wounded look, thanked Mum for the tea, and left in a huff. (This took him a little longer than expected – so it was probably more like a minute and a huff).

'Right then My Boy…' said Auntie, folding her newspaper and placing it on the table, 'I think that it's time for some lessons…'

Bannister, Rundell, Darwin, Strangler, Captain Brayfield and "Miss" Thwaite had been given the Royal Command to appear in the study of the Headmaster. Miles Bannister was staring at a yellow square which had been stuck onto the wall just above the filing cabinet. On the piece of paper was written "buy more Post-it notes". The Head gave a slight cough, and began:

'Gentlemen, I have called you here to inform you that I am at this moment awaiting confirmation of a very important visitor, who will be coming to the Academy after the Easter break, and who will be guest of honour at our Founder's Day celebrations. I am not of course, permitted at this time to divulge the identity of our guest, but suffice to say, their presence will put St Onans clearly on the map as the top educational establishment in the Country. It is with this in mind that I have chosen to press forward with my programme of refinements, with regard to the behaviour and standard of uniform for our students.'

The Masters looked at each other. They had heard similar speeches all too often. The bus of common sense was rounding the corner of inevitability, and was about to turn into the dead-end-street of revenue raising. They looked over at Dr Chambers for a clue, but

136

he merely rolled his eyes and returned to studying the papers in front of him.

'In addition to enhancing the general demeanour and appearance of St Onans...' the Head stated, 'Before we are visited by R-...by an important person, I require that the Academy be brought up to standard in the decoration department. In order to ensure that this happens Gentlemen, we must have adequate funds to hire in the services of various tradesmen. I have taken a long, hard look at the petty cash totals which we hold at present, and have found...'

(he nodded to Dr Chambers, who lifted a sheet of paper and read from it...)

'Erm...ninety-seven pounds and fifty-two pence, twenty-nine Euros, five Australian dollars, eight Polish Zloty, eleven foreign coins of unknown origin – and six washers of various sizes...'

'So you see Gentlemen, we are in the position of having to raise revenue in order that the very necessary work can be carried out. To this end, I have been in contact with some rather influential friends of mine, who happen to be the Directors of local Businesses. They have intimated that they will be willing to donate sums of money to St Onans, in return for being able to utilise some of our vacant advertising space'.

'Could you be a little more specific, Headmaster?' asked Rundell, from behind his bandaged nose.

'Let me explain...' said the smiling Head. He was the only man in the room whose face was not frozen in anticipation...

'It was explained to me at a recent meeting of my friends who are Fr- of my friends who run local firms, that it is possible to raise a large sum of revenue by allowing Sponsors to advertise their Company on the shirts of Football Clubs.'

'You want us to form a football team?' asked Bannister.

'Oh no, indeed I do not...' laughed the Head. 'I merely want you all to consider what unused and readily-seen space might be made available to a possible advertiser'.

'Sorry Head – I'm not with you' said Captain Brayfield.

Farmer leaned back in his chair, which made the predictable but yet acutely-embarrassing sound as if on cue…

'If we wish to look to the future – then we perhaps need to pay attention to what is already behind us' said Farmer. As a body, the assembled Masters turned around and looked at the wall…The Head gave a sigh of annoyance, and signalled to Dr Chambers.

'The Head is suggesting that we permit the advertising of local firms on the clothing that we wear' said Chambers.

'I am certainly not going to wear a football shirt!' declared Thwaite.

'No Gerald – ine, I presume the Head is referring to our gowns' said Chambers.

'Football gowns? – never heard of such a bloody silly idea!' said Strangler.

The Headmaster cast a rather angry glance at Dr Chambers, and shook his head.

'Now listen here…we can raise a lot of money. All we need to do is let the Firms put their adverts somewhere that they will be seen on a regular basis' stated the Head.

'Let's cut to the chase here shall we…' said Darwin, 'exactly where are these adverts going to be placed?'.

'The advertisements will be displayed tactfully, on the back of the gown of every member of Staff…' declared Farmer.

'Over my dead body!' shouted Captain Brayfield.

'Indeed… Bury and Sons, the local Undertakers, were one of the first Businesses to express an interest in the scheme!' said Farmer.

'Just who else is involved in this bloody fiasco?' demanded Strangler.

The Head again nodded to Dr Chambers, who scrabbled around on his desk, until he located another sheet. 'Ahh…so far, we have Dobney's Industrial Carpets…'

'Oh Lovely…that's just ruddy marvellous' said Rundell, 'So in order to get you some cash – I've got to walk around all day with "DIC" written on my back, have I?'

The other Masters seemed to find this exceptionally amusing. The Head was not pleased when he saw the grin on the face of Dr Chambers. 'Well I have a meeting at the Lodge on Friday night – and I intend to inform them that I have obtained consent from you all for the proposed scheme to go ahead' stated Farmer. Miss Thwaite raised a questioning hand...

'Head...would it perhaps be possible for the Sponsor to give us small badges with their logo on it?' he asked.

'Why would that be necessary?' said Farmer, 'there is much more space available on the back of your gowns?'

'I was thinking more along the lines of evening gowns...' said Thwaite.

Chapter Seventeen:

As the Police Officers entered the quad, they were forced to edge their car carefully and slowly around the massed column of pupils who were marching around the quad in silence, and who were carrying placards with various anti-establishment slogans written on them. Finally finding a safe parking space, Detective Inspector Mike Posta got out of the car and gazed around the austere enclosure of the Academy. It was strangely comforting to be back at the place, and he remembered some of the fun that he had during his previous stint as a "pretend" Teacher.

He closed the car door, and leaned against the vehicle whilst he lit a cigarette. A passing boy was carrying a placard which read "Defy the Snip!". Posta thought that the lads seemed a little too young to be holding a protest about Family Planning, but what the hell – this was after all, St Onans. He caught sight of a familiar face: it was a grinning and red face, which was attached to a body that was veering somewhat uncertainly across the quad. The face (and the veering) belonged to his good pickled friend Dr Gus Matthews. He strode up to the History Master, and shook his hand with vigour.

'Matthews!...Hello' he said. The Master attempted to focus on him.

'Same surname as m'self...who'd have guessed it! Hang on a moment – it's Michael Pasta isn't it?' said Matthews.

'Posta..' said Mike Posta.

'Pesto – that's what I said...' answered Matthews.

'Is the Headmaster in?' asked the DI.

'You managed to get an audience with old Vermin? My word! You are a lucky boy, Mr Pistol' said Matthews. 'Has the Farmer been a naughty boy then?'.

'Not that I know of. My lads have been called in because a car has apparently been stolen. One of the Masters telephoned us, and told us that it had "gone walkies" from where he had parked it' said Posta.

140

'Happens a lot, especially with Rovers…' said Matthews.

Posta watched as his friend weaved away unsteadily, and was fascinated to note that a local off-license was advertising on the back of Matthews' gown. Sponsors normally insisted that anyone who advertised their product or services actually used them. In the case of Dr Matthews, you would require a considerably larger gown in order to mention all of the alcoholic beverages which he sampled on a regular basis, or maybe something like a tent – a beer tent would be ideal…

When Miss Piggott had set eyes on Mike Posta she had panicked…She had a churning feeling in the very pit of her stomach. She began to perspire with tension. Had the Police somehow got wind of her plan? Or had she merely got wind? No, it was not possible. She had been so careful not to breathe a word about her intentions. Anyway, there was no chance of her being arrested for a crime which she had not yet committed. She would do exactly what she had done when her Sister had accused her of stealing her boyfriend, and called her a "Hussy" – she would brazen it out…

'Look Dick – all I'm saying is, is it possible?' demanded Professor Darwin. His colleague Strangler put his finger up to his lips and made a worried face:

'Well in theory, I suppose that it is possible. We know absolutely nothing about the life form which we encountered, apart from the fact that they are spherical in appearance. There is every reason to suggest that they would have some sort of evolved defence mechanism, and as with various animals on the planet – camouflage is a very effective method of dealing with any perceived threat. The trouble is, that we are a school, and in any school there are so many similarly-shaped objects – in the gym, on the sports fields, and all over the place…'

'That's a lot of balls…' said Darwin.

'Mock my theory as you may, but if one of the life-forms has come back with us through the Vortex and hidden amongst similarly-shaped objects, then we're going to have one heck of a job to find it – which we must do. We have no idea if the thing is dangerous or not, how it thinks, or what it might do when it gets hungry…'

'A sort of Teenager then?' said Darwin.

'I don't think that the concept of spotty, petulant, sulking spheroids rolling around the Academy venting their dimensionally-displaced spleens upon anyone with whom they come into contact with, is any subject to be taken lightly' said Strangler, chewing on the end of a handy pencil. 'What we need to do is to gather a squad of trustworthy boys, and mount a campaign to systematically check all of the balls which we come across. When they have been checked and found to be "normal", then we mark them with something. By a process of elimination, we are bound to come across the "intruder" sooner or later…'

'Yes – and it will be easy to spot a ball with a chalk-mark on it, if it happens to be chewing on a human leg at the time' said Darwin.

'The watchwords that spring to mind for our campaign must be "authenticate: isolate: eliminate"' said Strangler.

'How about "deny: ignore: hide: deny again?' asked Darwin.

'No Johnathan – that simply will not do. They're bound to trace the problem back to us in the end anyway. We get a team together right this instant, and start our hunt…'

Darwin had fallen silent, an odd grin on his face. Professor Strangler knew only too well how the mind of his colleague was apt to work in such circumstances. Before Darwin could speak, he added:

'If you are about to suggest that we name our search-and-destroy squad "Ballbusters", I am going to have to do something unpleasant to you - with this pencil…'

Darwin frowned at his friend. 'So we mark off all bouncy, round objects – right?'

'That is correct' said Strangler.

142

'Can I just clarify – does that, or does that not, include Mrs Bradley?'

'I don't think that you are taking this terribly seriously, are you…'

There was another short period of silence, and the butterfly mind of Professor Darwin could almost be heard as it ground together the mechanical cogs of all reason. The man raised a questioning finger (never a good sign), and mused –

'I was just wondering, cogitating if you will, on the subject of reproduction…'

'You've been warned about that sort of thing before…' said Strangler.

'I was thinking…what do you consider that their process of reproduction might entail? They obviously have some means of creating more of their kind: would it be through cellular division? Might they achieve it via absorbsion? Perhaps some form of complicated form of cellular osmosis? I wonder how we might distinguish the Male from the Female of the specie? (assuming of course, that they are not asexual or hermaphrodites). How would they advertise their "availability" during any breeding cycle? What exactly would a spheroid Boy look for in a spheroid Girl? It's fascinating, when you come to think of it!' exclaimed Darwin.

'Look – I can see exactly where this is all heading…' said Strangler, 'and if you are about to make any sort of statement which is likely to include the terms "Balloons" and "Page Three", then I shall be forced to have you sedated and removed…again'.

'I am merely exhibiting all of the questioning traits of a healthy and inquisitive scientific mind…' stated Darwin.

'You need to get out in the fresh air more…' answered his colleague.

Professor Strangler continued to chew thoughtfully on the pencil. His pensive silence was broken as he firstly detached, and then managed to swallow, the eraser on the end. As he coughed and spluttered, he tried to ask his seemingly unconcerned friend 'Do you think that this is a bit more than a two-man job? I mean, do you think that there might be anyone else on the Staff that would be willing to assist us?'

'Well I suppose that we could always try Thwaite?' said Darwin.

'If it doesn't concern Rounders or Netball – I doubt very much that he would have any interest' answered Strangler.

'Couldn't hurt to ask him though?' mused Darwin, 'where is he?'

'At this time – almost certainly in the Staff washroom. Very "regular" man, our Thwaite, you can set your watch by him. He will be in there now, performing his pollutions...'

'Shouldn't that be "ablutions"?' said Darwin.

'Not if you have ever had the experience of following him in there...'

In the Staff lounge, similarly odd conversations were underway. 'And now! Ladies and Gentlemen! I give you the Man who put the "ish" in "English" – the man who put the "say" in "essay" ...the geezer who puts the "Dic" in "Dictionary" – the One...the Only...Mr Royston "Huge-Bulge" Hyde-Jones!!...Yhaaaaayyyy!!'

'Just pass me my tea please, Loopy...' said Hyde-Jones, as his colleague Mr Newhouse continued to applaud him wildly. From somewhere within the room, Newhouse had obtained a pair of wooden-handled dish mops, and was performing an enthusiastic cheerleading routine with them.

'Give me an "R"...give me an "O"...'he began.

'Will you stop it, you mad impetuous fool!' laughed Hyde-Jones, as Newhouse performed unrehearsed star-jumps in front of him.

'Is there something that you wish to tell me, Royston?' asked Newhouse.

'No there is not, you cavorting nutter!' said H-J.

'Perhaps something that may be approaching?' teased the Music Master.

'Like what, exactly?'

'Perhaps something that begins with the letter "B" maybe?' Loopy replied, grinning.

'Ah yes – "B"ugger off and let me drink this tea in peace, you strange person' said H-J.

'I feel a Birthday coming on!' said Newhouse… 'and how old will the Birthday Boy be on that great day?'.

'I have no intention of disclosing that information – you do not have adequate Security Clearance Sir!' said H-J, in Mock-American CIA tones.

'Then I shall be forced to cut off thy head, and count the rings!!' declared Newhouse.

'Do please get some Professional help…' laughed H-J.

'Oh no…Thou hast a Birthday coming up my learned friend – and thou knowest that can only mean one thing…' said Newhouse.

Hyde-Jones hated to ask…but decided to, anyway 'And what, may God help me, is that?'

Newhouse adopted a sombre and serious expression…

'It means…PAR – TEEEEEEE!!' he screeched, frightening the other Staff.

'Oh no, not a chance…' said H-J, 'the only celebration which I would be prepared to consider, would be a small discreet affair, with proper jelly, ice-cream, and paper hats'.

'What I had in mind was an indiscreet affair, with proper Gelignite, whipped cream, and paper underwear!!' said Newhouse, enthusiastically. 'The occasion of your birth must be declared a National Holiday! There shall be feasting, fire-eating, tightrope-walking, and a parade of musically-gifted Sea-lions shall serenade thee on waterproof ukuleles, as buxom wenches in spangled tights ply thee with peeled grapes and cool drinks…'

'All of that in my little flat?' laughed Hyde-Jones.

'Well, as much as we can cram in – we'll have to keep some space spare for the Red Arrows and the extensive Bar facilities…' Newhouse answered.

'No – I just want a quiet drink, maybe' said H-J.

'With what I've got planned for you Royston, you'll be lucky to hear yourself think – never mind drink!' declared the Party Planner designate.

'I'm afraid not Loopy…you know how your celebrations have a habit of getting, shall we say, rather boisterous…' said Roy. He shuddered with the recollection of a previous Loopy-organised Birthday celebration, held at the Greyhound Racing track. Newhouse had fetched them drinks, and they took their places to watch the next race. The announcer had declared that the "Hyde-Jones Handicap Race" was about to start. Roy had thought that to be a rather nice touch. Newhouse had passed his friend a pair of small binoculars. As he studied the dogs speeding around the track in pursuit of the hare, he suddenly noticed to his horror that every dog in the race was wearing a pair of Hyde-Jones' own underpants…

'It will be an elegant and polite celebration of the birth of a very Dear Friend…' stated Newhouse, 'I shall ensure that you are treated wi-'

There was a very loud bang as a pale blue football-sized object smashed into the glass of the window. The Staff jumped with shock, Hyde-Jones spilling his tea into his lap. Newhouse raced to the window to try and see who had been responsible. He scanned the whole expanse of the quad. There was not a single boy to be seen. All that was visible to the Music Master was the pale blue ball, as it rolled away around the corner, and out of sight.

Chapter Eighteen:

Jedekiah stood at the top of the stairs which led down to the lower level of the cellar, gazed at the mirror-finish black fluid which filled the floor from wall to wall, and said a word which HoBi would have to slap his wrist for later...

'Well what can I possibly say?' he said, which was a touch ironic. 'Verily, thou hast certainly put thy great big clumsy size nine right in it this time, Obadiehard...'

'So it doth come to me to accept the blame again, as usual, doth it?' said Obadiehard, 'I tell thee without bias nor favour – it is always me that doest end up getting the blame...'

'Well only because it was thee that done it!' said Samuel.

Jedekiah smiled his enigmatic smile, as Obadiehard began to push his leather work gloves down the back of his trousers, in order to shield his bottom.

'Chastise not the boy, Brothers. Doest the word of HoBi not tell us that the unfettered deeds of the young mayest be likened to the joyous leaping of the forest deer?' he asked.

'No, don't think so, Elder...first time I've heard that bit...' said Samuel.

'Ah...well...yes, it might be one of my own sayings, now I come to mention it' said Jedekiah. 'Cracking phrase though – doest thou not think?'.

Obadiehard pulled the gloves back out of the rear of his trousers, as it looked like he might not need the safety padding. The three Groundling men continued to gaze at the shimmering black lake before them. Occasionally, the drill-hole would throw out a spurt of oil, which would fall back onto the surface with a "gloop". It was Lemuel who broke the silence with a shout... 'Got it!' he exclaimed, 'don't you see? HoBi has sent us this sign as a way of securing our future for...for the...er...well, for the future!'

'How so, Brother?', asked Jedekiah.

'We shall be rich! And we shall share these riches according to the will of HoBi with all the peoples of the Earth, that their lives shall become better. Once we have built the refinery we shall-'

'-Just have to stop thee right there for a moment...' said Jedekiah. 'A modern oil refinery occupies an approximate area of three thousand seven hundred acres of land. What we have at the moment is a cellar which doth measure twenty-two feet and three inches, by fourteen feet six – can thou see a bit of a problem starting to emerge here?'

'We couldst always knock through?' suggested Obadiehard.

The look that he got from the Elder suggested that he might need that padding after all...

It was an altogether different type of refinement that Nicky was in search of. Auntie had pushed back the furniture in the front room, and commandeered his music equipment from his bedroom. As the room had swirled to the loud sounds of a Strauss waltz, Auntie had ignored the bruising of reluctant feet on her shins, and had begun to instruct the boy in the art of ballroom dancing. By the end of their first session, Nicky didn't feel that might win any trophies any time soon, but he had begun to feel just a little bit of confidence starting to settle in. He hoped that this confidence might last longer than the bruising caused to Auntie's feet.

He had also attempted to turn "detective" in relation to the loathsome boyfriend of the lovely Jozza. He had made various undercover enquiries concerning their relationship with some of her St Gertrude's friends. It seemed like the smarmy little git had told them that he ran a local prestige car dealership. Further investigations had produced the evidence that he was only twenty-one. So he had either done very well for himself in a very short space of time, or inherited the Family business from Daddy, or won the lottery and decided to set up in the auto trade. This would explain why Nicky had seen him pick up Jozza in a succession of different coloured cars – all fast, all luxurious, and all very expensive. It wouldn't explain though, why he was such a smug little tit. Well he could get ready to move over – as Nicky was about to begin the fight back to win his lady. Now that he could Waltz, well "Hot Rod" could do something beginning with "F", and he didn't mean "Foxtrot".

This Friday there was going to be a "Rock Night" at the village Youth Club building, which was opposite the pub. All of the village lads would be there, and Nicky had put the word out to his Academy boys. It should be a good evening, with decent loud music, good company, and a further chance to keep an eye on Jozza, and make sure that she didn't get up to any bad habits – like carrying on with that pencil-legged, pony-tailed, sunglasses-wearing weasel…

Nicky had another plan. This was not plan "B", so much as plan "J", for Jealousy. Whilst up at the local "if you want it, then we've got it – if you can't see it, then chances are that you don't need it anyway" shop in the village, he had been approached by one of the village girls. This was quite an unusual event for Nicky, and for a few seconds, he felt rather embarrassed. The girl that had come up and spoken to him was attractively shy, very pretty, and softly-spoken. This was Victoria Ellison, a cousin of the famous "Squiddy" Squire from the village. Victoria had everything that could be wished for in a girl: she had a brilliant sense of humour, good manners, superb shape, an absolutely radiant smile, and real vision. She had vision all right…the young lady could probably visualise Lincoln on a clear day – as she was just over six feet tall.

'Hello Nicky…' she purred, 'Will you be up at the dance on Friday night?'

'Ah…errm…yeah, I suppose so' answered Nicky, articulate as ever.

'Do you perhaps have a spare ticket? I'm really sorry to ask, but my friend Tracy is desperate to go, and the tickets seem to have all been sold…' she said.

'No problem – I'd be happy to give you one' replied Nicky.

As the girl turned away giggling, with a brief 'thank you', the boy felt his face begin to audition as a tribute band for a post box. Oh my God – he had just actually said that, hadn't he! What if she told anyone else what he had just said? What if she told all of her friends? What if she told the whole vill- oh no! what if news of his indiscretion filtered back to the ears of Jozza? In truth, he didn't think that Victoria would say anything, but the same could certainly not be applied to her friend Tracy Thorpe...Tracy was one of the girls that caused his Mum's eyebrow to raise at the very mention of her name. She had (even at the tender age of sixteen) managed to acquire "a bit of a reputation" in the village. She and her other school friend Charlotte ("the Haystack Harlot") were well known to be shall we say, rather flexible in the matter of their affections. Mind you, having said all of that, the two girls were never short of friends, always in high spirits, and totally unconcerned about any slur on their character. Well good for them, thought Nicky – and he was absolutely terrified of the pair of them.

Tracy was the subject of a rumour. The gossip in the village was that she was involved in a torrid and intense physical relationship with the keyboard player from the local band "Funderthuck". Nicky didn't pay much attention to what he had heard – it was common knowledge that Tracy faked all of her organists...

Charlotte "Charley" Draper had a completely different approach. Born into a very good family, she was always being given lectures by her Mother, who insisted on twittering instructions at the girl if she ever even thought about going out to meet a boy.

'Now if this boy takes you out for a drink, well that is fine – Mummy will not worry about that. If he wants to hold your hand, well that is alright, as Mummy will not worry about that either. If the boy takes you home in his car, and parks up in the lane, Mummy will not be too worried about that. If he wants to kiss you, well I suppose that is perfectly natural, and Mummy will not worry. But Dear Charley – if the boy tries to get on top of you, then you must not let him! – because My Dear...Mummy will worry!'

When Charley arrived home at one-thirty in the morning, with the strap of her dress hanging off one shoulder, Mother had interrogated her daughter as to what had been going on.

'Well Mummy, we went out for a drink, and I thought "well Mummy won't worry at this". He wanted to hold my hand, and I thought "well Mummy wouldn't worry about this either". Then he offered to drive me home, and he parked up in the dark lane. We got into the back seat of his car, and he wanted to kiss me. I remember thinking to myself "well Mummy won't worry about this". Then he did try to get on top of me, like you said he might...'

'Whatever did you do?' asked Mother, horrified.

'Oh it was alright, I climbed on top of him – and let his Mummy worry!!'.

There is a colloquial saying that declares that "A Wise Man knows his Onions" ...

Yes, he does, or at least he ought to. It would indeed be a Foolish Man that would ever purchase a toffee-onion. In the case of Professor Johnathan Darwin, this statement was true in every respect. He did indeed know his onions. He knew them all by name. He had grown them lovingly from seed as part of an experiment to demonstrate to his pupils the effect known as "positive geotropism". Over the weeks of growth, the boys would observe how the green shoot of the onion began to grow, and curve upward toward the sky in search of sunlight, even when planted upside-down in its pot. A brief but productive excursion into the world of DIY cloning had led to a batch of onions that didn't just respond rapidly to the effects of gravity and sunlight – but could also tell you why.

There had been a row of nine of the edible bulbs in a tray on the laboratory window cill. Now there were eight onions, and one onion-sized hole where the ninth should have been. When he came to think of it, Darwin could only remember having actually planted eight seeds when he originally set up the experiment. Where was the larger one that usually sat at the end? There was obviously a thief about in the Academy. He was truly appalled at this act: hadn't he tried to make up an interesting experiment for the boys? What sort of person would saunter into his laboratory and just help themself?

His onion had been stolen...well, honestly, it was enough to make you cry.

Professor Strangler had given discreet instructions to all of the boys that had been with him and his colleague Darwin on the recent foray through the Vortex. The hunt for the "intruder" was now on. The task had been made all the more urgent due to the fact that there had been yet another "incident" in the gym. During a PE lesson, a boy had run the length of the gym and placed a medicine ball on its allotted spot, ready to be picked up by the next member of his team, whose task it was to run with the ball back up the gym to the starting marker. As the second boy had bent down to lift the ball – it had leapt viciously into the air and hit the poor boy full in the face. As the pupils and the Master rushed over to attend to the injured lad, the ball had quietly rolled away into the corner. Once at rest, it had assumed the size, shape and colour of a basketball.

When the PE lesson was over (the victim of the attack having sat out the rest of the session with a large amount of tissues stuffed into each nostril, to stem the flow of blood), the boy in charge of putting away the equipment had gathered up all of the balls. He stacked them in the gym store area on the appointed shelf. He grabbed one of the basketballs and began turning it around so that the logo on it was facing the same way as the others. He noticed that the wording on the ball was wrong, not really words at all, just an approximation of what words might be, if written by someone who was completely unfamiliar with the language. He picked out the ball and turned it again – it was then that it bit him...

Nursing a rather nasty wound to his finger, he wished that he hadn't fiddled with his balls.

Reverend Vernon Farmer stood on the sunlit lawn outside his study. Today, he cut an imperious figure as he cast a long shadow in the crisp morning sunlight. In celebration of his pending ennoblement, he had insisted that his long-suffering wife made one or two changes to this normal day-to-day Headmastering attire. His teaching gown was now edged with crimson, and the tassel on his mortar board was now gold. He was engaged in a daydream as he cast out seed and bread for the birds. He imagined that he was distributing alms to the poor, and cast the riches out with a wide sweep of his arm, punctuated by a royal wave or two…

He enjoyed feeding the Academy ravens daily, in the knowledge that their continued presence kept his own personal ivory tower from crumbling. There was the old legend that if the ravens ever deserted the environs of St Onans, then the ancient edifice would fall. There was an equally popular rumour that if the huge black birds did ever decide to vacate the premises – then everyone's car would need a lot less regular cleaning.

'CAW!...CAW!...CAW!...' rang out the throaty call, echoing around the lawned garden as the sound bounced back from the ivy-encrusted walls, as he scattered the food for the birds. Keith, the leader of the motley crew of ravens (although that is really an unkindness), stared down from the rusted cast-iron guttering, nudged his fellow raven, and said: 'I really do appreciate all of the food you know…but why does the bloke always insist on making that silly bloody noise when he feeds us?'.

Across the immaculately-manicured lawn, and just past the heavy oak door of the Headmaster's study, was the equally ancient portal of the Academy office, and where could be found the equally ancient Miss Emilia Piggott. On her desk, next to the novelty tissue dispenser in the shape of the Pope, and slightly to the side of her silver-plated cake tongs, sat a very cold cup of tea. The chair was empty. The occupant of said article of furniture was over at the far wall, where she was standing in front of a small mirror. She was talking to herself...

'Perhaps this one...no, too formal. Maybe I'll try this one again...ah...looks a bit on the droopy side. Where did I put – ah yes...oh no, that one won't do at all. Somewhere in the box, I'm sure that I've got...oh yes!...now that is perfect. Yes – that's the one...'

It may have shocked an invisible observer (or possibly not, depending on your family background, and which drinking establishments you favour) to note that she was in fact trying on a selection of false moustaches...

Chapter Nineteen:

The pressures of having to organise and take part in a hunt for an alien life form, which he might just have been responsible for letting loose in the Academy, was beginning to tell on poor Professor Strangler. For several nights now, he had not been able to get more than a few minutes' sleep. He was having very vivid and terrifying dreams, and just to make matters worse – he now thought that he had picked up some sort of weird virus. Sleep deprivation can do strange things to an already strange mind, but this recent turn of events was particularly worrying for him.

He had begun to wake up with a start…When he had thrown off the covers due to the heat of a fever, he had suddenly noticed a squadron of tiny aircraft, which were circling his bed, and then landing on his stomach – only to take off again and repeat the cycle.

Worried out of his mind, he had gone straight to see his Doctor. He had explained the odd phenomena, and the Doctor had listened patiently, whilst making notes.

'What do you think is wrong with me, Doctor!' Strangler had nervously asked.

'I'm not too sure – little aircraft did you say?' asked the Doctor.

'Yes, tiny ones…have I caught some sort of weird virus?' said Strangler.

'Well possibly yes…' said the Doctor.

'Should I stay away from the Academy? Do you think it's infectious? Is there any possibility that it could be contagious?'

'In my opinion…' said the Doctor, 'The virus may not be contagious. You may just be a carrier…'.

When Uncle Joe smelled the faintest aroma of a money-making business idea, there was really no way that he was going to give up, until he had extracted each and every possibility – or until he was instructed to do so by the Police or the Authorities. In the cosy confines of his shed, surrounded by what remained of his various "inventions", and an ever-growing mountain of threatening letters, he was still dreaming up various ideas as a continuation of his Yiddish-themed escapades.

He had wandered down to the area of town where The Lad went to school, and had sat in quiet contemplation with a drink, in a rather pleasant club called "The Vaults". He had engaged in conversation with a tall, well-spoken man, who had informed him that he was one of the people that ran the establishment. The club was very busy, even for midweek, and Joe was impressed by the range of food and drink on offer, and the friendly demeanour of the staff. It wasn't long before the Uncle brain began to whirr into action...He could see, as he looked around him, a ready-made outlet for his Jewish microwave meals – not to mention the hundreds of boxes of tea that he hadn't been able to shift so far. Joe had gently tested the water with his new friend "Jed", and found that he was very open to any idea which might benefit more social inclusion for any race or religion...Everything which Jedekiah said in their conversation after this point could be filed under the heading of "Too Late". Joe had cast out his line, and the Elder had nibbled on the bait, and was altogether too polite to spit it out – not an easy feat by any means, when you have an Uncle Joe frantically reeling in the line from the other end...

With Jedekiah's conversational radio now switched from "transmit" to "receive", Joe went in for the kill –

'So what I were thinking My Son, is that since you're doing so well here, you might as well rake in a bit more profit by catering for persons of the Kosher persuasion. Down the end there, we can open up the space for a nice little cocktail bar, catering for our Jewish friends. We can serve my food as bar snacks, and I've got sweets we can put out in nice little bowls, and I might be able to lay me hands on some special tea, for them who don't fancy an alcoholic tipple. Ho yes, I can see it all now Jed, me old mate!! – this is going to be a real little earner, you take a tip from me...'

'We have a five-foot neon sign outside on the wall, (very tasteful mind…), and hey presto! Moysher's yer Uncle! – people will be flocking in from miles around, just for the pleasure of enjoying a "Kosher Kocktail" or two – at *Bar Mitzvah* …'

A delighted Uncle Joe had left the club with a contract hastily written on the back of a napkin: Jedekiah had left with the beginnings of a migraine…

There is one in every school. Well strictly speaking, this applies only to academic institutions which have Teenage Males in residence. At some indeterminate point within the educational career of the schoolboy, they become acquainted with one who has appointed themselves as custodian of much sought-after reading materials. I refer of course, to the section of the unofficial library marked "Adult Interest" …

At St Onans Academy, this supplier of the suggestive, this vendor of vice, this loaner of the lewd, this purveyor of porn, was one Mark Davis – the unopposed and highly unofficial "King of the Dirty Book" at St Onans. Rather than a mere flogger of filth, Davis took his role extremely seriously, and thought of himself as a source of scientific reading material for his classmates. His various wares could be loaned out for very reasonable rates, and Davis himself was careful only to rent out magazines to boys who met his strict criteria of age, urgent need, research, and who were not likely to do themselves any lasting damage to their eyesight. The funds which he had accrued from the Perfects alone, would probably enable Davis to purchase a modest but comfortable time-share property abroad. His highest-grossing publication was the ring-bound and laminated luxury copy of "Bum's the Word". This was the only magazine available from Davis that had a waiting list. The major selling point of the publication was that in the centre pages, it heavily featured a young "model" making her adult feature debut. This was a young lady by the name of Lucretia Dipper, who would shortly go on to be known throughout the Academy by the shorter title of "Matron" ...

Now Nicky had not had an altogether sheltered upbringing, far from it. He had been subject to the usual contact with the female of the species that proves to be instructional in later teenage life. However, there was the prospect of a date with the lofty Victoria looming over the horizon, and the last thing that Nicky wanted was to have her think that he was some sort of inexperienced idiot – if indeed circumstances should proceed along a certain line. He would seek the advice of his friend Davis. He thought that it might be a good idea to at least give himself some idea of what a Fair Maiden looked like, when she was not wearing her Fair Maiden costume. He daren't actually rent a copy of one of Mark's dubious magazines, because he knew exactly what might happen if he did.

When girls become women, well that is fine, and all is as it should be. They blossom into wondrous creatures of mystery (apart from the ones who blossom into screeching Harpies – bellowing down their mobile phones in the Post Office queue). It is when the woman becomes a Mother, that certain terrifying changes take place. Mothers are wonderful, they provide you with the finest care, love, and support in everything that you do. Until as a boy, you reach a certain age, that is...

There is a point in the life of Mum, where the brain sends out the signal to begin the operation of little-known gland, which is hidden deep within the Mum brain. This tiny but deadly biological feature is designed specifically to wreak havoc upon the psyche of a young boy (there is a female application too, but this seems to be entirely modified by the "disappointment" hormone). Picture this scenario: you have just come back into your house for tea. You may not yet have spoken a word of greeting to anyone. Mum will look at you, perhaps from her nerve centre of the sink, maybe across the kitchen table. She will look you in the eye and say:

'And what have you been up to?'

You are now powerless. You will crumble under the influence of a biological trait that you were completely unaware of. Resistance is useless…as your brain attempts to write a script for your young mouth to recite, the ink in the theoretical pen will run dry. You will hear yourself as you give details of times, places, and names of any co-conspirators who have joined with you in committing whatever heinous act of naughtiness you have taken part in. You will confess all. You may just have enough brain function left to ask yourself – 'but how did she know?'. I will let you in on the secret. In her DNA, Mum has a tiny but lethal strand which is known informally as "Mum Radar". The correct biological term for this is MIG – or "Maternal Interrogation Gene". All Mums have it – and you cannot escape it.

It will go like this…

'What were you doing up at Harvey's Plantation?'

'We weren't up at the Plantation – we were up at Pettit's Barn' (dammit!)

'Why were you setting fire to things?'

'We weren't setting fire to anything – we were riding on Pettit's tractor' (dammit!)

'What have I told you about hanging around with that Haynes Boy?'

'He wasn't there Mum – it was just Me, Mike, Squiddy, Pete and Tracy' (dammit!)

'So why were *you* driving the tractor then?'

'I only turned the key, and I had to take over because Mikey couldn't steer properly'

'So you did drive it then? (dammit!) and who is going to pay for the damage?'

'It was only a bit bent at the front – Mikey says his Dad will-(dammit!)

'I'm not allowed out again, am I?'

'Not in any true sense…'

See – told you.

This is why a Mum can silently creep up into the attic and catch you when you are trying to dismantle the dog. She didn't think it was "a bit too quiet" when you were upstairs, about to hang-glide out of the front bedroom window: oh no, it was her little friend the MIG that tipped her off. The terrible side-effect of the gene is that it can often operate when you are out of the house completely. This is why Mums have the skill of "finding" things at the back of cupboards, and in pockets, and especially – under beds.

Thus – there is no way that Nicky would risk bringing any dodgy magazine into the house. He could just about get away with *Classic Rock* magazine, if the girl on the front cover was not displaying too much of her talents. If that were the case, then Mum would give looks of disapproval, and Auntie would no doubt make an observation along the lines of 'She wants to be careful that she doesn't trap 'em in her guitar strings!'.

Just to further complicate matters, there had been a telephone call from his Academy bandmate John. It would appear that by some magical twist of fate, Nicky's band had been asked to do a "spot" at the Friday night Rock dance. Wow! This could be their big break – or a chance to get a big break in the leg department if they were judged to be crap. The village crowd were known to be rather critical, and could turn nasty if the performance of an artiste was deemed "not up to scratch". Nicky remembered one band who had turned up, where the lead singer had insisted on playing a long solo on the flute. He also remembered the rumours about how long it had taken the staff in the A&E department of the local Hospital to remove it…

Oh my God!!, what about the drum kit? He couldn't play a serious gig with only half a kit? There was no way that Mum or Auntie would be able to lend him any money with which to buy new drums…what could he do? Just then, Uncle Joe knocked at the door. Despite having very recently entered into a business partnership with Jedekiah (Joe would inform him of the fact later), Uncle seemed a bit down. 'What's the matter Joe – have the Police finally caught up with you?' asked Auntie.

'Nah...I turned on the Cloaking Device on the tank when they showed up, and they didn't spot it when they looked in me shed. It's something the Missus said...'

'Did you have another row?' asked Mum.

'Oh no, nothing like that – she just happened to casually mention that she thought that I was going a bit thin on top.' said Joe.

'It's just premature scalp widening...' said Auntie.

'Yeah, that's what I thought – but she went on and on about it. She said that instead of spendin' all me money on me business ventures – I should go and have a transplant'.

'Well what's wrong with that, sounds sensible to me?' said Mum.

Joe frowned – 'Well I told her flat, I did, I said that I would look like a proper pillock, if I 'ave to walk around with a kidney on me 'ead...'

To fill the embarrassed silence, Nicky took Uncle out into the back garden, and told him about the planned gig up at the Youth Club. To the boy's total amazement, Joe fixed him with a steely gaze and said 'Well then...you'd better come round to me 'ouse now. I 'ave something which might just be of use to yer. I wuz savin' it for yer next Birthday – but it sounds like you are going to need it a bit sooner!'

Nicky made his excuses and left with Uncle Joe. After the short but heart-stopping drive through the village (some of which was on all four wheels), they shot up Joe's drive and parked outside his shed. Uncle opened the shed door with his secret combination (and a screwdriver, which he would really have to return to Mr Melkins one of these days) and pulled Nicky in after him. Joe motioned to the boy to remain silent. He picked up an old television remote control with an egg whisk nailed onto it, and began to wave it slowly around every surface of the shed. 'Won't be a minute Lad – I just got to sweep the place for hidden listening devices' said Joe.

'But that's an old TV remote, with an egg whisk stuck onto it Uncle' said Nicky.

'Aye Lad – and just you keep thinkin' that…' said Joe.

When shed security was to Joe's liking, he grinned at Nicky, reached down in front of his workbench, and pulled a lever. The shelves and tool racks on the far wall slid sideways, revealing a larger storage space beyond. Joe gave a whoop of glee, and began to lift out various short cylinder-shaped objects, placing them in a line in front of the bemused boy. He instructed Nicky to take off the coverings from the objects.

'Got this from an old mate of mine who owed me a few quid…' said Joe, 'He used to play in a Big Band in the Sixties. Shame really, he could have gone far, if it hadn't been for his terrible habit…' said Joe.

'Was it drugs, Uncle?' Nicky asked.

'No – he used to fart nauseatingly in confined spaces…' Joe answered.

Nicky carefully removed the wrappings from the line of cylinders. When he had uncovered them all, he stood back and gazed at them in utter disbelief. What Joe had stored away was a Premier drum kit…There were two 22-inch bass drums, there was a 10-inch tom-tom, a 12-inch, a 14-inch, and two floor toms – one 16-inch-deep, and the other 18 inches. All in a shocking salmon pink sparkle finish. There was a forest of stands and hardware, and even a proper drummer's "throne". A crash from the back of the storage space told Nicky that Uncle Joe had located the cymbals.

'There ye go Son!...it's all yours' Uncle told him. 'Now you can really show the buggers how it's done on Friday night!'

'I…I…I don't know what to say Uncle…I really can't accept it – it's just too much. Can you please let me just borrow it? I'll pay you for it out of any money I earn…' said Nicky.

'No you bloody well won't. Look: your Ma and her Sister 'ave been bloody good to me and my Missus over the years, an' I know that ye ain't got a pot to piss in at the moment. You'll take the kit with my blessing. I want to see ye like yer 'eroes Cozy Moon and Keith Powell an' that lot. You can rehearse in here if ye like – it's soundproofed so as I can test me jet engines when I needs to. Now let's lock up and get you back for yer tea' said Uncle.

As they stepped through the connecting door into the other half of the shed, Joe called out 'For God's sake mind you don't walk into me tank – I told you that the Cloaking Device is still switched on…'

Nicky smiled to himself, and called out 'Don't worry Uncle – I'll be careful'. Joe was certainly a very surprising and generous man, even if he was given to telling the odd little white lie, and making up the tallest stories that anyone had ever heard.

He was still smiling as he hit his head on something cold, metallic - and invisible…

Chapter Twenty:

Rumour is a really sneaky little devil. Oh yes indeed it is. No matter how much you may have paid for those brand new double-glazed windows, or however much you forked out on that high-tec draught excluding system that you saw on the television advert – rumour will always find a fissure or crack through which it can leak out. The problem will be made worse by the fact that it will become a Family affair. Once rumour has found a way out into the fresh air, it will bring along with it its siblings known as Gossip and Speculation. Following closely behind them will be the Cousins Loose Talk, Hearsay, and Whispers. The sound that they all make as they merrily trot out to make a general bloody nuisance of themselves in public, will be Tittle-Tattle…

And so it had come to pass…that some daft oaf (or of course, Oafess, or even Oaferina) had been just a little bit careless in the mouth department.

The effect of the gossip had been remarkable upon the Staff of St Onans. The first symptom of the sickness had been an outbreak of severe politeness between the Masters. There were so many "No, I insist – after You's" at the tea urn, that break times were over before any of them actually got to drink anything. The exception to this was of course Dr Matthews, who as usual, came fully prepared and stocked up in his own preferred beverage department.

Every member of the Staff began to assume that they were the person whose good works were being rewarded with an Honour, and their behaviour toward their colleagues and pupils suddenly began to reflect that thought. Missing homework was dealt with by means of an admonishing wag of the finger, rather than a swift entry on a detention slip, or use of a handy cane. Matron continued her use of corporal punishment (on request), but removed the VAT from her hourly charges. How thoughtful…

The changes had even managed to filter down through the bedrock of tradition, and drip upon the head of the Reverend

Felchingham. His "private war" with his spiritual tormentor Stan was still in full swing, but the Rev thought that it might be a good idea to look upon his ghostly nemesis with an altogether more kindly eye. He decided that he would ease up in his constant search for methods of ridding himself of Stan, and perhaps even attempt to reason with the angry old man. He had visited yet another "Psychic", in an attempt to contact the world beyond the veil, and try to calm Stan down a little. The Psychic had tried to make contact with Stan – initially by means of the "automatic writing" method. No good had that turned out to be...The poor lady had been startled when she saw what her "guided" hand had written on the note pad, whereas the Rev had almost predicted what single word Stan would write. He was not wrong.

Feeling rather let down and dejected again, the Rev had gone home having achieved nothing.

'I don't know why I bothered...' he had mused to himself, 'I mean – expecting a Psychic to be able to read my mind...what on earth was I thinking'.

The Rev had later been subject to yet another revenge attack from Stan. He had plugged in his car sat-nav to recharge it. In doing so, he noticed that a destination had already been selected, and a postcode typed into the unit. It was not one that the Rev instantly recognised – nor any place that he might have wished to go. He used his computer to check out the code that had been entered. The result was surprising, or to put it another way, completely unsurprising, if you were at all aware of Stan's *modus operandi*.

The post code set was for a village. It was set up to take the driver of the vehicle to a village near Bolton in Lancashire. A more detailed investigation by the Rev, uncovered the exact name of the village in question.

Nob End

The Rev was sure that he heard a throaty chuckle coming from the kitchen...

Miles Bannister the Mathematics Master was getting very little sleep. His rest was being constantly interrupted by the disturbances supplied by his spirit guide and leading Authority on Everything, Mrs Elsie Noakes. Since she had first heard about the possibility of a Knighthood in the offing, she had decided that it should without question be her boy Bannister who should receive it, and that she should by default, also receive the Honour. This had led to the daily and nightly routine of poor Miles being consistently interrupted by queries from Elsie as to what she should wear, what she should chat about when meeting "A Royal", and requests to bring along her good friend Mrs Wormall to the Investiture ceremony.

'You must find out exactly what the Queen will be wearing, Miles!...' she had insisted, 'I was thinking about wearing my best pearls – and the last thing that I want to do is embarrass Her Majesty by clashing...'

'It's four o'clock in the morning Dear Lady – do you think I might be permitted some sleep?' Miles had asked, after being woken up for the fifth time.

'Yes Dear, of course Dear – it's just that...What's that Gwyneth?...Oh, I'll ask him...Miles Lovey - there will be a toilet within easy reach for Mrs Wormall at the Palace, won't there?'

'Yes Dear Lady...I'm sure that there will be – dozens of them. With gold seats...'

'Oooooh! I don't know about that Miles, you know that Mrs W has to be *very* choosy about what she sits on, because of her "problem" ...' said Elsie.

'Oh dear...I've lost it' said an exasperated Miles.

'Lost?...what is it that you've lost Dear?' asked Elsie.

'The will to live...'

Gideon Rundell had an inbuilt contempt for Pupils. His dislike of them was born out of the fact that they did not seem to share his love and enthusiasm for the noble and ancient Latin tongue. They seemed impervious to the perfection of the Roman Empire, which had shaped so much of the world in centuries gone by. Even his fellow Tutors showed no interest or knowledge about the cornerstone of his own personal existence. True, he had seen Newhouse the Music Master wearing a tee-shirt bearing the legend "*Poto Ergo Sum*", but "*I drink, therefore I am*" did little to advance the cause of the language of Rome…

Having drunk the wine of gossip straight from the grapevine, as it were, even he had decided to adopt a gentler approach toward his charges. Having now removed the bandages following his recent nasal surgery, he had espied a boy having great difficulty getting the top off a bottle of fizzy drink in the quad. Rundell had made a great show of striding over in order to assist the boy, with a Fatherly "Here – let me help you" being delivered. The boy was most surprised at the sudden change in demeanour from the normally stern Latin Master. Rundell had been even more shocked than the boy, when the bottle cap had exploded upwards and hit him full in the face…

He had staggered away, clutching his handkerchief to his bleeding nose, and muttering '*Et Tu – Irn Brute*?' to himself.

There was a small group of three members of the Staff who had heard the rumour, hadn't believed a word of it, and quite frankly couldn't give a bugger at this particular moment. Roy Hyde-Jones, "Loopy" Newhouse, and Dr Matthews were hunched over a table in the Staff lounge, engaged in that supremely educational pursuit of playing "Dungeons and Dragons". Matthews was in fact playing his own version of the game – which he had entitled "Dry Gins and Flagons" …He was already well ahead on pints.

Professors Darwin and Strangler had heard the rumour, thought about it, dismissed it, and filed it under "Far too busy to bother with such nonsense at the moment". They were in fact genuinely too busy with their search for the stowaway from another dimension that was causing such mayhem within the Academy.

Strangler handed his colleague a brand new mobile phone, and told him 'I got you this Johnathan – we need to keep in touch at all times in case we locate the ball-thingy assassin. I know you don't like these things, but for the sake of safety, we need to be in touch at the drop of a hat'.

Darwin regarded the phone with a suspicious eye... 'That was most thoughtful of you Dick. Yes, I despise the wretched things, but I take the point – I won't knock yer'.

Madame Dreadfell paid absolutely no attention to any form of gossip. She paid so little attention to it that she had run up a total of over £5750 on her credit card, as she plundered the High-Fashion shops for clothing which might be more befitting for a Titled Lady. She had begun to turn up at the Academy wearing huge and very luxuriant furs – so much so that some witty person had witnessed her arrival in said coat – and called out 'Bloody Hell!...here comes Chewbacca!'

Bell-Enderby the Art Master was convinced. It was going to be him. He knew that it was going to be him. There was no way that his contribution to the world of Art could be overlooked or ignored. Had he not just recently finished a superb artwork in a local church depicting the Stations of the Cross? Well yes, there had been comments, but then great works of art always attracted criticism. Yes, some of the ladies depicted may have been...over-generously endowed in certain areas, but everyone who saw the work made comment on it. He had also designed, sculpted and cast the new bronze for the Council Chambers. It was a sculpture of that local Dignitary, the former Lady Margot DeMande. The Council had asked him to sculpt a Bust – and by God, he had given them one.

Matron had thought that the whole thing was quite sweet. Her "clients" over time had included well, a fair few High Court Judges, Magistrates, Councillors, a large number of Lords, and the odd Lady. If her career in "Public Service" was about to be recognised (and hopefully, some of her Titled Clientele would not be), then that was nice. She would go about her normal daily duties as she usually would. She enjoyed her job, and she was certainly not "strapped for cash" – although some of her Clients frequently were...

168

Miss Piggott had smiled to herself when she had heard the news. If she were to be the recipient…well, that would be the perfect cover. Who could possibly suspect the owner of a Title to do what she was planning to?

Albert Brooks, completely in keeping with his job and responsibilities, was having a field day. As far as Albert was concerned, this was just another slap in the face for the Working Classes – as the Toffs patted each other on the back, and handed out the silly hats. He could not care less about any of those jumped-up cretins being given an Honour. He had worked long and hard, and there was something which he would soon be anointing them with, so let's wait and see what Milord thinks to that.

The attitude of the boys of St Onans had been altogether more relaxed. There was much talk and mainly good-natured banter between the lads as to which member of the Staff they thought most deserving of a Title. One thing had been entirely predictable…Within seconds of the rumour going public, Weatherill had opened up a book (quite a feat for a boy who claimed to hate having to learn…). With his trilby hat which bore the legend "Honest Dicky" on the front of it firmly in place upon his grinning head, he was very busy raking in money from the entire Academy – all wanting to place a bet on their "favourite". As with everything that he did, Weatherill absorbed himself completely in his new role. He stood at the side of a large poster, and was shouting:

'Come on Fellows! – come and 'ave a little flutter on yer Favourite! Long odds, short odds – they're all odd at St Onans! You won't win it – if you ain't in it! Go on all you Third Formers – 'ave a quid on who gets the Gold Lid!'.

'I'd like an each-way on the Matron…' whispered one of the older boys.

'You and me both Mate!' replied Weatherill.

'What about Brayfield?...' called a voice.

'Twenty-five to one!' called back Weatherill.

'Those are crap odds…' said the voice.

169

'Odds? – sorry, I thought that you wanted to know the time' said Honest Dicky.

'What's the odds on Thwaite?' asked a boy.

'Well now... he says that he isn't – but we reckon he is!' declared Weatherill.

'I should be doing this!' said Mark Davis, 'I am more of a Role Model to the lads'.

'You're more of a Rolling Model, Davis...' laughed Weatherill, as he took in another bet from a shifty-looking Prefect. 'There yer go Guv - that's twenty-five to one on "Barmy Bannister" in the Title Stakes at St Onans – an' good luck to yer!'.

'I could at least be Treasurer...' said Davis, hopefully.

'Not a chance my Son!' said Weatherill, 'I daren't trust the finances of my lucrative business venture to someone who self-medicates with Jammie Dodgers! I shall cut you in at a preferential percentage, if you loan me the "Matron Special Issue" at a discount...'

'Five Quid?' enquired Davis.

'One Fifty...'

'Three Quid?'

'Done!'

'Yeah – I have been'.

Chapter Twenty-One:

Nicky had decided that an approach to the "Licentious Librarian" that was Mark Davis, was probably not the best idea. He simply didn't want to look like some sort of fool in front of his friends. He had always thought that dubious magazines always came from under hedges…His village mate Squiddy still did the occasional paper round, and so Nicky had asked him, as casually as he could, if he ever had to deliver any "specialist" publications in the village. Of course, Squiddy had laughed at him, but without malice. He had passed Nicky a magazine entitled *"Citizen Cane"*, which was for Mr Pennery at number 26, and told Nicky 'Just have a look in there Mate! – there's some real gymnastics going on in that one…'

Nicky had looked, and then looked again. He saw plenty of "Leo" – but very little in the way of "leotards". It occurred to Nicky that his friend Squiddy had lied about the sporting content of the magazine…The discipline which was featured had very little to do with the Parallel Bars. There seemed to be only the one bar which was featured prominently – and that was mostly pictured horizontally.

Miss Piggott was ready. Every check which she had needed to do had been completed, and then re-checked, just to be sure. It would now be only a matter of hours before she set off on her adventure. She giggled to herself as she remembered that she was probably about to become a criminal. She didn't care. The Easter weekend was fast approaching, and she would have to do so much, in a short space of time. For Emilia Piggott, it was certainly going to be a long Good Friday…

Back at home, Nicky's Mum was gazing wistfully out of the back kitchen window. Auntie came over and joined her Sister in her observations. It was a while before she spoke…

'I see Mr Taylor is on the lawn again – poor old soul'.

'Yes, I went out to have a word with him as soon as I saw him lying there' said Mum.

'Did you find out who he is this week?' asked Auntie, casually.

'I went and asked him - apparently he's The Mendips this week...' answered Mum.

Mr Taylor was one of their more fascinating neighbours. After a fall from the roof of his bungalow three years ago, he had begun to assume various different personalities and identities. There was one big difference though. Not for he the sash and white breeches of Napoleon, oh no. He spurned the polished high boots of Wellington. Winston Churchill or General Montgomery were not on his list of characters to impersonate.

Mr Taylor had taken to becoming well-known English Hills...

'He can't stay there – we really need to move him' said Mum.

'No – you can't, we'd get into terrible trouble!' said Auntie.

'Why?' asked Mum.

'Because he's a National Heritage Site...' said Auntie, straight-faced.

The two Sisters stood gazing out at the prone Mr Taylor, as they sipped a cup of tea.

'I have to admit – he does look picturesque...' sighed Mum.

'I can't wait until he decides to be The Cotswolds' said Auntie, 'I could just do with a nice relaxing holiday...'

They watched the resting man silently. Suddenly, Auntie peered intently at the figure on their lawn, and asked 'Is that a tattoo that I can see on him?'

Mum picked up a pair of binoculars, and focussed... 'Oh yes, it is. Well spotted'.

'What's all that about then, do you think?' Auntie asked.

'Ahh...right – I think that must be the tattoo left over from when he was the Berkshire Downs'.

'What do you mean?'

'Uffington – you know, the White Horse?' said Mum.

Auntie pondered... 'Do you think that he would want me to go out and give him a quick run over with the lawnmower?'

'Best not...' said Mum, 'You might knock off the little bench and fountain that he has balanced on his stomach. He's also got a small waterfall running off his fringe'.

'Why has he got all that stuff all over him?' asked Auntie.

'He says that he's a local Beauty Spot...' said Mum.

Nicky was now getting ready to worry about the gig at the Youth Club on Friday night, but before he got around to that – there was a much worse horror to contemplate. Thursday after school would be the dreaded first round of the Ballroom Dancing lessons.

The suit that had been loaned by Uncle Joe had finally been allowed back into the house. The fresh air seemed to have dispelled the mothball fumes from every inch of the fabric. Mum had cleaned and pressed the suit, which Nicky had to admit, now looked quite stylish. No doubt when he put it on, he would resemble someone who had just had a head transplant.

In the assembly hall of St Onans, a throng of haughty young ladies, and a tribe of educated monkeys from the Academy, were sipping cooled drinks prior to the commencement of the hostilities. The girls of St Gertrude's presented the image of a group of mannequins, all dressed in ridiculously expensive clothing, and awaiting delivery to an extremely up-market shop. They stood in a haute-couture huddle, the braying of their upper-class voices ringing out across the hall. Nicky regarded them with suspicion, and wondered why they had not sent their Maids to do all of the actual dancing for them. Most had been delivered to the Academy by ludicrously expensive cars, some even chauffeur driven, with the uniformed man holding open the door for them as they made their elegant entrance. The nearest that Nicky could hope to get to a Rolls, were the ones which contained sausage on the table behind him.

His own group of friends were busy eyeing up the competition. The boys had all made the effort as instructed, and turned out in their dinner suits. It was strange to witness the transformation from casually-worn uniform, to looking like a bunch of actors about to audition for the part of James Bond. Remarkably, the boys had scrubbed up pretty well. The looming Jackson looked tall and elegant (not that he had much choice in the matter), Davis had somehow managed to tame his hair into an actual style, and Calderman appeared to have come direct from a ball held at the British Embassy. Merry was a credit to the suit hire shop.

They were all awaiting the entrance of one particular friend. He would not disappoint…The door at the end of the hall opened, and in strode a vision. There were gasps of astonishment as the figure casually let the door close behind him. Weatherill smiled enigmatically as he handed his top hat and coat to a shocked Mr Thwaite – who took them from him as if in a trance. The boy was attired in a white tuxedo, complete with gold embroidered waistcoat and white silk scarf across his shoulders. He slowly removed his white gloves and handed them to Thwaite – passing the astonished Master a small tip as he did so. He looked around at the two groups and smiled. Now "ready for action", he walked over to Nicky and his friends, helped himself to a "nibble" from the table, and said 'Wotcher, Lads!'

He had been in the hall for a matter of moments, but was already drawing admiring glances from the girls of St Gertrude's – not least, from their Teacher Miss Trimble, their chaperone for the evening. This was the trouble with Weatherill, he could wear something utterly outrageous and inappropriate, yet look as if he was correctly dressed, whilst everyone else had turned up in their pyjamas…

Kendy didn't look at all nervous. He stood almost vibrating with energy. Nicky sidled over to his friend, and quietly asked him 'You look a bit excited Jon, have you done anything like this before?'. Kendy smiled at him, 'Oh yes, on Alta Media when we reach appointment age, we take part in something very similar – it's all part of our mating and courtship rituals…' Nicky was rather taken aback… 'Well I don't think that we are expected to go quite that far Mate – it's just a bit of dancing'. Kendy was still looking glassy-eyed at the collection of young gels opposite, 'The ritual is all a precursor to selection of a life-partner, and if the female accepts our appointment, then we can go on to perform inter-cellular union by means of physical junction at a time of our choosing – in private, of course…' Nicky raised an eyebrow in shock, 'Well I really wouldn't try any of that stuff at the moment Jon, 'cos that Miss Trimble looks as if she might have a pretty mean right hook on her!' he cautiously advised his amorous alien friend.

Mr Thwaite and Miss Trimble were anxious to get the session started, and introduced their "guests" for the evening, who would be instructing the trainee dancers in the skills of the terpsichorean muse. This turned out to be a pair of dancers who were "resting" from their regular employment as part of Summer theatre shows at the coast. They were introduced to the group as "Raymonde, and his partner, the lovely Alana". Now whatever she might be, the "lovely Alana" was definitely not the partner of Raymonde in any Biblical sense. He wore a tight-fitting one piece dancing suit, and was as camp as a row of Boy Scout tents at a Jamboree. There was no way of ascertaining if Alana was in fact "lovely" either – as she was plastered in such a thick layer of orange-hued makeup, that seeing who was actually beneath it, and visualising their true facial qualities, was impossible.

Thwaite explained that they would be dancing to modern music rather than older, more traditional tunes, in order to make the kids feel more comfortable. He was really disappointed – he had wanted the group to dance to the strains of Glenn Miller and his Band, but the CD had mysteriously gone missing. The boys would be instructed by Alana, and the girls by Raymonde, to begin with. Having mastered the basics of Ballroom, they would then get to choose a partner (in the dancing sense, of course) and trip the light fantastic as their Instructors looked on.

It had all gone well, as the would-be dancers took their lead from the "professionals", who partnered them until they had mastered the moves. Calderman had provided an early shock. As the lovely Alana had placed his hands in the correct positions, he had whisked her spinning and twirling across the hall floor – to the open-mouthed astonishment of herself and the watching crowd. Eventually, he spun her back to the centre of the hall as the music finished. Breathlessly, she thanked the boy, and gave Raymonde a "How come you can't dance as well as that?" look.

Nicky was impressed… 'Bloody hell Calders – I never knew that you could dance!' he said.

'Well, it's your fault if you never ask me…' laughed his nimble-footed friend. He leaned over and whispered into Nicky's ear, 'Kemble's Dance Studio – ten quid an hour, a bit expensive, but at least I won't make myself look like a complete tit…'

Now had come the point where the boys got the girls. Over by the buffet table, Mr Thwaite had already got the girl, and was firing questions at the lovely Alana as to where she bought her makeup, what brand of tights she wore, and just what kept those massive false eyelashes in place…

Nicky found himself paired up with an attractive but snooty girl called Katherine Heath-Cliffe. As they danced carefully across the floor, Nicky attempted to engage her in conversation. With the concentration that he needed to prevent his nervous feet from committing an act of GBH upon hers, the interaction between them seemed to be very hard work. It was made worse by the fact that she seemed only to want to give one-word responses in answer to any of his questions, such as 'Nyhaah…' or 'Realleahh?' He gave up.

Light relief was provided as another twirling couple spun past, which included the grinning Merry as the male half of the duo. The girl dancing with Merry was much taller than him, and was chatting away in her cut-glass tones as they danced. As they passed Nicky and his partner, he heard the young lady enquire 'Eayand..what exactly does hyour Papa do for a living?'.

Merry answered 'Oeuew Yhaah… he's something in the City, don'tcherknow…'.

'Hyand hwhat is that?' asked the girl…

'I dunno – a speed camera, I think' said Merry.

The girl that was dancing with Nicky decided that she could speak after all. She had been staring intently at Mr Thwaite, and had obviously decided to and then ask, what she thought was a pertinent question…She was both fascinated and somewhat horrified by the fact that the man was wearing red silky trousers, matching court shoes, a lacy blouse and bright pink lipstick. His thick moustache had thrown her completely, as had his elegantly manicured pink nails.

'Euuew…I say' she began, 'That Chappie of yours over thaare, that Master. He looks as if he is…I mhean…is he – is he one of those Trans-'

'-sylvanians…Yes, he is' added Nicky, swiftly. 'They do have their own funny little customs…'

The fascinating discourse had come to an end. For the next dozen or so tunes, Nicky stared at the wall, and she stared down her nose. Eventually, Miss Trimble had announced the last dance for the group, which was to be the "Bossa Nova", but would be performed to a rock melody, rather than a more traditional tune. When it was over, Nicky turned to Weatherill and said 'Meet the New Bossa – the same as the Old Bossa'.

'I tell you what…' declared Weatherill, 'We won't get fooled again!'.

To finish the evening's torture, the last dance was to be a "showpiece" put on by Raymonde and the Lovely Alana. All of the trainee dancers stood around as the two went through what must have been a well-rehearsed show routine. At the end of the piece, Raymonde stood some distance away, and Alana faced him with as much of an adoring look as she was able to fake – and then set off toward him at a run. He caught his dancing partner as she leapt, holding her above his head. All eyes were on the couple as the music reached a crescendo. This was unfortunate, as at that precise moment, a three-foot pale blue translucent ball came crashing out of nowhere, knocking Raymonde and his smiling partner into the air – and flattening the rest of the people like skittles in a bowling alley…

As the screams began to die down, and as attempts were made to revive Mr Thwaite who had fainted, Nicky grabbed hold of Calderman's lapel, and told him 'If you've got your mobile on you – get hold of Darwin or Strangler...tell them that we've located our Intruder!'

Chapter Twenty-Two:

With the spectre of Ballroom dancing now just a fading and hilarious memory, Nicky had other worries on his mind. Good Friday was approaching with the stealth of a Ninja, and he knew that he would soon be expected to perform in front of the potentially life-threatening crowd at the village Youth Club dance. Although rehearsals with his band had gone reasonably well, he was still a little nervous about the capabilities of his other band members when place into a "combat" situation. Anthony the bass player was a constant source of worry. Although competent enough on his instrument, the boy was more than a touch nervy at the thought of performing in public. He also had a rather sloppy attitude when it came to guitar maintenance. When he had broken a string on his bass, rather than replace all of the strings as any other player would have done, he simply replaced the broken string using the speedometer cable from his pushbike. The sound was quite frankly horrendous – but he could at least tell at a glance, just how fast he was playing...

Well as far as he was concerned, Nicky was ready...He had put in hours of practice with and without the full band in readiness for their show. He had pounded the kit with confidence – and when not actually behind the new drums, he studiously rehearsed licks, fills and rolls on cushions in his bedroom, watched by his most severe critic...Dave the Chicken.

He had the tools, and he had the talent. He was ready.

Yes, he certainly was ready – ready to kick the lavatory door open. Time, tide, stage fright and diahorrea wait for no man. Well at least if the audience did storm the stage, he had enough drums now to hurl at them, and hopefully keep the baying wolves at a safe distance until the Riot Police showed up. Unless they had been already waiting outside the venue and heard the band. They might decide to join in...

It was too late to panic now – the gig was tonight.

Nicky had been careful to invite as many of his Academy crowd as he could, in the hope that they might provide him with a kind of sympathetic "Rent-a-Crowd". Being Good Friday, there was no school today, so the band had made the most of their free time, and set up the gear in the village Youth Club well in advance of the doors opening. There had also been time for another quick rehearsal. Anthony the bass player had broken another string. This time the daft but enterprising amateur musician had replaced it with a length of thick wire. His bass might have been considerably easier to play, had he removed all of the barbs first.

They locked the doors of the Youth Club behind them, and left the venue until later, with Nicky still sweating from the exertions of the rehearsal. 'See you back here at eight o'clock sharp' he called to the rest of the band. Anthony the bassist would probably find it to be very sharp indeed.

Nicky walked down the side path of his house, and around to the back door. As he turned the corner, he noted the figure lying prone on their lawn. He went into the kitchen. Mum was feeding Dave the Chicken... 'I see Mr Taylor is back' said Nicky. 'Who is he today?'

'The Chilterns...' answered Mum.

Miss Emilia Piggott (or maybe even soon-to-be "Dame" Pie-Gott, who knows?) had long since loaded the last of her equipment into the hired car. It was an Estate car – in other words, the last person to have hired the vehicle, had returned it in a state...She was singing along to the radio as she drove toward the coast. She had already decided to dress herself in a man's plaid shirt and jeans. There would be plenty of time in which to put on the wig and the false moustache later – her meticulous planning had seen to that. It was rather ironic that when she had tried on the various fake moustaches, the adhesive from them had actually succeeded in "waxing off" the one that she already had.

She glanced over briefly at the map which was laid out on the passenger seat, smiling happily to herself as she pictured the seat occupied by a passenger – the one that she was on her way to collect.

Detective Inspector Mike Posta had gone back to the Academy. There were no Staff or boys in residence (apart from one or two Boarders, whose Parents were overseas, and who had to sit out the Easter break at school). His idea was to have a hunt around for any clues which might help him to solve the mystery of the stolen car. He had interviewed the owner of the car, a Dr Julius, at some length. He had found the Master to be a thoroughly unpleasant and generally weird sort of man. When giving his statement to Posta's team of Officers, his exaggerated hissing when he spoke had made Posta feel as if he should feed the man with a dead mouse. The Master tended to hold his unblinking eye contact for just long enough to be uncomfortable. As Posta had shifted in his seat, the head and shoulders of Julius had followed him like a snake. The way that the man moved was also unsettling. When he left his office, Posta had watched the man walk up the path (more to ensure that he was actually leaving than anything else), and had been rather disturbed by the way in which he seemed to ooze, rather than walk.

The area where the car had supposedly been parked had been roped off by Police tape. In the middle of the rectangle, some witty boy (he assumed) had placed a large grey canvas sack, with the word "SWAG" stencilled heavily on it in black ink. A few minutes of scanning the ground intently produced nothing in the way of clues. It was as if the car had just been "lifted" away by some giant hand. Would Aliens have abducted an aged Hillman Imp for its scrap value? Maybe there was a car boot sale out near Alpha Centauri that was selling a nodding dog and a pair of yellow fluffy dice? As usual at St Onans, nothing was going to be in any way what could be classed as "normal". If there was any evidence to be had, well it must be well buried…

Uncle Joe had turned up again, but this time it was to drop off the steam iron which he had repaired for Mum. 'Do ye fancy a quick run into town, Lad?' he asked Nicky. 'Depends how long we are going to be Uncle; I've got my gig tonight' the boy answered.

'Shouldn't be more than a few minutes, I've just got to pick up a couple of bits for the car from the Dealer, and collect a cheque for the anti-gravity device work that I did for the MOD' said Uncle.

Nicky agreed to accompany Joe on his quick sortie into town. He enjoyed the unpredictable conversation of his Uncle, and the trip might take his mind off the nerves that were starting to build up. The drive into Granchester centre was a swift one. Joe was convinced that his partial colour-blindness gave him a special dispensation to ignore all colours of traffic lights. It was not surprising that any mechanic making repairs to Joe's car, would find his brakes to be in perfect condition. This was because Joe didn't use them. He handled the Zodiac like a stunt driver, and considered that braking was for the people that didn't wish to get to their destination as soon as possible.

The car screeched to a halt outside the Prestige Car Dealership, blocking the forecourt completely. 'Shan't be a mo'...' said Joe. He disappeared inside the showroom. Nicky stepped out of the car, ignoring the angry stares of several drivers who wanted to gain access to the driveway. Out of the corner of his eye, he saw several really expensive-looking cars parked to the side of the main building. There were one or two low, sleek, and very sporty models. Even when they were parked, these cars looked fast. Someone was shouting from the side office – 'Oy!....Stop daydreamin', you lazy little Sod – an' get that Alpha Romeo washed if you want to borrow it later on!'

Nicky listened in sympathy – some poor apprentice was no doubt getting it in the neck from the Boss. He looked over toward the parked sports cars. A scrawny figure in ill-fitting overalls emerged from the office, with a bucket and chamois leather in hand...

No – it couldn't be, could it? Nicky hid himself partly behind Joe's car and peered over the bonnet like a soldier on surveillance duty. Yes...it was! The youth that the Boss had shouted at was all too familiar to Nicky's eye. It was "Red Car Rodney"! So, that's why the smarmy show-off kept turning up to collect Jozza in a selection of flashy sports cars! He was borrowing them from the Dealership...He wasn't a car dealer at all – the lying bugger was employed to wash

182

them! Nicky was still staring at the youth when Uncle returned to the car. He jumped back into the Zodiac – hiding himself down below the window as they sped off with a roar of the engine. There was just enough time for him to give a little wave to the carwash youth – just enough to let him know that he had been seen, and that his duplicity had been uncovered. Now that the raw truth had been revealed in all its sordid glory, that car might not be the only "Romeo" that would end up getting leathered…

Nicky was so horribly pleased to have discovered the dirty secret of his rival, that he almost forgot to be nervous about the evening performance. He had had a bath, a careful shave (you never know), and had laid out his "stage gear" for tonight. His friend Jim Jackson had turned up at the house. The boy was a bit early, but Nicky was pleased to see him. Mum had answered the door when he had knocked, and had stared up at the tall lad…and then up a little more. Since he seemed to have been able to fit his lofty frame through the door, Mum thought that the least that she could do was to feed him. This was not a process that it was wise to adopt if Mark Davis showed up – the boy could strip a house of anything edible in minutes, leaving a trail of devastation like a swarm of locusts had just dropped by for tea…

Soon after Jackson's arrival, Weatherill, Merry and Kendy made an appearance. They were made welcome (especially by Auntie – who had really taken to Kendy). The lads sat in the kitchen and took up their hobby of mocking each other. Jackson had insisted that he had recently found out that his new neighbour was in fact the Easter Bunny.

'Really?…THE Easter Bunny?' Kendy had asked.

'Yeah, really – but it's not how you think' said Jackson, gloomily.

'What do you mean?' asked Merry.

'Well, turns out that his real name is "Chris", and to be honest, he's a bit of a Tosser…' Jackson confided to the boys. 'Doesn't speak to anyone, doesn't recycle, accuses us of poisoning his lettuces, and claims to have something called OCD'.

'Is that "Obsessive Compulsive Disorder"?' asked Kendy.

'No…' said Jackson, 'It's "Congenital Dyslexic Syndrome" …'

Okay then…Special Bath completed: hair suitably threatened: stage gear in bag: drumsticks sanded off: teeth cleaned…that was everything – now it was off to the gig.

Just as Nicky was going out of the door, Auntie called him back. She handed the boy a small white paper bag, inside which seemed to be a smaller box. 'Take these with you just in case…' she told him conspiratorially, 'They might come in handy, in case you er…in case you happen to get lucky with a young lady'.

Nicky thanked her, gave her and Mum a kiss for luck, and set off to the top end of the village. The plan was to meet up for an illegal pint up in the village pub, where he and his friends could sit at the back of the "snug" and not draw attention to themselves. The Landlord Douggie always operated a rather relaxed attitude toward the underage consumption of alcoholic beverages. If the village Teenagers behaved themselves, and kept their trousers on, well, that was alright with him. He didn't interrogate any of them to produce their ID, and didn't shout too loudly if they ended up getting so plastered that they couldn't remember who they were anyway, let alone when they were born.

The lads took up their station in the pub. Jackson had caused much merriment for the regular drinkers, when he had overlooked his height – and struck his head on the oak beam over the bar counter. Calderman sipped his pint and said 'I'm really looking forward to this'. Merry agreed, 'Yep – it's good beer innit!'. His friend donated him a sharp cuff to the back of the head. 'What's that you're fiddling with Shep?' asked Calderman, as Nicky fished the paper bag out of his pocket. Nicky passed the bag to his friend: 'Auntie said that these might come in handy – if I "got lucky" tonight' he said. Calderman peered into the bag. He opened the little box inside, without removing it from the bag, and said 'Ah…you do know that there's only three in there, don't you?'. Nicky looked over into the opened box, 'Should I use all of them at once do you think?' he asked. 'I suppose you could – if you want to be *extra* careful…' answered his friend.

Nicky thought that it was very considerate, and typical of Auntie, to have given him some Fresh Breath mints…

As the boys continued their excited buzz of conversation, a figure entered the snug. He walked up to the tiny bar, ordered a pint, paid for it with what seemed like a ton of loose change, and then knocked it over himself. As the youth turned around with one dark leg and one lighter one, Nicky recognised him… 'That's Liam from "Funderthuck"! he whispered to Calderman, 'What's he doing up here?'. Nicky couldn't resist approaching the dampened boy at the bar. Everyone from miles around knew the band "Funderthuck", nearly everyone he knew had seen them perform live, and they were, he had to admit – bloody good. He tried to be as casual as he could, in the presence of a musician who was almost a "local Celebrity". (The Rock and Roll image might have been slightly better, if the guitarist didn't look as if he had just pissed himself…) 'Hello Liam – how's it goin' Mate!' said Nicky. The Rocker looked up at Nicky as he tried to mop himself with a beer towel from the bar.

'Yeah – good thanks…well, it was until I spilled me beer down me leg. I heard that there was a local band on at the Youth Club tonight, so me and Crusty thought that we would come and check 'em out' said Liam.

Now Nicky felt the panic really beginning to rise…not only was he about to perform in front of most of the kids from the village, but now he was going to be scrutinised by members of the top local band – who would no doubt be watching his every move. He hoped that the bolts on his drum stool didn't come loose during the show, although stool loosening of an entirely different nature was more of an immediate concern…

Hi – Ho, Hi – Ho…it's off to the gig we go. The boys made their way across the road to the Youth Club. There was already quite a crowd outside the Club, milling around at the bottom of the wide iron steps that led up to the entrance door. As they made their way through the throng, Nicky was spotted by Victoria Ellison, the well-known local beauty and Radio Mast. She, her impressive stature, and her friend Tracy, all came rushing over to Nicky.

'Hello Nicky – I can't wait to see you on stage!' she giggled excitedly, 'Isn't there something that you wanted to give to me?' (there was a loud choking noise from Merry...). Nicky blushed slightly, and handed over the two much sought-after tickets which he had promised her. Her friend Tracy made a bee-line for Ian Calderman, who was swept away from the group and almost dragged up the stairs and into the venue by her. Once inside the club, it took their ears some time to adjust to the volume of the music which was blasting out of the PA system, plus the animated chatter of the crowd. There were no bar facilities inside the club, but there was a steady stream of "refreshments" finding their way in from the pub across the road, via the rear fire escape doors. The lads settled into a corner. Victoria had other ideas, and immediately settled herself very close on the seating next to Nicky. Liam and Crusty from "Funderthuck" were holding court across the dancefloor – where they were being chatted to and swooned over by some of the local female population. Merry had placed a bottle of beer in front of Nicky, and as he nodded his thanks to his friend, he noticed a couple who had just entered the club. It was none other than Jozza, arm-in-arm with that rodent with the red car...Nicky grinned, and turned to his friend Kendy. He asked him to go over to the DJ, and get a request played. Kendy returned a few seconds later, and told Nicky 'He said that he will play it next...' The DJ was as good as his word. He introduced the next record just as Kendy had instructed him to...

'And now, we have a very special request for a guy called "Rodney" ...This one is for you Rod – and I hope that you enjoy it!' Red-car Rod turned around in surprise, and began looking around the people near him and Jozza to see who had requested him a song, but was greeted by a lot of shrugs.

As the strains of "*Car Wash*" by Rose Royce boomed out, Nicky and his crowd all raised their drinks in salute to Rodney, then collapsed in a heap with laughter. Red-car Roddy was not sure whether to be angry, confused, embarrassed, or all three at the same time. He stormed off into the corner, as Jozza gave him questioning looks of disapproval. Nicky gave her a wave as she looked over into their corner. He hoped that she had taken notice of the fact that he was accompanied by the statuesque Victoria, and having seen them together, he hoped that she would not be amused...As the beam of disco light swept over her, Nicky noticed for the first time that she was putting on a bit of weight. Her normally elfin shape seemed to have filled out alarmingly during the last few weeks, and she was not wearing her purple-tipped hair in a Punk style, which he thought was rather strange.

Unbeknownst to the boys inside the club, there had been a minor scuffle outside. The local Morris Men had chosen to stage a protest outside the venue. It would seem that they were opposed to "young upstarts" taking over their normal rehearsal venue with their "Heavy Mental Music". They had formed a picket line, whilst some of the Troupe danced and capered up and down the line of punters waiting to get into the club. The "Fool" of the Troupe (although it would be very difficult to single out one fool amongst the rest of them) had skipped along the line of people waiting to get in. He had managed to skip just as far as Billy Sharpe. Billy had taken great exception to being hit with a bladder on a stick, especially as he was with his new girlfriend. The jingling idiot had persisted in bouncing around him, until Billy had reached the end of his admittedly short tether...

With a cry of 'And a Rilly – Dilly bloody Dildo to you too Mate!!' he had performed a very vital public service.

The group of Morris Men had scattered as Billy exacted his revenge on his tormentor. An ambulance had been called by a public-spirited observer, who had witnessed the unfortunate incident in all its glory. The Paramedics found it very hard not to laugh as they loaded the Morris Man with the black eye, face down onto their stretcher. As he was lifted carefully into the vehicle, the bladder was still bouncing on the stick which had been inserted in his "Jilly – Jolly – Jacksie-o"…

Chapter Twenty-Three:

The evening had been great so far. The lads were enjoying themselves, and the wide selection of good, loud Rock Music that was being played by the DJ. There had been only one "casualty" so far, when Merry had decided to get on the dancefloor and gyrate to the strains of *"Pinball Wizard"* by The Who. Attempting to copy the windmill guitar actions of Mr Peter Townshend, Merry had failed to leave enough clearance between himself and another dancer. He had floored the poor boy with a single swing of his arm. When the chap had regained consciousness, Merry had insisted that he accompany him over to a seat, where he had provided him with a pint by way of apology.

Calderman had still not been sighted since Tracy Thorpe and her naughty reputation had led him off somewhere. It was either a case of "Missing in Action", or "Missing – in Action". Jackson was being pursued by a rather horsey girl by the name of Lucinda Oddley-Brown, who had pinned the poor lad in the corner, declaring her undying love for tall men, and smelling slightly of saddle soap. Nicky was now getting ready to take his place on the stage. His band would be going on in a few more minutes. He had decided to try and fend off the attentions of Victoria by getting Weatherill to chat to the girl. She had initially seemed quite pleased at the attention given her by the tousle-haired attractive boy in the baseball cap. This had gone slightly awry, when Dick could not resist asking the leggy beauty 'Do Tall Girls lie down longer?'. As she had swung her arm at him, he had ducked. The blow missed Weatherill, and hit the boy that Merry had knocked unconscious earlier. Merry did the decent thing – and took his beer back.

Kendy was making new friends left, right and centre (or if you counted Tracy Thorpe – left, right, and centrefold…). His easy-going manner and innate charm were warmly welcomed by the village kids. As he had looked around the club however, his extra-terrestrial sense of inquiry had been triggered. 'Who is that boy over there?' he had asked. He was informed that it was a village lad named "Benedict". This was not enough information for our friend from Alta Media...

'Why do the girls not seem to like him?'

'I'm sure that they do, at least some do' said Nicky.

'Why is he holding the hand of a boy, and not a girl?'

'I think that he likes boys...'answered Merry.

'So do I! – my friends at the Academy are all boys'.

'Ah...yes...well, they are "Special" friends'.

'But you, and Calderman, and Merry, and Weatherill, and Jackson, and Trevill are all my Special Friends...'

'Yes, that's true, but... (how can I put this?) we're not "friendly" in quite the same way...'

Kendy looked most bemused. 'I shall go and ask him...' he declared.

He marched off and went to speak to Benedict, but found him busy, talking to a friend. Not to be deterred, Kendy did the next best thing, and made his enquiries with one of the many female members of the boy's group. Kendy returned. He sat down and sipped his drink. There was a long period of quiet contemplation before he finally spoke:

'What exactly is a "*Sausage Jockey*"? asked Kendy...

The band got changed into their stage gear in the tiny toilet at the side of the stage. The room was so small, that if there had been one more layer of graffiti on the walls, then a person would have to have walked in sideways. John had tuned up his guitar, and Nigel had been told what the meaning of "tuning" actually meant. They edged out of the gents, and stood at the side of the stage, eager to begin, but nervous. Nicky felt a tug on his sleeve, and there was Auntie in front of him...'What are you doing here Auntie?' he asked. 'I've come for the cake-baking competition, you silly bugger!' she replied, 'Did you think that I was going to miss out on your first gig? I thought that I would come and lend you my support – you could wear it if you get an encore!'. Nicky suddenly had a great idea... 'Auntie, I don't suppose that you would fancy helping us out with a little problem, would you?' Auntie eyed the boy suspiciously. 'And what might this "little problem" be, exactly?' she said. 'We need someone to play the harmonica in the last number, only our Singer has just dropped his down the toilet, and we haven't got a replacement' pleaded Nicky.

Auntie gave him her slyest of sly grins, and said 'Well it just so happens…'

As the strains of a Black Sabbath song faded out, the DJ took the microphone, and announced: 'Ladies and Gentlemen – will you please welcome…the Act that you have all been waiting for…Zip Fastener and the Studs!'. Much to the band's surprise, they were greeted by a massive roar from the crowd as they took the stage. They launched straight into their first song *You Shouldn't call the Doctor-(if you can't afford the Bills)* by "Doctor Feelgood". It was tight, it was loud, there were crunching guitar chords and twirling drumsticks – and best of all, Anthony didn't fall over. The song ended with a classic "burn out" and a terrific roll right around the sparkling pink kit by Nicky. As he hit the snare for the final beat, he bounced a stick off the snare drum and up into the air – where it stuck into the ceiling tiles above the stage.

The audience went mad! 'Bloody hell…' thought Nicky, 'I didn't know that we were that good?' As their Lead Singer chatted to the crowd before the next number, Nicky scanned the front row of the audience, who were pressed right up to the front of the stage. He grinned, as he saw all of his Academy friends right at the front, and the tower that was Jackson, a couple of rows back. Victoria had squeezed herself in between his school mates, and was staring at him intently. So, it was on with the show. The band got stuck into a version of *Summertime Blues* (the "Who" version), and then led straight into *Shakin' All Over* by the same bunch of Gentlemen from Shepherds Bush. Nicky put in another "stick throw", only to find that the drumstick ended up joining its friend, stuck in the ceiling above him at an alarming angle. They played *Doctor, Doctor* by the band UFO, and *Messin' with the Kid* by the Irish Guitar Legend Rory

Gallagher. It was all going brilliantly. Then, Nicky noticed a problem…

He had secured his bass drums to the stage by means of small wooden blocks, which were supposed to prevent the "spurs" of the drums slipping forward in play. They had come loose. With every kick of his bass pedals, the drums seemed to be dancing forwards across the stage toward the crowd – and he was forced to grab the edge of the drums and haul them back when the beat would allow him to do so. More alarmingly, as he glanced to his right, he noticed that the drum riser that the kit was sitting on, had begun to lean down suspiciously. He did his best to alert Merry, who was their unofficial "Roadie" for the evening – but couldn't make himself heard above the volume of the band. Merry was tweaking the surprise "set piece" of pyrotechnics for the last number of the show. He had rigged up thunderflashes, smoke generators, strobe lights, and a couple of meaty-looking Roman Candle fireworks, which would give a spectacular effect for the last number.

The trouble with Merry was that he had absolutely no experience in pyrotechnics or stage effects. In other words – he had no idea what he was doing, what he had done, or what his battery of "surprises" might produce. Had he looked up the word "Detonation", then he might just have held back a bit on the gunpowder…And maybe just one smoke generator would have been sufficient…

Time for their master-stroke. Nicky called for the microphone, and announced 'And now – by Public Demand…Will you please welcome our Very Special Guest, the Blues Legend – "Howling Legs Shepherd"!!' Auntie strode onto the stage: she took the spare microphone and held it to the harmonica in her hand. She was wearing dark glasses, and a bandana hastily supplied by Weatherill. She turned to the band, 'Okay Man…Four Bar Blues in A – break eight middle, back to four and out on Coda…Hit it!' Nicky gaped at his Auntie, until she said 'One, Two, Three – FOUR!', and they were off and running.

She was superb. The band played *Ice-Cream Man* by Van Halen, with Auntie supplying the R&B soulful Blues like someone who was born on the Bayou. Smoke drifted across the stage, and Roman Candle thingies did fiery coloured Roman things as they played. When they nodded to her to take a solo, she fell to her knees and made the little harmonica sing. The number ended with another roar of approval from the crowd, as the band applauded their brilliant guest musician. Auntie gave the crowd a two-handed Rock salute, and hurled her bandana into the crowd, where the front rows began to fight for it.

Merry was now stamping on the electrical power board, as some of the expected effects had failed to work. Nicky was worried that at any moment now, the drum riser was going to sink like the Titanic, and tip him and his kit off the stage. The crowd were going wild, and demanding an encore. 'But we don't know any more songs!' wailed Anthony, 'We only rehearsed a few numbers for this show'. John the guitarist said 'You don't know the songs that we *did* actually play – so what's the difference!'. They decided to repeat *Summertime Blues* and then call it a night. As the powerchords crashed out, Nicky's kit decided to make another break for freedom. He managed to keep playing, but the angle of his legs now threatened a severe rupture, and several more sticks now hung over his head like thin wooden stalactites. Everything suddenly went into slow-motion...

The drum riser gave up its struggle with gravity and collapsed. Nicky's right-hand bass drum went with it, taking out three cymbal stands in the process. At the same moment, Merry's delayed special effects decided to go for broke. The thunderflashes decided to thunder, the remaining Roman Candles declared fiery war, the smoke generators all decided to try and compete with one another, and the stage was suddenly filled by noise, light, smoke, and hastily-fleeing musicians. The DJ dived for cover, and hid trembling under his stack of CDs. Nicky was enraged...well this had buggered up everything. He was going to look a complete prat in front of his friends, half of the village, and the lads from "Funderthuck". This was it then – the final humiliation, he might as well forget a career in music. He stood up and kicked the remaining bass drum off the stage and into the crowd, and then hurled over the floor toms. It was at that point, as he stood centre stage, surrounded by fallen drums, fizzing fireworks, and wreathed in smoke, that the drumsticks in the ceiling all decided to fall on him…

He went to storm from the stage, slipped on drumsticks under his feet, fell over, got up, fell over again, then dived for the safety of the gents' toilet. When he emerged, it was to a scene of total chaos. The crowd were trying to get out of the doors. The room was entirely filled with smoke, but he could just about make out the animated figure of Merry, as he tried to extinguish the fire which had caught hold of the curtains. Nicky grabbed a fire extinguisher and helped his friend to at least get the curtains under control. Nothing else seemed to be alight, so he grabbed Merry and made a break for the exit door. Just outside the door was Victoria. Slightly smoke-stained and breathless, she was nevertheless trying to urgently suggest to Nicky that there was still time for him to join the "Six-foot-high" club.

The crowd were all at the foot of the wide iron stairs which led down to the car park. Some were laughing, some were coughing, but all seemed to be wanting to congratulate the lads on a really brilliant show. Auntie was over in the corner of the car park, hastily signing autographs…Some concerned resident had called the Emergency Services, after seeing the thick smoke pouring out of the hall. There were now two Fire Engines in the car park, as well as an Ambulance, and three Police cars. The Police were busy dealing with a minor scuffle which had occurred when the disgruntled Morris Men had tried to re-enter the venue. They had been beaten up again by public-spirited locals, and there were many torn straw hats, ripped white shirts, and bent bells in evidence.

Nicky was approached by Liam and Crusty from "Funderthuck". This was what he had been dreading: they would be bound to make some very sarcastic comments about his band's performance. He was therefore shocked, as Liam put a Brotherly arm around his shoulders, and said 'Bloody hell Man! – that was brilliant! That's what I call proper Rock and Roll'. Nicky grinned, sheepishly. Crusty pointed at him – 'Look, We'll get straight to the point...We are looking for a new drummer and bass player for the band. We met up with your Teacher, Loopy Newhouse – what a cool Dude that bloke is! and he told us to come here and check you out. We need a drummer sharpish, 'cos we've got gigs coming up all over the place...Do you fancy joining the band?'. Nicky was dumbfounded: 'What – after that performance?' he stuttered. 'Well Liam and Me thought it was wicked. We think it's the best night we've had in ages' said Crusty. 'But why do you need a new drummer?' Nicky asked. 'Well you see, Spider has got a serious problem with drugs...' answered Liam. 'Oh, I'm sorry to hear that' said Nicky, 'Is he getting help?'. Crusty laughed – 'Oh it's not what you think, Spider is going off to be a Trainee Pharmaceutical Chemist, and he won't be able to do that and play drums for us'. Nicky decided to go for it: 'Yeah – I'd like to join...and I know where I can get my hands on a tasty bass player for you as well'. Liam nodded, 'Brilliant – we'll be in touch. Let your Mate know about the Bass job going, will you?'

Nick felt that he just had to ask... 'How come you are replacing Dave the Bass player as well?' Crusty laughed – and Liam answered 'Oh, Dave, yeah – well Dave is just a turd...Now just before we go – can I ask you a favour?'. Nicky didn't know how he could possibly help, but was very eager to do so, whatever it might be. 'Yeah, of course' he said 'What do you want me to do?'. Liam leaned forward conspiratorially, and whispered 'Is there any chance of getting your Auntie's autograph for us?'.

Hang on – where was Kendy? In all of the excitement, Nicky had failed to notice that the boy was missing. Was he still inside the hall? The Firemen had raced up the metal stairs, and through the billowing smoke. They had shone their lamps into the hall, and had been amazed to see Jonef Kendy and Lucinda Oddley-Brown waltzing around the smoke-filled dancefloor. The two of them had been hastily ushered out of the hall, with the boy loudly going on about "Inter-cellular union", or at least that's what it had sounded like.

Nicky's Mum had turned up to collect him.

She surveyed the scene before her. The crowds had been shepherded away from the car park, and were crammed onto the pavement on the opposite side of the road. Cars were being carefully directed around the site of the incident. Some were being carefully directed into the pub car park by the Landlord. Fire engines stood in the yard outside the club, as their crews ran in and out of the building with hoses, axes, and breathing apparatus. The Ambulance was backed up onto the pavement, and various Police Officers were still attempting to break up a small riot involving several irate Morris Men. From overhead, came the sound of a Police Helicopter, as it circled low over the scene and shone down its bright spotlight.

His Mother smiled as she saw her Son emerge from his group of friends.

'Hello Love' said Mum, 'How did it go then…?'

Chapter Twenty-Four:

The first of the sirens had not gone off until she was well inside the perimeter fence.

It had begun to shriek out its piercing warning as she had leaned the long metal ladder on the top of the fence, climbed up until she reached the point of balance, and then fallen in an untidy heap inside the wire…

Now all she had to do was locate the unit in which her target was sleeping.

With the absence of pupils cluttering up his nice tidy Academy, Reverend Vernon Farmer had decided that now was the ideal time to bring in a crack team of Decorators to "spruce-up" the premises prior to the visit of the "Very Important Person". Biddle and Company ("Cut Price decorations for people who resent having to pay too much") were not so much of a "Crack Team", but rather more like a team who did their work as if under the influence of crack…They had begun to re-paint the Old Block, commencing in the top corridor. Work had progressed as far as the wall next to the classroom of the Divinity Master, when a problem had reared its water-based head. Not one of the team of decorators could understand it, and despite threats which ranged from the docking of pay, to extreme physical violence, no-one was able to find out who was doing it. So far, they had re-painted this one particular section of wall six times. Each time another coat was completed, they would move on down the corridor, and onwards down the stair well. After a cup of tea or nine, they would return to put a second coat over the wall – and there it would be…

Someone was repeatedly painting a word in capital letters on the wall, and a large black arrow which pointed to the classroom door. If they over-painted the word on the left hand side of the door, it would swiftly reappear on the right. They had tried to thwart the invisible graffiti artist by taping large plastic sheets to the wall on each side of the door. When they returned to check, the same word and another arrow had been daubed above the door in similarly large and insistent letters. One of the team had suggested leaving a camera in the corridor, left running to record any tampering with their work. They had done this. When they came to check the camera, they found that not only had the lens had been painted over, but the word had once again renewed itself on the wall, in fact on both sides of the door this time. Whatever stealthy method they employed, when they returned to the same room in the same corridor, there would be that word…

KNOB.

Young Jason was starting to get a bit spooked, and had sworn that he had heard a throaty chuckling from down the corridor. He didn't like it one little bit. Undercoat and glossing he could handle, but things at this School were starting to get a bit "Occult" for his liking. When you are only on Minimum Wage, the cost of Garlic, Holy Water, Bibles and Crucifixes can really eat into your take-home pay.

When the smoke had cleared, and the casualties had been bandaged up and sent on their way (not counting the Morris Men, who had been arrested and charged with Loitering, Public Disorder, Affray, Breach of the Peace, and "Going equipped to make a General Bloody Nuisance of Yourselves"), Nicky, Auntie and Mum had returned home in triumph.

Mum had celebrated in style with tea and sandwiches, and Auntie (still in her dark glasses) had sat at the kitchen table and demanded 'Where is that Boy, with my Latte?' Nicky was worried: they had only been back at home for about forty-five minutes, and Victoria had already telephoned the house five times. Mum had found a note, which it would appear had been pushed through the letterbox by Uncle Joe.

'Oh no, would you believe it…she's been at it again!' said Mum.

'Who has, and what?' enquired "Howling Legs".

'Have a wild shot in the dark' said Mum.

'Only if it's at that bugger Seaton…' said Auntie.

'Joe had to go down to the Police Station earlier on this evening' Mum began, 'Cousin Sheila has been detained again…'

'What is it this time?' asked Nicky.

'She's been arrested for collecting washers' said Mum.

Auntie and Nicky looked at each other, 'Seems a bit harsh doesn't it? Just for a small thing like that?' said Auntie as she stirred her tea.

'The note definitely says "collecting washers", look…' said Mum, proffering the note for inspection.

'There were apparently two Window Cleaners, some bloke from the local Car Cleaning unit, some poor lad who does carpets, and a curious youth from a nearby Health Spa…'

'The dirty little devil!' exclaimed Nicky.

'Quite the opposite, so it would appear…' said Mum.

Uncle Joe had also made reference in the note, that he was thinking of resurrecting his career as a Showbiz Manager, and once again entering the world of Stage and Screen, where he would promote and publicise his varied catalogue of acts. Nicky made a hasty mental note to keep Uncle Joe as far away from "Funderthuck" as was humanly possible.

There was unlikely to be too much of a problem at the moment, as the only "Act" that Uncle had on his books to promote, was The Amazing Mrs Betty Kibble and "Disney", the whistling cat…

There may well be a God after all. It could possibly fall to Mankind to accept the existence of a Supreme Creator, who casts his or her watchful eye over the affairs of our little species as it scurries around and busies itself with the matter of how best to blow itself off the face of the planet. One thing must be abundantly obvious, and that is that the same Creator, or Creatoress, is possessed of a particularly warped sense of humour.

It is written that God sees every tiny sparrow that falls. Full marks for observation then: but it might have been of more help, to either catch the poor bird, or perhaps have prevented it from falling in the first place. One can only assume that the Creator has far too much on his or her plate to be bothered with the minutiae of everyday events. When you are the Managing Director – well of course, you have to delegate. There may well have been a Divine Board meeting at which the decision was taken (over tea and really, really nice biscuits) to set up a separate Observations Department which would take over the ultimate responsibility for everything in the Falling Sparrow area. Obviously, their brief would extend out to include all other Species, and this would include Mankind. They would see and record when one of us falls. The results might even be filmed, and played back at Celestial Board Meetings, to add a little levity to the proceedings – a sort of Heavenly "You've Been Framed", for Angels.

This would entirely explain the creation and purpose of black ice...

The Observers with the wings would have been highly entertained by the antics of Miss Piggott, as she attempted to navigate her way toward the main buildings of HMP Fenland. She had abandoned the ladder, leaving it on the perimeter fence where it had become stuck, and had edged her way toward a collection of low brick-built structures some distance away from the main block. The screaming siren had been turned off by Prison Officer Whelks, who had assumed that it had been triggered by pigeons as per usual, and who had emerged angrily from a fire exit, flapped his arms wildly to scare off the perching birds, and then gone back inside to resume watching the football game on his small television. Miss Piggott had seen his emergence from the building, and had thrown herself flat on the ground. When it appeared to be safe, she had risen up like Venus from the sea – or rather, had risen up from the runner bean patch of the Prison vegetable garden. She now crept toward the low brick wall that she had spotted, trailing various lengths of garden twine and bean shoots. Upon reaching the low wall, she pressed her back to the brickwork commando-style, then hurled herself over the wall in one quick action. Not the best decision that she had ever made...

As she landed on the other side of the wall, she was immediately aware of two things. The first fact that came to her attention was just how soft her landing had been. The second point that came to her notice was just how much the reason for her cushioned fall smelled of pig. The pigs in the sty hardly bothered to look up at the strange figure as she fell into the manure heap. They assumed that the short person in the ill-fitting jeans, plaid shirt, overly-large boots, false moustache and wig, was one of their regular visitors. Since there didn't seem to be a swill bucket in evidence, they merely grunted their piggy disapproval of having their rest disturbed. Emilia levered herself up and out of the evil-smelling mud. The wig and moustache were now irrelevant, as she had very effectively camouflaged herself from head to foot with what she had landed in. She squelched her way to the opposite wall angrily, and attempted to climb over the brickwork, all the time being snuffled at by a huge sow who had come over to investigate the chances of the stranger having anything edible about their person. Miss P found that the covering of mud and manure, however supposedly good for the complexion, did nothing to help with the climbing of a wall. She was unable to get any purchase on the wall, and slid down several times, as the sow continued to harass her for titbits. It was a certainty that she would be marooned within these foetid walls, if she didn't come up with a solution. The trouble was though, the pungent piggy aromas were making it much more likely that the first thing that she would come up with, would be her lunch...

Making an instant decision, she waited until the snuffling sow pushed its way between herself and the wall, and then she made her move...She lunged at the top of the wall with her hands, whilst using the broad back of the sow as a step. This time, she was able to lever herself up onto the top of the wall, but in doing so, she also left her rear unguarded. Peggy the piggy had taken great exception to being used as a ladder, and had turned and lunged at the area of denim which was disappearing up and over the wall. She grabbed the ample seat of Miss Piggott's trousers. Miss P was already rolling over the top of the wall at this point, but as Peggy held on firmly, she completed the rest of the roll minus a very large amount of trouser. As she stood upright with as much dignity as she was able to muster, she was given another shock, as the huge shape of Peggy the piggy stood upright on her own side of the wall – now wearing the wig that had fallen off the head of Miss Piggott.

Wigless, false moustache now under her left ear, half-naked from the waist down, and covered in rather-too-fresh manure: Miss Piggott wondered if this was really the way that Tom Cruise usually did it?

The combined Educational Tour-De-Farce that was Professors Strangler and Darwin were once again locked in deep discussions, as to how they might prevent any further attacks by the spherical nasty from the who-knows-where.

'It would help if we could find out what it wants' said Strangler.

'What it wants, is a damned good kicking...' answered Darwin.

'Good idea old Chum – assuming of course, that you don't mind losing half of your leg in the process' said his colleague.

The two men looked at each other, then Darwin picked up a long wooden ruler, with which he made a vicious stab at a globe of the world on his desk. 'Better safe than sorry...' he mused. Strangler took the ruler from his friend, and gave the globe another couple of prods for good measure. 'We have got to come up with a way of trapping the thing, containing it somehow, and then getting it back through the Vortex to where it came from' said Strangler.

'We could always make a translucent blue ball of our own, and place it somewhere near to the Vortex. When our little matey sees what it thinks is one of its own kind – it may decide to come out of hiding and investigate. When it does – Kapowee! We can lob it back through the Portal a bit sharpish…'

'And if it checks out the decoy, only to find that it's made of paper, and decides that it isn't too pleased about it, then it might be us that gets the "Kapowee" instead' said Strangler.

Darwin nodded grimly, and picked up the wooden ruler again. 'We have to find the damned thing first. Right! Got it- we make a ball of our own. We place it near the Vortex with as many other balls and spherical-shaped objects as we can lay our hands on. Then, when the little bugger gets curious…' He began to tap on the globe again, in the rhythm of his words, 'We – can – simply – boot – the – little – Ba-'

He never got to finish the sentence…As the ruler came down to tap the globe for the seventh stroke, it was swiftly bitten in half. As the splinters of wood filled the air, the two men jumped back in alarm as the "globe" made a rapid rolling exit out of the door.

Captain Hercules Brayfield was rubbing down his horse, who he sometimes thought of as his only true friend, and certainly the only one that ever really understood him. As the docile yet massive creature turned its noble head to observe him, Brayfield wondered just why it had taken the Powers that Be so very long to recognise his contributions to Education, and the maintenance of the correct standards of behaviour. His long-suffering Wife was wondering why on earth the man always found it necessary to groom his horse in their living-room...

When he was done with things Equestrian, the Captain set about polishing his Cavalry sabre. So, there was to be a Knighthood handed out, was there? Well then, there was no question at all who the recipient would be. The only question in his mind was why had it taken them so long? He had built his career on terrifying his students into submission, fending off the unwanted advances of the Modern Age, and fending off Johnny Foreigner in all of his filthy, scheming guises. He would receive the Honour with humility and good grace, after which he would immediately gallop on his charger to the white cliffs of Dover – and issue dire threats and English scowls at the

Devils across the Channel. (Unless it was wet of course – in which case he would probably take the car).

Back in the confines of his spacious, yet Spartan flat, the Reverend Felchingham was also pondering the rumour which had reached his ears. Before today, he had been certain of one thing. He was absolutely sure that whoever the recipient of the Honour was going to be – it would not be him. Presumably, the body which collated information pertaining to any future planned recipient of any Honour would have at very least done their homework on the candidate. He was not naïve enough to assume that the dreaded Stan would not have poked a spectral interfering finger into the pie. He dared not even hazard a guess as to what the filling of said pie would be, but he could visualise only too clearly exactly what word would be written in pastry letters on the top of the crust…

A surprising and altogether cryptic letter from his Bishop this morning had thrown him into a state of confusion. However many times he read and re-read the letter (which was in the Bishop's particularly spidery and indecipherable scrawl), it seemed to be hinting that "Old Bish" had heard about some award or other, that was coming to the Reverend, and that it would also be rather a "feather in the cap" of the Church for one of its representatives to be recognised. Bearing in mind the fact that the Rev had been trying for so many years to push his students over to the Dark Side, he felt that on the whole, it might be better for him if they failed to recognise him – and he was able to slip out of a back door quietly.

His mind had gone back to the time when he, recently ordained as a Clergyman, had roomed with friends of his. They had been very strict Presbyterians, and as part of their creed would shun any and all forms of comfort – insisting that suffering and hardship focussed the mind, and brought them closer to God. The furniture and beds had all been constructed out of concrete. Yes, those had been hard times indeed…

He had confided his worries to his friend and colleague Miles Bannister. He utterly failed to take in the fact that should you confide anything to Miles, then you automatically confided the information to Mrs Elsie Noakes, his unofficial "Spirit Mentor" and all-round gossip merchant. To share a secret would usually entail the recipient of said secret responding, "I promise not to tell a Living Soul…". That's where Elsie Noakes had the advantage…She and her multitude of friends were Souls who were not, in the legal sense, living. Once Elsie had the information, well…it would have been spread from horizon to horizon before lunchtime. There would not be a single winged, harp-wielding contact that didn't know every single aspect of your business. Once Elsie had picked up her celestial telephone, you were wasting your time trying to block nuisance calls.

The initial conversation had begun quite normally, until Elsie had listened in on the Party Line. There had been a high-pitched shriek of delight, and Elsie had joined in the conversation… 'Oooooh! Well Reverend, I think that's lovely – just imagine…a friend of Miles and Myself getting a title…I must tell Mrs Wormall…she'll be wanting a new hat for that, I just know it…I wonder what sort of brooch they will give you – I hope it's one of those nice pointy gold ones on a red ribbon…honestly – I can hardly believe it! Just imagine Reverend – they're going to make you into a Nob!'.

The Rev put his head in his hands, and in the distance, he heard a deep throaty chuckle…

Chapter Twenty-Five:

Auntie had asked Nicky to help her out with some little job which she had to do that evening. Since she had helped him out with her show-stopping performance at the club the other night, he was more than pleased to help his Aunt in any way that he could. Besides, she had "that look" in her eye when she had asked him, and he knew that meant that she was up to something.

She had gone out to the shed, and had returned with some items in a carrier bag. As she came back into the kitchen, she asked him 'Did you know that there's a tall girl doing her best to hide behind next door's garage?' Oh hell – it was Victoria again. When she had been talking to Nicky at the dance the other night, she had obviously omitted to tell him that one of her hobbies was stalking…At a height of over six feet tall, she might also want to throw in a side order of looming, with perhaps a loitering sauce.

When he had checked that the lovely Vicky had fled the scene, Nicky and his Aunt made their careful way up the track that ran along the bottom of their garden. Four doors up the lane, they came up to a small white van. 'What are we doing here, Auntie?' Nicky whispered, as his Aunt produced tape, a stencil, and spray paint from the carrier bag. 'Just a small job that I wanted to get finished whilst the weather is good…' said Auntie. 'Here – hold this up on the side of the van will you'.

She placed the stencil onto the rear door of the van, placed a piece of tape at all four corners, and sprayed over the template. She waited a few moments, while the paint dried a little, then carefully removed the stencil. The stencil, tape, and spray can disappeared back into the carrier bag. She walked away a little distance, then turned back and said 'Oh yes…a rather neat job – if I do say so myself'. Nicky looked back at the rear of the vehicle. There was a medium-sized sticker on the glass, which asked "How's my Driving?", and gave a contact telephone number for any complaints. Now below it, covering both rear doors in neat block capital letters was the statement "*The driver of this vehicle has a face like a Baboon's Arse*".

Auntie had giggled to herself all the way home. Nicky felt that he just had to ask the question. 'Auntie – why is it that you dislike Seaton so much?'

'I took an instant dislike to him'.

'Why?...'

'It saved me having to waste time later on'. She laughed again.

'Right, I'll tell you a bit about old Seaton...' she declared, as they got back to the house. 'Years ago, he used to be a Copper, and he was a right jumped-up little git then. He thought that the uniform gave him some sort of authority over who he thought were the "lower classes" in the village. Well, when you were only a toddler, I had a car. Seaton hated anyone having anything that he hadn't got, and made it his business to make life miserable for anyone who had. Every time I was out in the car did that bloody man pull me over, and go over every inch of the car looking for anything which he could give me a ticket for. So after this had gone on for about six months, I was starting to get pretty fed up with the officious little git and his tricks.

One night, I was coming back from visiting one of the girls from work, and I was doing about sixty-five miles an hour down the back lanes, when I see the old flashing blue lights behind me – and just as I expected, it's that idiot Seaton in his patrol car. He pulls me over to the side of the road, then swaggers over to my car. He tells me that he is going to book me for speeding. He asks to see my driving license. I told him that I've never had one. He grinned and said 'Oh dear – well I've got yer now then...' He then asked me to produce my MOT documents. I told him that I never bothered with the MOT – as the car runs perfectly well without it. He shakes his head again, and says 'This gets better by the minute'. Then he wants to see my Insurance – I told him I never use it. He found this really enjoyable, and keeps scribbling away in his little notebook. He then says 'Can you prove that you are the registered owner of this vehicle, Madam?', and I told him 'No – I can't, because I nicked it about an hour earlier tonight…I don't know the registration number either – so you might as well bugger off!'

Just then, another car pulls in behind him. It's his Sergeant from the station. 'Good evening Sergeant' he says, 'I'm just about to make an arrest'. The Sergeant looks at him and says, 'What for, Constable?'. 'Driving a stolen vehicle, no Driving License, no MOT certificate, no Insurance on vehicle – for starters, that is. This lady has readily admitted each and every one of the offences' says Seaton.

So I calmly walk over to my car, reach into my glove compartment, and take out all of the documents. I spoke to the Sergeant…The registration of my vehicle is VTO667K, here are my ownership documents, along with my Insurance, License and MOT certificates. The Sergeant looks at Seaton, who seems to be having trouble closing his big mouth – 'Do you have some sort of problem with this officer?' he asks me. I answer, 'well yes Sergeant, he seems to have some sort of vendetta against me for some odd reason. He has accused me of all of those offences – which you can see I am clearly not guilty of…And it wouldn't surprise me if the nasty little bastard tries to accuse me of speeding as well…'

'Wow – then what happened?' asked Nicky.

'He went to work for the Water Board' said Auntie. 'And I sold the car'.

'That's a bit of a shame Auntie' said Nicky.

'Not really, I bought myself a lovely new hunting rifle' she said, 'Oh, and maybe a couple of other little bits and pieces…'

'Such as?' asked Nicky.

'Nothing much – just a bazooka, night-vision goggles…oh, and a crossbow.'

Captain Brayfield raised the blade in his outstretched hand, so that the sunlight glinted along its pristine length, and pointed it skywards in a gesture of bravery and defiance… 'FOR ENGLAND – AND SAINT GEORGE!!' he proclaimed, in the voice of the Crusader.

'For God's sake – will you just put the bloody butter on the toast…' said his Wife.

Nicky felt like he was in complete turmoil (a specialist lubricant only found in schools, during certain periods of the Academic year). Everything seemed to be going so well for him, and yet he still felt full of a kind of churning angst. He had just been asked to join the best and most accomplished local band around, and yet to further his musical career, he knew that he would have to let his former band members down by informing them that he was leaving. He had spent many troubled hours, weeks, and months trying to work his way into the distant affections of Jozza. She had spurned his amateurish advances in favour of some lying little toe-rag who washed cars. Now the tables seemed to have been turned – and he had a girl who was actually pursuing *him*. The trouble was, she was doing it in quite a disturbing manner. She was apt to turn up in the most unlikely of places, and on a regular basis. It was getting harder by the day to avoid her…but then, did he really want to? He might as well forget all about Jozza, and walk off into the sunset with Victoria, the towering lovely. This image suddenly gave the poor boy even more worries – as it was far more likely to be the case that the Amazon Vicky would hurl Nicky over her shoulder, and stride off back to her cave with him.

Nicky had even tried to enlist the assistance of The Desk. If the answers to his Teenage forebodings were to be found anywhere, then The Desk would be the place. He had put a brief note in the top drawer. He had waited. The response had been both swift, and rather sarcastic for an antique piece of furniture. His "One-Stop-Shop" for advice had replied by means of a little note which had read '*You really are a miserable little Turd – stop whining and buy yourself a ladder…*' Who needed a Therapist's couch, when you could get help of that quality eh?

Nicky vowed then and there to get his own back, and hide his Mother's beeswax furniture polish.

There were other people who were having just as confusing a time as the Teenage Would-be Rock Star. Oh my word yes…One such poor unfortunate was edging her way along the wall of the canteen block of HMP Fenland at this very moment. She knew that her ultimate target was near, so near that she could almost smell him. Actually, that was not true in any sense, because what she could smell strongly was the farming product that had recently left the digestive system of a lot of pigs. The actress Ursula Andress had risen out of the surf in her white bikini like a Goddess, in the early James Bond film *Dr No*. No Goddess (as far as Miss Piggott was aware) had risen up half-naked out of a heap of piggy poo, trailing runner bean stalks and string, and provided an iconic silver screen moment. She ducked under the open canteen window with her customary excellent timing, and received the dregs of a cup of cold tea over her head, as it was tipped out by one of the canteen staff.

As she fumbled her way nervously around the corner, she was amazed at what she saw...

Gerald Goodwill was leaning nonchalantly against the outer wall of "E" Block, smoking a cigarette. Miss Piggott was both elated and disgusted – there was her beloved Gerald, but to see him indulging in such a filthy and disgusting habit was...was...well, it was worse than gaining illegal entry to one of Her Majesty's Prisons, dressed (half-dressed, that is) as a man, in a false moustache, covered in string and runner beans, and topped off with a thick layer of pig manure. Maybe.

Goodwill blew out a languorous smoke ring, and casually turned to the bizarre vision that had come into view...

'Emilia...how very nice of you to drop in, whatever it might be that you have evidently seen fit to drop into' he said.

Miss P rushed toward him, but Goodwill raised his hands in a gesture of dissuasion:

'Please no, I've just had this uniform cleaned...' he told her, pouring cold water on her desire to hug him.

'Oh Gerald...' she began, 'I've come to take you way, I just cannot bear the thought of leaving you in this dreadful place for another moment, I have a car waiting – and it's parked around the back. No-one saw me come in. I got over the fence, and sneaked through the farm buildings, and I've disguised myself, and I've come to get you out! I've got a flask and sandwiches for you on the back seat…'

'I see…' said Goodwill, pulling slowly on the cigarette, 'Why did you not just drive to the front entrance and park in the Prison car park?'

'I didn't want to be seen by the security cameras…'

'My Dear Lady, this is what I believe is usually termed an "open" Prison establishment. Since my blasted incarceration within this cursed unit, I have come to realise that certain things such as security and procedure would seem to be approached with a certain, shall we say, relaxed attitude. Your ingress would not have been recorded by the cameras at the front of the building in any case…'

'Why is that, Gerald?'

'Because My Dear, the Prison Guards have turned the 24-hour recording CCTV cameras around. I believe that they have done this in order to ensure that the cameras get a good view of the bathrooms of the Nurses' Accommodation opposite. I am given to understand that the "zoom" facility in particular of the cameras is rather good – really, they are such a bunch of Scamps! In truth, should we decide to do so, we could merely walk right out of the wretched place. The Shift turnaround occurs at round about this time, and I doubt very much if any of the highly-trained staff will have the presence of mind to keep a keen eye on the cameras, unless it is to check on Nurse Atkins as she towels down after her shower, that is.'

'So let's walk out together then, Gerald' Miss P urgently suggested.

'Ahh…if 'twere only that simple, My Dear' laughed Goodwill.

'But you just told me th-'

Goodwill held up his hand. Around his wrist was a black canvas strap, attached to which was a chunky square device like a very old and cheap digital watch…He explained:

'We are all forced to wear one of these perfectly beastly devices at all times. They apparently send a signal to a central computer, and record the location of each and every wearer. Should a signal fail to be received, or be seen to be outside the perimeter, then an alert is sounded immediately. All units have to be inside the main block during shift changeover, in order to prevent the poor Officers having to tax their brains by being asked to count heads'.

Miss Piggott regarded Goodwill with the same look of abject pity which is normally employed by Inuit peoples who answer a knock at the front door of their igloo- only to be confronted with a double-glazing salesman... 'Well, can't you just slip the wretched thing off your wrist?' she enquired.

'A simple solution my Dear – but alas, not a practical one...' stated Goodwill. 'You see; the device has a heat-sensitive insert that will detect if the wearer removes the tag for more than a few seconds'. The mud-splattered face of Emilia Piggott lit up – 'I have it!' she declared triumphantly, 'If we take off the tag – and re-attach it to someone else before it registers any movement, then we can escape without the system knowing that we are gone'. Goodwill raised a quizzical eyebrow: 'And whom did you have in mind to act as the recipient, may I ask?' Miss Piggott pointed triumphantly at the pigsty wall, where the huge sow was still watching proceedings with a grunting disinterest. 'There!' she said, 'I shall release you from this hellish torment by means of attaching the tag to the pig!'

This was working out a lot better than Goodwill could ever have hoped for. Not only could he see the door to freedom wide open – but fate had provided him with the perfect stooge with which to make good his escape. He smiled at Miss Piggott. 'Madam, you display not only great beauty, but great planning abilities' he said. Under her coating of manure, Miss Piggott felt herself beginning to blush hotly. Goodwill continued... 'If I may ask you one small favour: since you are already, shall we say, somewhat "camouflaged by nature", it might be a better idea if you were to take the tag over to the pig and attach it,

212

whilst I go and collect the vehicle – I shall meet you in the front car park, just in front of the barrier'.

Miss Piggott gladly agreed. Greasing the wrist of Goodwill with the contents of a small tin of lip balm (which she just happened to have concealed about her person, because let's face it- no prospective felon wishes to be seen with cracked lips), she slid the tag from the arm of her hero. She placed it on her own wrist, admiring it for a second, as a girl might admire a brand new engagement ring for the first time. She hurriedly passed Goodwill the keys to the car, which he carefully took from her fingers with a look of mild disgust on his face.

'Bless You, my Brave Heroine!' he declared 'I shall go and get our transport, whilst you attach the bracelet to our porcine friend over there'. Without a backward glance, Gerald Goodwill scurried off around the corner of the building. Miss Piggott squared her shoulders, and quickly marched over to the pig sty wall. This time, she sought out the heavy metal gate, and was just about to open the latch, when she was suddenly grabbed by the shoulder of her shirt and lifted bodily up and over the gate. Peggy the piggy had seen her coming. She liked this new visitor, as she smelled the same as she did. Still wearing the wig at a jaunty angle, she decided to give her new friend a really piggy welcome.

Officer Keane was anything but. When tag FN6263NP1/L had shown up to be outside the main building after shift handover, he had drawn the short straw and been forced to go and collect the errant inmate from the farmyard area. He had approached the pig pen carefully, not wanting to get any mud on his highly-polished boots, or ruin the knife-edge creases in his uniform trousers. As he looked over and into the pig pen, he was astounded to see what appeared to be one of the prisoners attempting to fit his security tag onto the leg of Peggy the pig. There was a tremendous wrestling match going on in the oozing mud – and the pig was already ahead by two falls. As the contestants rolled and tumbled, it became rather difficult to ascertain exactly which one was pig, and which one was prisoner. He reached for his walkie-talkie, which he fumbled in his haste, and dropped into

213

a heap of all-too-fresh manure. He then reached for his whistle, giving a mighty blast. Peggy the piggy was the only one of the two mud wrestlers to stop and look up at him. The other contestant was still face down in the mire, with Peggy sitting in triumph on top of her.

'RIGHT – YOU!...OUT! NOW!' he screamed at the top of his voice.

Miss Piggott ("Pie-Gott") arose slowly, like the Creature from the Black Latrine. Peggy ("Peg-Gee") sat bolt upright in her wig, awaiting further instructions.

Officer Keane barked his commands at the completely unrecognisable Miss P without bothering with the merest hint of punctuation...'Rightyou'orriblemangetyerarsebackinsidesharpishcoz theGuv'noris gonnatearyouanewoneforthislittlecaper...'

Poor Miss Piggott was pushed back inside the prison door, protesting her innocence, and leaving a trail of something which would really benefit the roses. She was held by two more prison Officers, in front of the sterile-looking "reception desk" where the Officers gathered to drink tea and observe the Nurses across the road. 'Take your hands off me this instant!' demanded a smelly yet furious Miss P. 'I am not one of your prisoners – I am just visiting'.

'In *our* pigsty, in *our* yard, wearing one of *our* tags – yeah, 'course you are...' smirked one of the Officers as Miss P struggled. They forced her arms behind her, and she heard the click of a set of handcuffs. At that moment, she happened to glance up at the bank of security screens at the back of the desk. There were three screens that were not displaying views of the Nurses' Accommodation. She stared in horror as she saw Gerald Goodwill calmly driving out of the prison in her hired car, casually waving out of the open driver's window...

214

Chapter Twenty-Six:

Uncle Joe ground his teeth angrily, as he paced up and down the living room carpet at Nicky's house. Mum was rather perturbed by this, as Joe clearly had his own carpet at his own residence, upon which to pace, and grind his teeth (should he wish to do so). His "side-venture" as a Show-Business Impresario was not going at all well. He had been very badly let down by one of his acts last night. Despite his better judgement, he had taken on a semi-professional club singer by the real name of Doreen Pyng. She was an ex-nightclub entertainer, now semi-retired, and unfortunately only semi-tuneful. The lady now strutted about the stages as a Tribute Act to one of the biggest singing legends ever to emerge from Wales.

Joe had booked Doreen to appear as the main act at the local Working Man's Club, on their "midweek talent night". She had given it her all, under her new Joe-suggested stage name of "Shirley Bassley". The former Nursery Nurse had taken the stage in her gold sequinned frock, and delivered her show-stopping song "Diapers are Forever" …

Joe had turned up, just as the first of the Police cars was leaving.

He had stood in the shadows of the Club doorway as he reminisced… 'That takes me back' he had mused. Unfortunately, it had not taken him back quite far enough: he was spotted by an eagle-eyed Club Member, and had to make a break for it across the Bowling Green and over the main road. In a nearby bus shelter, he came across a bruised and breathless Shirley Bassley, her dress looking particularly battle-weary for a Wednesday night. 'What the bloody hell went wrong in there tonight?' Joe had demanded. 'I've no idea lovey' she replied, 'I don't understand it – the audience were with me all the way'.

'I know – I think you lost them at the corner of the Post Office, I saw the trail of sequins leading off behind the houses' said Joe.

'Do they want me back next week?' asked Doreen, hopefully.

'No...' stated Joe, quite firmly. 'And they don't want you to re-varnish the entrance either'.

'Sorry?' said Doreen.

'I think that the exact phrase used was "That Woman is never to darken our doorstep again", if I heard them correctly' said Joe.

'Do I still get paid, Joe?' she asked.

'Look, Shir- I mean Doreen: we both got out alive, let's call that a generous bonus shall we?'

Joe gallantly put his Star Performer into a taxi, and paid the driver to drop her off.

(Beachy Head would probably be favourite...)

Yet again, poor Uncle was forced to try to remember if he had ever inadvertently trodden on a Fairy somewhere in his chequered past. He must have somehow upset the natural order of things, which had led to the spelling being amended to "ordure", in relation to every area of his Business affairs. He had been ecstatic when he had finally finished writing his Stage Musical for the West End. He remembered being bitterly brought back down to earth, when his Wife told him 'Not to make such a song and dance about it'.

He was also troubled with the thought of how he could possibly shift a hundred and fifty metal embossed signs which warned "DO NOT TOUCH" – all printed in braille. He sat at his kitchen table and gazed at the glass of water into which he had dropped a couple of much-needed soluble aspirins. Half an hour later, and still with the beginnings of a raging migraine, he noted that just to annoy him, the tablets were both still fully intact. Unless things picked up dramatically, then that glass would illustrate his life perfectly – a picture of insolvency. There was still no reply from his Jewish Business Consortium, to whom he had recently unveiled his latest brilliant idea. With a view to providing a product which would be greatly appreciated by Jewish Ladies of "a certain age", he had branched out into the lucrative world of Cosmetics. He had spent weeks developing a skin cream that really did reduce the appearance of wrinkles. He himself had tried it – it worked. Joe just couldn't understand why the group of (let's not be shy about it) extremely wealthy Jewish Businessmen had not leapt at the chance to finance his new product - "Oil of Oy Vey".

It was a time of portents and omens…The local newspaper had been full of reports of strange sightings and occurrences. A woman from a neighbouring village had reported seeing a flock of wood pigeons repeatedly circling her garden. The reporter on the News Desk had been, in her opinion, unnecessarily rude and abrupt to her when she had telephoned in with her sighting. He had called her a "timewasting old bat", and informed her that her sighting was nothing out of the ordinary – and not to bother them with such trivia again. She had been so angry at the attitude of the man, that she didn't bother telling him about the Sat-Nav that the pigeons were carrying when she spotted them.

The local Vicar had telephoned the local Radio Station, and breathlessly recounted the weird sight that he had just seen. It appears that he had witnessed a cloud, which was *exactly* the same shape as a large ball of cotton wool…and he had pictures to prove it.

One of the young Postmen claimed that he had seen the face of Elvis Presley, which had mysteriously appeared on the cover of one of his Father's old vinyl albums *Jailhouse Rock*.

Mrs Evadne Whipskin, a self-professed Clairvoyant, Psychic Reader and Kitchen Fitter, claimed to have had a series of unsettling dreams – in which she was approached by various breeds of dog, all asking her if Poodles were in fact members of some strange canine Religious Cult.

Reginald Cramper (War Hero, ex-Casino Croupier and boiled egg expert) had begun a systematic campaign of letter writing to the Press. He besieged the in-trays of the papers with an avalanche of letters, all demanding to know why, if that structure on the High Street was called a "Bus Shelter"- he had never, ever seen one with a bus under it.

A village Farmer had made a frantic telephone call to the Police, after finding apparent Alien interference with his crops. He had been out in one of his biggest fields, using equipment to break up clods of earth. He had found that some mysterious and unworldly force had created a straight rectangular pattern of lines in the soil behind his tractor. It had proved to be a harrowing experience for the Farmer…

There had also been various reports in the press that a large pink Hippo had been sighted running across the Market place on a Saturday. Auntie had put forward the hypothetical scenario that Cousin Sheila just may have taken up streaking again…

Nicky was more interested to know just who the long, lean figure was, that Auntie had spotted lying in the long grass at the end of their garden - observing the house through a pair of binoculars. Even the normally reliable (if a touch on the cryptic side) Desk had not been able to provide any immediate answers. Nicky had placed a written question into the small drawer, which had been answered with the following phrase – *"All our Mystic Operators are currently dealing with chocolate bunnies and eggs, and are unable to answer your written submissions directly. Please direct any queries of a deep or profound nature to drawer three- where they will be answered as soon as an Operator becomes available. We would like to apologise for the temporary delay, and any subsequent inconvenience which this may cause, but hey! – we've got stuff to do, you know how it is…".*

None of this was any use whatsoever to a boy who was urgently seeking the answers to some pressing questions (and in the case of Victoria- it was highly likely to be her that would be doing the pressing, given half a chance). His musical career did seem to be on the rise, with his "promotion" into the Premier League of local Rock. His mind however, was still tormented by the thoughts of Jozza, and why (having witnessed his performance at the Youth Club) she had not made contact with him. As far as he was concerned, he had put one over on the Carwash Cretin- at least enough to make her re-think her decision as far as Boyfriends was concerned. He had seen her walking past his house at least three times since the dance, and yet she had not so much as cast a glance over the hedge. Perhaps he mused, she was happily settling into the joys of a long-term relationship with the idiot. She had looked quite content when Nicky had seen her go past, and he couldn't help but surmise that such a level of contentment might just have something to do with pies. The previously sylph-like girl did seem to have extended a touch around the waist department, and on more than one occasion, he had observed the object of his desires munching away intently on what he thought had been a bag of large pickled gherkins. Such ponderings were getting him nowhere – he would have to bite the bullet and ask the Desk for answers again, assuming of course that the Magic Pixies who provided all of the answers were not away from their desks having extensive dental treatment after their apparent chocolate binge...

As nonchalantly as he possibly could, Nicky approached the polished leviathan and leaned against it. Whistling rather tunelessly, he casually flipped down the lid of the desk and opened the small top drawer. He placed a note into the drawer which simply read "What's the deal with Jozza?" He then strolled out into the kitchen, and poured himself a casual glass of milk. Auntie eyed him suspiciously 'And what might you be up to then, young Feller-me-lad?'

'Nothing really Auntie, just waiting for something, that's all' he lied, spilling the first mouthful of cold milk casually down his tee-shirt.

Auntie was staring intently at a small pot of cream. She shook her head sadly, and said 'Honestly, the price of this stuff...no wonder the Co-Op staff all have three holidays every year. Mind you, I supposed that the price is justified – because the cows must find it a real bugger to squat over these little pots...'

Nicky thought it best not to comment on Auntie's opinions concerning the Dairy Industry. He sidled back into the living-room, set down his glass, and approached the desk. He was for some reason, extremely nervous about what the Desk might have given him by means of an answer to his question. It seemed to him to be one of those awkward instances where you needed to know, but didn't really want to know, although you had a perfectly good reason for wanting to know what it was that you were dreading to find out. Even if you found out that what you were told was not what you really wanted to know, you had to know, sort of.

He opened the top drawer of the Desk. Inside was the usual neatly-folded note of reply. Nicky extracted the note from the drawer with all the care of a bomb-disposal expert, not even daring to breathe until the drawer had been slid securely home. He slowly unfolded the note. Here was the regular immaculate copper-plate writing. So- now to see what wisdom the Desk had dispensed...

He was baffled. He read the response four times. The note merely stated:

"Mum's the Word..."

Brilliant, he thought - now I apparently need some sort of special Security Clearance to be able to obtain a sensible answer from a damned desk. What next? Would I have to complete a Retina scan before I was able to operate the steam iron? Would the television only permit me to watch it if I can supply copies of my fingerprints, and give the correct nine-digit password? What would happen if he put in the wrong password? He had heard so much about ID theft recently, that Nicky was beginning to panic that the Authorities might choose to come round and repossess his fingers. He needed to get a grip...This might be somewhat problematical though, if the finger collection did in fact take place.

"Getting a grip" was not a phrase that was in regular daily use by the Staff of St Onans, and certainly not in the context of Reality...As far as some of the more outwardly eccentric Masters were concerned, they merely regarded reality as a word which occurred in their dictionaries, somewhere between "re-assess" and "rectum". Professor Richard Strangler for instance, was quite likely to put all his time and effort into developing a device which would counter the effects of gravity- in order that he could float up and dust the model Spitfire that he kept on the top shelf of the laboratory cupboard. He and Johnathan Darwin the Biology Tutor had made the decision that in order to capture and return their "visitor" (whereabouts currently unknown...), other Masters should be let in on the secret. They had been very choosy as to who they had told about the wonderful Vortex and its properties. Had they been just a tad more choosy, then they might have considered the fact that certain individuals might just be ever-so-slightly tempted to "have a go" on the Interdimensional Funfair ride. There really should have been a sign placed at the side of the Vortex, which read "You must be a minimum of this Sane to ride..." If such a sign had been put in place, then one thing was certain – there would be no queue.

One of the first potential travellers on the Disorientated Express had been the Reverend Felchingham. When the principles and workings of the Vortex had been discreetly divulged to him, you might just have assumed that a "Man of The Cloth" would probably have wanted to travel back in time and meet his Hero, Jesus Christ. Unfortunately, our Rev was cut from a different cloth entirely. He had put on his "concerned" face, and had listened to what Darwin had told him about travel across the interdimensional interface. No- that's not true at all, he had let the technical stuff fly right over his head, completely ignoring words like "trapped", "danger" and "disintegration". The Rev had plans...he knew just where he was going to travel to, and who he needed to see.

On a pretence of returning a borrowed coffee cup to Strangler, the Rev had made his way into the back room of the Physics laboratory. Finding the ante-room door open, it had been a simple matter to lock the door behind him, flick the switch to the "On" position, and set off through the Vortex on his little voyage of discovery. Bless him- he even took a packed lunch.

Armed with a copy of a book by the person with whom he hoped to make contact, the Rev had stepped cautiously through the glowing portal in the back room of the laboratory. Finding himself outside an imposing grey stone house, he carefully edged his way to one of the front windows and peered inside. From the appearance of the decorations and furniture, the Vortex seemed to have deposited him in exactly the place that he had wanted to be. He straightened himself up, brushed his robe down to remove dust and stray candle wax, and walked toward the front door which was painted in a deep black gloss with a grotesque carving of a demon for a knocker. The thought suddenly occurred to him that his appearance in Clerical robes might not be well received by the man that he had come to visit. In preparation for any doorstep confrontation, and to prove his allegiance to the "Dark Side", he held up the battered, fire-damaged and very goat-chewed copy of the *Malleus Malefecarum* in front of him as a talisman to ward off ev- well…to ward off whatever it needed to ward off, as he wasn't exactly too sure at this moment in time.

Little did the Rev know that he would shortly receive a shocking revelation from the occupant of the house, and that further terror would chill his very soul in the form of a message that the man was to give to him…

'I greet thee, Priest…' said the stout man who opened the door. He too, was attired in black robes.

'I bid thee entry to my Temple. I am the one whom you seek.
I am Crowley - Aleister Crowley…'

Chapter Twenty-Seven:

The Rev returned to the ante-room of the Physics laboratory, a sadder but a wiser man – much like the famous ex-sailor in the old poem, who had a jar of Ancient Marinade tied around his neck and some sort of personal problem regarding his water…

He had been given information, and a hand-written parchment which Crowley had demanded that he follow to the letter, under pain of eternal damnation. He was angry at the former, and utterly bemused by the latter. He scurried off to the darkened sanctuary of his classroom, where he could examine the scroll in detail. Once seated at his desk (and having locked the door securely behind him) he fished in his drawer for the paper bag containing the apples which he had bought for a lunchtime snack. They were his favourites, a tasty, if oddly-shaped treat by the name of "Knobby Russets". He glanced at the supermarket receipt as he withdrew the first apple. Taking a bite, he was not really surprised in the slightest to see that the till system had abbreviated the purchase transaction…it stated "KNOB".

Seemingly from inside the paper bag, came a throaty chuckling…

Oh to think…it had all begun so innocently.
'Happee – Birthday to Yoooo…
Happy Birthday tooo Yooo…
Happy Birthday Oh My Deeeaar Roystoonneee…
Happy Birth-a-day, a- to YOOOOOOO!!!'
Thus had sung the completely over-excited Music Master Mr Newhouse, as he urged all of the Staff to join in with the song, spraying them and the Birthday Boy Roy Hyde-Jones with a magnum of champagne. There had been shouts of horror, gestures of distaste, screams of delight, and a rush by Dr Matthews to attempt to capture as much of the flying fluid as possible in his open mouth. Roy the

English Tutor had accepted the cards, gifts and best wishes from the Staff with his usual slightly-embarrassed good humour. He was more embarrassed when his friend Newhouse had wrestled him to the floor of the Staff lounge and planted a great big sloppy wet kiss on his cheek. The rest of the Staff had applauded, crying 'Speech!!'.

That had been yesterday. That had been before the party. That had been before the full force of the Newhouse Intergalactic Celebratory Experience had been unleashed upon the Birthday Boy.

Now it was the day after the party before. It was going to be some time before Roy Hyde-Jones would be able to achieve anything which would even remotely resemble the function of speech…

Roy had winced in pain as the light had attempted to crowbar open his pickled-onion eyes. He was immediately concerned that during however long he had been unconscious for, some creature had removed them, gone to the toilet over them, and then put them back into his head. He could feel a sharp pain in his left cheek. Delicately and carefully probing his back teeth with a shaking finger, Roy produced a small purple and yellow cocktail umbrella…He laid back on the carpet and began a mental inventory of all his body parts. The checklist produced nothing that seemed to be broken, dislocated, or otherwise attached to anything surprising or unpleasant, so that was a bonus to begin with. He sat upright- achieving ninety degrees of lift at the third attempt. From the kitchen area of the flat he could hear the melodious singing voice of his friend Newhouse, warbling a complicated ditty which involved a Swedish Lady, some fresh fruit, a stepladder, and a goat. As the jack-hammer inside his head began to go into overdrive, Hyde-Jones flexed his hands. No injuries there- good, because if that loon in the kitchen didn't stop singing, he would need both of his hands in good working order to throttle him with.

Newhouse appeared at the kitchen door. He was a vision of complete and utter normality, and looked as fresh as the proverbial daisy. The Music Master gave his recumbent friend a huge grin, and said 'Ah…welcome back to The Land of the Living, oh Great Royston-type person. I have prepared some breakfast in your honour…Ladies and Gentiles- may I present…A Full English!!' He swept a plate of fried delights onto the table, as Roy held up a hand in abject horror.

'Oh my God – how can you possibly do it?' asked Hyde-Jones.

'Oh, it's not hard Roy, I just fry it all up in a really good non-stick pan, and whack it onto a plate…' declared Newhouse.

'Not the food you madman, I mean…just how the hell are you feeling?' asked H-J.

'Well Sir…' began Newhouse, 'Nerves in my fingers send sensory impulses up the synapses and up into my brain…'

'I mean, how the blue blazes can you be so…be so…bloody cheerful?'

'I practise a lot…' answered the smiling Newhouse.

Roy Hyde-Jones regarded his friend as he attempted to take a seat at the table. Good grief- the man was completely untouched by the debauchery and over-indulgence of the previous night. And just to add insult to liver injury – the man was sitting opposite him, drinking a PINT, for heaven's sake. Roy felt that he should perhaps start with the basics…

'Can I just check, Loopy…' he whispered, 'What planet is this?'

'Why…'tis the very same one that we were on last evening Royston – but slightly redecorated in certain areas. Once you have eaten up all of your breakfast like a good boy, and perhaps a hair of the Werewolf that wee'd up your leg- I shall let you come out with me and explore it'.

Like slowly and gently prising apart the stuck pages of an ancient Encyclopaedia, the events of the previous evening began to re-appear in the mind of the English Master, each dreadful scene more embarrassing than the one before it. He remembered that the night had begun at a local "Kosher Kocktail" bar, where Newhouse had insisted that he be treated to a dizzying selection of the brain-numbing concoctions which lurked menacingly behind the bar. Unused to exotic drinks in such quantity, Hyde-Jones had been forced to ask his friend to explain what each of the lethal liquids actually contained…

'Socks on the Beach?' he asked, 'What's all that about?'

''Same as "Sex on the Beach" mostly' replied Newhouse, 'But with this one, if you overdo it- then you will end up paddling, trust me...'

There had followed a startling array of sweet-tasting and highly-flammable cocktails, which were all served up in celebration of H-J's birthday. "Man-Hat-On" had turned out to be a variant of the famous cocktail *Manhattan*, but served with a hard hat. *Singapore Sling* should really have been slung a very long distance away for safety reasons. In honour of a Gay friend of theirs, they then moved on to *Pink Jims*. Newhouse then toasted his friend with a cocktail of his own devising, a little thing which he had christened a *Harley Wallbanger*. Loopy explained that after about four of these, it was quite possible to be able to ride your American motorcycle through any wall of your choosing. They had settled for a borrowed pushbike – it had worked a treat.

Newhouse then set up the partygoers with a large glass of lager, into which he dropped a smaller shot glass full of lazy amber fluid. As the glass sank to the bottom of the larger receptacle, it began to fizz and bubble alarmingly, especially when he had added a large shot of vodka to the mix. 'What the hell is this?' Roy had slurred. 'This is one of my very own favourites!' declared a proud Newhouse – 'I call it the *3D and E...*'

'Could you be a little more speck – a little more spesh – shpecifical?' slurred Hyde-Jones.

'Why certainly, my cute little Birthday Person!' grinned Newhouse. 'It is my creation which I call the *Drambuie Depthcharge Double-Ender*. It is a singular delight, which bestows a sense of well-being and general loveliness upon the recipient – BUT I must warn thee, can have certain "repercussions" upon the over-imbiber of same. Partaken in sufficient quantity, the beverage may result in prolonged sitting on the white porcelain, whilst utilising the cistern lid to catch anything prematurely ejected from the top end...'

'Sounds asbol – abblu – abs'lutley bloody lethal!' declared H-J.

'Nonsense Royston!' said Newhouse, 'Matthews has already tipped four of 'em down his neck'.

All eyes had swivelled around to view the History Professor, who grinned hugely, and raised his glass to the rest of the party-goers.

When the shelves at the back of the bar had been efficiently diminished to the point of no return, Newhouse had leapt to his feet excitedly and declared that the entire group should immediately re-locate themselves to his flat, where they could get down to some serious drinking. What a good idea this had seemed at the time, and the unsteady huddle of guests had lurched their way into the residence of the Music Master. For poor Hyde-Jones, most of the events which occurred after this point were still more than a little hazy...

The crowd of guests, some invited, and some collected along the way, made their way to the elegant and slightly decadent residence of Mr Newhouse. He ushered them all inside, saying 'Mind the donkey, he doesn't like being disturbed until he's finished eating...' They all laughed heartily, assuming that "Loopy" was having one of his little jokes. He wasn't...

Newhouse gently guided his friend into the living-room. They ducked as a young lady in a cerise leotard with garish makeup swung over their heads on a trapeze... 'Do be careful Brenda!' said Newhouse, 'You're going to get sequins all over the trifle'. She was deftly caught in mid-air by her partner Gunther – who had a sausage roll firmly gripped between his teeth as he gripped the ceiling light fitting with his feet.

It wasn't long before the party got into full swing – (including Brenda and Gunther).

Despite the loud Rock music which was causing the double-glazing to vibrate in harmony to *Keep Yourself Alive* by Queen, there had been the barely-audible chiming of the doorbell. Newhouse had skipped merrily to greet the new arrivals, weaving his way carefully around Dr Matthews, who was at present laying on the hall carpet, and demonstrating the correct etiquette which should be followed when downing a Yard of Vodka.

At the door stood an unrecognisable figure. Newhouse first assumed that the neighbours had made an official complaint about the noise – and had sent round some Legal Representative who would slap a "cease and desist" order into his hand. The vision was Female – very obviously so. She stood before him in a slate-grey business suit, with an immaculately-tapered skirt which reached below her knee. Under the suit was a white silk blouse with frilled edges, done up to the neck and pinned with a delicate cameo brooch. Newhouse noticed that the extremely high heels that the Lady was wearing raised her a full two inches above his own impressive stature. Her hair was pinned up in a tight bun at the back, and black-framed Business spectacles completed the look of the Boardroom.

'Hello My Dear…' she purred, 'I have a little something for the Birthday Boy'. As if by magic, Hyde-Jones wobbled his way out of the living-room, and appeared at the elbow of the Music Master. 'You wanted the Birthboy – the DayBirth – The Brith…Oh Bugger – It's Me! 'Smy Birthday…Innit!' he slurred. The figure handed Newhouse the black leather bag which she was carrying, and gently eased him out of the way, leaving an open space between herself and the giggling Hyde-Jones.

'May I wish you very many Happy Returns, Roy' she said, in a seductive whisper, 'I couldn't let the day go by without making sure that the Birthday Boy had something to open!'

Without warning, she reached up and gripped both of her shoulders with her hands, and then tugged firmly downward and outward in one swift movement. The business suit surrendered its Velcro fastenings, and fell to the floor to reveal a black leather studded bra, suspenders, and the skimpiest pair of briefs that could ever have been sold without a printed warning…She shook out the bun, and her hair fell around her head like a fiery mane. As she slowly removed the glasses, the transformation was complete. Both men stood transfixed with their mouths open – having suffered an instant overdose of Matron. Even with the thick carpet of the hallway, you could clearly hear the jaw of Mr Newhouse dropping...Things were made worse for the men's' trouser departments, when from behind the Matron stepped a similarly-clad Goddess, but with white leather "embellishments" and blonde hair. The two ladies took up station on either side of the stunned English Master. 'This is my Swedish friend Irena...' said Matron, 'She normally works for the O2 Company, but she wanted to come with me tonight to wish you a Happy Birthday – I hope you don't mind!'.

Roy Hyde-Jones tittered drunkenly as the two barely-clad lovelies took a hold of both of his arms – 'So she's the...she's the...(hic) that means she's the famous O2 Irena!!'...

They all had to quickly flatten themselves against the wall, as from nowhere, a man in Victorian swimming costume with an enormous walrus moustache sped past on a unicycle, whilst carrying a silver tray of vodka shots and assorted canapes. The cyclist saluted the group, and turned the corner into the living-room, passing the smiling figure of Dr Matthews as he did so. As he came to a halt in the room. The wheeled butler was astounded to find that he was looking at rows of vodka shot glasses which were completely empty...

Roy had been kidnapped by the pair of ladies, and escorted giggling to the master bedroom. Newhouse had left them to it. When he next passed the door, he was sure that he had heard the sound of a party squeaker. How it was being used was anyone's guess...It was quite a long time later that the English Tutor emerged from the bedroom.

Roy was in great need to answer a "call of Nature" – which in truth was more of an urgent telegram. Another scantily-clad temptress was busy playing the pinball machine in the hallway. He edged his way around her, and squeezed into the bathroom. He was not the least bit surprised to see a dolphin cavorting in the large sunken bath. It was juggling with what appeared to be two eggs, a novelty bar of soap, one cowboy boot, and a travel guide for the city of Prague. A very creditable job he was doing too, thought Hyde-

Jones, as he edged toward the toilet. Sitting in the bath with the dolphin, and applauding enthusiastically, were three naked (apart from their gilded caps) members of the Granchester Girls Brass Ensemble, still clutching their instruments to prevent water getting in. Roy wondered just how much more bizarre things could get…and then he noticed the orang-utan who was sitting on top of the toilet cistern, engaged in what sounded like a very angry telephone call to his Agent.

Back in the kitchen, Mr Thwaite had been shocked to the core of his being to witness Bell-Enderby the Art Master, who was kneeling in front of a topless and frighteningly well-endowed lady, whilst holding up a plastic container of semi-skimmed milk. He was holding up the container in front of her, whilst she struck the top of it continuously with her ample breasts. 'What on earth do you think you are doing?' Thwaite had shrieked… 'Oh, I was just getting this young lady to help me to prove a theory' explained Bell-Enderby. 'You see, when I was a young lad, my Nanny always used to tell me that tits used to be responsible for pecking the tops off the milk in the morning – but now I'm beginning to have my doubts: you see, this poor lady can't seem to achieve the same effect at all, in fact all she has managed so far is a couple of nasty bruises…'

Newhouse had to step in, when the game of Naked Twister which was being played in the guest bedroom had got a little out of hand. Bannister had joined in most enthusiastically with the members of the Female Brass Band, but had become entangled dangerously in the trombone slide, and now had his foot firmly jammed in a French Horn. Newhouse began to laugh heartily, as in the corner of the room, he saw the bottom halves of Dr Matthews and the Conductor of the Brass Girls protruding from the chocolate fountain which had been set up on a table. Their heads were immersed in the deluge of delight which was flowing down the sides of the fountain. As the smiling Matthews came up for air, Newhouse asked 'everything alright in there Doc?' Matthews gave him a calorie-loaded grin, and replied 'Oh but yes indeed Dear Boy! – I managed to fill the thing with liqueurs!!'. Newhouse dipped in a finger and tasted the mixture. There was no denying it – the man was a legend...

The next day, it had all seemed like some weird dream caused by too much cheese before bedtime, at least that is what Hyde-Jones hoped – when he recalled some of the evening's more lurid events.

'I mean to say Loopy – just who on earth would ever think of bringing a Llama to a Birthday Party?'

'Hmmm...I'm thinking – possibly an Inca?' said Newhouse. 'Might have been my own fault actually, I think I told Thwaite to make sure that Inga the Swedish Barmaid came to the party – perhaps he misheard me?'

'And on the subject of unexpected guests – who was it that organised the Stripper to attend?'

'No-one Royston: that was Mrs Beasley my neighbour, she's always a really great "joiner-in" at parties- really gets into the spirit, bless her'.

'She must be eighty-nine if she's a day!' said Hyde-Jones.

'And still working, would you believe!' laughed Newhouse.

'Where's that?' asked H-J.

'At the local Strip Bar. She's been there for years- and trust me, she's still got all of the moves. These days, she's more of what you might call a "Delapidancer", but she can still work that feather boa' said Newhouse.

'But were all of those cartwheels really necessary?' asked H-J, 'and what about the baby oil, the whipped cream, and that banana!'

'Yeah, sorry about that...is your eye alright now?' said Newhouse.

'I didn't know where to put my face when she did that thing with the satsuma...'

'Be fair Royston- it does count as one of her "Five a Day" ...'

'I was amazed, I mean to say...some of the things she was able to do, especially at her age...I couldn't believe it when she put her ankle behind her ear, and started juggling with her dentures...is she always that flexible?'

'Well no, no always…she can't do Fridays as a rule, it's her bingo night…'

'And what about old Matthews, what happened there?'

'Well when we started to run low on booze, I sent him out for supplies' said Newhouse.

'A very wise decision, and exactly what did he come back with?' asked H-J.

'Four bottles of vodka, a case of scotch whisky, eight bottles of wine, and some mixers' said Newhouse.

'And…?' said H-J.

'Ah yes – and the Granchester Girls Brass Ensemble…but you must admit- they were bloody good mixers!' stated his friend.

'And whilst I recall…who was the tall girl in the sequinned dress?'

'More detail please?'

'The one with the Zapata moustache and the pipe…'

'Ah yes of course- that was our friend "Pink Jim"… nice bloke'

'Yes indeed, one hell of a handshake on him, I can tell you that. He certainly enjoyed himself after Mrs Beasley taught him fire-eating'.

'Pity we had to ask Bell-Enderby to leave early though…' mused Newhouse.

'I suppose so…' said H-J, 'but with all those young ladies in residence, we just couldn't trust him not to take a quick trip down Mammary Lane, now could we…'

'What did Bannister mean when he said that he really liked your "golden bidet" in the bathroom?'

'I really couldn't say, but I did have to slip that girl from the band a few quid to get her tuba properly cleaned, just in case…'

'The girls all seemed to enjoy playing pool with Mr Thwaite, didn't they?'

'Oh yes, but I think that he took exception to them continuously putting the blue chalk on the top of his head…'

Hyde-Jones carefully bit into a sausage as if it might explode, and thought whilst he chewed.

'And Loopy – who was that bloody weirdo in the purple velvet smoking jacket: you must remember...the prat who was standing in the sink without any trousers on, and shouting at the mirror about the woeful command of the English Language that young people have today, whilst trying to draw cartoon faces on a bunch of grapes...?'

'That would be you, Royston...' grinned Newhouse.

The two friends finished off their breakfast in silence, punctuated by sharp intakes of breath from Hyde-Jones, as more barely-legal incidents from the previous evening came back to him. Eventually, the English Tutor was provided with a small glass of water, in which something medicinal was effervescing and spinning around in. Newhouse brushed his friend and colleague down. Roy Hyde-Jones was staring at the glass, as the clods of bubbles rose.

'What goes "Plink-plink-fizz" ...?' he mused.

'Elton John – in a bath of acid!' laughed Newhouse.

Both Masters put on their jackets. As they walked up the passageway to Loopy's front door, the Music Master suddenly placed a hand flat to his forehead, and declared...

'Oh my Dear Boy!...how can I ever apologise to you. Please do forgive me...'

'What's the problem Loopy?' asked H-J.

'Now look...There are people in New Zealand and the Samoan Islands for whom the sun has yet to rise on the new day. For these poor unfortunate beings, they have yet to realise the vital importance of this new dawn...'

'I'm not really following you, Mate' said H-J.

'In the farthest outposts of Humanity, they have no idea that it is now, for them, a time of great celebration...' Newhouse declared.

'How do you mean?' asked a still bemused Hyde-Jones.

'We must celebrate with these tribes as they mark the occasion of your Birthday!!' said Newhouse, grinning hugely. 'Let us begin our joint celebrations at the nearest watering-hole and raise a toast tour far-flung Cousins in Foreign Parts'.

'My Cousin lives in Newark...' said H-J.

'Sounds Foreign enough for me!' said Newhouse.

The English Master knew that there was to be no escape from another session of liquefied brain damage. He was spun around by his friend, and pointed in the general direction of the nearest Public House. He shook his head (as gently as he could, until the aspirins kicked in) and smiled.

'There was something that I wanted to mention, Loopy' he said.

'Ask me anything, oh Teacher of Linguistic Treachery...' answered Newhouse.

'Well I don't know if you noticed it – I mean, it's only a minor point, but did you notice at all that there was a Volkswagen Beetle parked in your living-room?'

'Ah yes – that will be Effie Beasley's car'.

'Can I ask please...how did it get there?'

'By safe driving, and good parking' answered Newhouse.

'Good parking indeed...' said Hyde-Jones. 'How do you think Mrs Beasley got it in there?'

'By her usual method of driving carefully and considerately at all times' answered Newhouse.

'And that is commendable. But does anything strike you as well...ever-so-slightly odd about her parking?' he asked.

'Such as?' queried the Music Tutor.

'Well such as the fact that your flat is on the first floor, for instance?' said Hyde-Jones.

'Honestly Royston – you do surprise me sometimes...' said Newhouse, as he held open the door to the bar,

'She *has* been on an Advanced Driving Course...'

Chapter Twenty- Eight:

It was a complete and utter load of balls. The hastily-convened "Task Force" of Staff and Boys had spotted, investigated, and carefully prodded every spherical-shaped object within the environs of the Academy. Pages of checklists had been pored over time and again, and although somewhat nervously, the conclusion was being drawn that just maybe their unwanted and violent "visitor" had managed to go back from whence he, she, or it had come from. There had been no outbreaks of spontaneous globular violence for quite a few days, and Messrs Darwin and Strangler were beginning to feel the relief of having got away with something that could in very real terms, have rolled right over the top of them. Instructions had been issued to each and every Pupil of St Onans, that should they wish to bring into the Academy a ball of any description – then it MUST be indelibly marked with an appropriate pen. In true St Onans fashion, this had led to a great deal of misunderstanding- and much entertainment in the showers following games.

Above the rectangular confines of the quad, Keith the Raven and his gang sat on the edge of the stone parapet wall, and pondered the apparent fate of their missing colleague Boris. Their friend was missing from his usual perch at the end of the wall. Some well-meaning builder seemed to have replaced the large concrete ball that had been absent from its plinth for the past few years. Around the ball was strewn a collection of black tattered feathers, but of poor Boris, there was no sign…

'Should we gather up the feathers and maybe hold a funeral?' asked Gareth, one of the Raven clan.

'Can't stand funerals…' said Quentin, his friend 'I just don't think that black suits me…'

Black too, was indeed the mood of the Reverend Felchingham, as he recounted his recent experience of travelling through the Vortex in search of Spiritual bedevilment from his hero Mr Crowley. He was utterly despondent as he recounted the sad tale of his meeting to his colleague Miles Bannister… 'And you say that things didn't go entirely to plan?' asked Bannister, in his usual caring manner. 'No Miles, they certainly did not' stated the Rev sadly, 'Quite the opposite of what I had hoped for in fact'.

'Did he listen to your views and opinions?' asked Miles.

'Oh indeed he did – and then added an opinion of his own…' said the Rev.

'And this is what has upset you is it? Did his ideology not match that of your own?' he asked.

'He had a very direct and forthright opinion, which he felt necessary to direct at me personally' declared the Rev.

'Would it help to share the details?' asked Bannister.

'No – I doubt it' said the Rev.

'Oh come now old Chap, I can't possibly see what he could have said that has upset you to this extent. Why not tell me, I promise not to tell another living soul, and remember- a problem shared is indeed a problem halved, or so they say…'

The Rev stared dejectedly at the floor. Bannister tried to lift his spirit:

'Why not get it off your chest old Chum, you'll feel much better if you tell me'

'He laughed at me…' said the Rev.

'Well that's not too bad now, is it – there are worse things that he might have done' Bannister said.

'S'not the worst bit…' mumbled the Rev.

Bannister motioned with his hands that the Rev should tell him the rest.

'And…?' he queried.

'And he said I was… a Knob…' whispered the Rev.

From seemingly all around the two men, came the sound of a deep, throaty chuckle. It went on for some considerable time before finally fading into silence.

Certainly not black, but definitely edging toward the more fluorescent purple end of the colour chart, was the face of the Headmaster, Reverend Vernon Farmer. The reason for his consternation and barely-supressed ire, was twofold: there was the fact that his Secretary Miss Piggott was still absent from her post, and the fact that another terrifying missive from "The Palace" had just arrived.

Despite his normal bluster and brag, the Head had not plucked up enough courage to force himself to open the imposing buff envelope – instead delegating the task to his Deputy, Dr Chambers. He slit open the envelope rather reverentially, opening it with great ceremony, and began to read the contents…

'Well Man…what does it say?' screeched Farmer, quite startling his Deputy, who dropped the letter into his tea, and had to hastily wipe off a generous serving of China's finest. The Head couldn't wait – and neither could the hands, because he snatched the paper from the fingers of Chambers, and began to tremble as he read the words…

'Dear Sirs: Her Majesty the Queen is pleased to inform you that your Academy of St Onans of Granchester will receive a visit from Her Majesty's Husband, His Royal Highness the Duke, on the occasion of Founders Day, Monday May 9th. His Highness will be pleased to hand out in person, such awards which have been earned by Pupils of the Academy as part of his Award Scheme. His Highness will also be pleased to present written confirmation of personal summons to appear at the Palace, to individuals who have been nominated to receive Honours in Her Majesty's Birthday Listings. Please be advised that His Highness will require sufficient space in which to land the Royal Helicopter, should he choose so to do, and provision should be made for the parking of five Royal vehicles. Please be advised that no special dietary requirements should be made on behalf of His Highness on the day, although it would be preferred that suitably private and accessible toilet facilities be made readily available. Her Majesty notes that you will be happy to confirm your acceptance of these details by immediate return of post.

Yours Faithfully, Sir Bernard Cranleigh-Home KGC DSO and Bar, Secretary of Honours to Her Majesty Queen Elizabeth II...

(Post Scriptum – pray remember to affix a stamp to the envelope this time, as having to pay a surcharge in order to get letters really gets right up Her Majesty's nose)'

Farmer sat in stunned silence for a few moments. He suddenly jumped upright in his seat, as if someone underneath the desk had found the "on" switch. 'My God!!' he stuttered 'Th-that gives us less than four bloody w-weeks in which to get the place sorted out...right Chambers- get the Decorators back on the telephone, and get Brooks in her sharpish – oh, and that Finucane Cleaner woman while you're at it...'

'I'm not sure it would be terribly acceptable to re-paint our Cleaning Supervisor, or our Grounds Keeper, come to that, Headmaster...' said Chambers.

'No, you idiot! – I mean I've got to – we've got to – well damn it all to bloody buggery...someone's got to, and quick – before the Duke gets here!' shouted Farmer, 'Get Dr Julius in here as quickly as you can'.

Chambers gave a look to the now panicking Headmaster, and scurried off to summon the members of Staff as instructed. It was some time before Mrs Finucane arrived, smelling slightly of floral disinfectant. The strange Dr Julius had already slid into the Headmaster's study, and was sitting hunched and hawk-like in a corner chair. Not long after, the sound of heavy boots was heard as they stamped purposefully down the corridor, and the heavy door swung open...

'What's tha want naah then, Vermin?' asked Brooks, in a voice thick with pure Yorkshire annoyance. 'Tha allus manages ter want to see me as soon I gets sat on t'closet...'

'Thank you for attending so very promptly' declared Farmer, 'I need you to ensure that the statue of St Onan is safely fitted, as soon as possible. In four weeks' time, we will be having a Royal Visit, and I do not want any little mishaps or incidents to ruin the day...'

Brooks eyed the man, and replied 'Well I've got 'ee all set up and ready, so there's no need to worry. But just you do me a bit of a favour – and keep bloody Rat boy over there in the corner well out of my way, or I'll 'ave his arse on the end of the fork I uses on me cricket pitches...'

Dr Julius looked down at the floor. His habit of lurking around in unwanted places at unwarranted times of the day and night made Brooks' fists itch. He felt certain that if he put down a big enough trap, with enough poison on it, then it was a certainty that he would catch Julius before very much longer. No-one in the Academy (apart from the Headmaster) actually liked Dr Julius, and in truth, there was absolutely nothing to like. After a few minutes in his slimy presence, you began to feel the urge to dash off and have a really good hot shower. When Mike Posta and the other Police Officers had finished interviewing Julius about his missing car, even they had given the cleaner at the Police Station a large tip – with an instruction that the interview room was to be thoroughly washed down and disinfected... Twice.

Quite a long distance away, somewhere out towards the East Coast, in a room that smelled of furniture polish and unpaid fines, stood Miss Emilia Piggott. She stood defiantly as the Magistrate gave his summation of the case against her...

'Whilst I would like to be able to say categorically that the case against you in respect of attempting to aid and abet the escape of a Prisoner detained at Her Majesty's Pleasure is proven, I cannot with the utmost certainty prove that your statement that you were merely visiting the Prisoner is not true. Your car was indeed stolen by the Prisoner – that much, we have CCTV evidence of: but I fail to comprehend why you would make a visit to one of Her Majesty's Prisons dressed in Male apparel, looking like some ghastly extra from a Western Film. I understand that you have stated that you were on your way to a "Line-Dancing" class? And if that is indeed the case, then that would seem reason enough to place you behind bars. Alas, neither cross-dressing, nor lack of common sense- not to mention pig wrestling, can be interpreted as punishable offences...I mean, if that were the case, then there would be a long line of High Court Judges waiting to be locked up (there were titters around the courtroom). I have therefore decided that you be bound over to keep the peace, for a period of twelve months. You will also pay the Veterinarian's bill of £58.76 for the removal of the Prison tag from the pig. You may now leave this Court, Doh-see-doh...' stated the Magistrate.

That was it then...Piggott was on her way back.

Confusion reigned supreme at the desk of Dr Chambers the Deputy Head. He had just opened a letter which informed him in large, jolly typescript that he had won a "Round-the-World Cruise" in a prize draw. What really confused him, was the fact that when he had checked as to who had sent him the letter, it had been sent from the Flat Earth Society.

His next allotted task was to sift through the badly-written pieces of paper which had been deposited in the Academy "Suggestion Box". One or two of the suggestions were very specific indeed, and contained quite painstakingly drawn and detailed diagrams...

And there were other letters which demanded his attention...A letter from the Academy Financial Overseers stated that they would no longer be prepared to go through the books and verify the costs of monitoring food quality for the kitchens. Very well then, that was one expense that could be deleted from the Balance Sheet. There really was no accounting for taste...

The loathsome Dr Julius was making his presence felt throughout St Onans, at the direct command of the Headmaster. He had been instructed to seek out and report back on any plans which might be overheard, concerning acts of Rebellion or disobedience. The Head knew that his iron rule was despised throughout the Academy, but he saw his rules as paramount – and not merely any old iron. This seemed to suit Dr Julius to a tee, as he enjoyed nothing better than sneaking around the place, and taking in any stray tit-bits of bad behaviour which might come to his attention. His favourite pastime was gaining the confidence of the boys, and having done so, turning their comradery against them when the opportunity presented itself. His lack of moral scruples made him the perfect "Fifth Columnist", and should he pick up any useful gossip from the Pupils – then he swiftly became a Gossip Columnist too. Whenever groups of boys would gather together, you would see them automatically check over both shoulders, just in case Julius was lurking somewhere in the vicinity. There was a strong rumour amongst the boys that since the man had landed at the Academy, the rat and mouse population had drastically reduced almost overnight. Gossip amongst the Pupils had stated that he had been regularly seen setting traps in the Boarding House, and waiting patiently whilst clutching a knife, fork, and serviette.

Nicky and his classmates were all in the Old Library. They were ostensibly there for a revision period in preparation for the forthcoming Term Exams. Calderman had suggested using some of the older History books to look up all about the Germanic origins of the Royal Family, as it was now common knowledge that a Royal Visit was imminent. This had seemed like a good way of distracting them from the more boring subjects which they were supposed to be revising, and so had been readily agreed upon. As with any gathering involving the usual mates, there was the regular good-natured banter taking place. It had been suggested that Davis should climb the tall library shelves and collect the ancient, heavy books containing Ancestries and Royal lineage. Nicky had pointed out that those book shelves were over a hundred years old – and hadn't they suffered enough? Davis had laughed, declaring: 'I will have you know...that I have recently got down to my proper fighting weight!'

'Yeah – proper fighting weight for a Sumo Wrestler!' said Merry, causing much uproar.

'Just watch it Merry ...' warned Davis, wagging a finger at his friend, 'I am training in Martial Arts...'

'Why bother? – you're already a Black Belt at "Hand-to-Ham" combat!' laughed Jackson.

'How dare you Sir!' said Davis, in mock-outraged tones, 'I'm learning that noble defence Art of K...oh bugger, what is it called? – I know it starts with a "K", I think...'

'Kentucky Fried Chicken?' ventured Trevill, and they all fell about laughing again.

Davis proved them all wrong, by sweeping aloft and gathering up several old and dusty tomes. The books were brushed off, and laid on the bench tables of the library. Calderman was the first of the friends to find what he was looking for... 'Oh Wow!' he said, turning a page, 'Yeah – our Royals are all descended from the German Family of Saxe-Coburg'. There was a scramble as the rest of the friends huddled around to see the Family Tree in the book. One boy however, had not rushed over to join the group. Kendy had remained at his table, where he was staring intently at the book which had in front of him – turning it this way and that, as if to get a better perspective on the photograph which he had found. Nicky noticed that his friend had not moved, and called out to him 'Hey Jon – what're you doing?'. Kendy looked up. Nicky could tell by the look on his friend's face that something was amiss. The boys ambled over to where their Alien friend was still staring at one particular image in the book. Whilst searching for facts on the history of the Royals, Kendy had opened a page which was displaying images of the Second World War. The particular photograph that had caught his attention was of a row of German SS Officers, pictured in front of some kind of rocket-launching device in 1940. The photograph had been taken somewhere in Eastern Europe, at a secret testing location. The faces all bore the confident smiles of an Army that knew that Victory was certain. All but one, that is. One face scowled at the camera through small round spectacles, with a look of reptilian malevolence.

The boys stared at the photograph...then at each other...then back at the image on the page.

'No...it couldn't be' whispered Merry.

'It bloody well is...' said Davis, 'unless he's got an identical twin brother...'

Chapter Twenty-Nine:

What the boys had seen in the library book was still troubling Nicky when he got home that afternoon. He had always heard it said that "The Camera Never Lies", but the sense of dread and unease which he was feeling made him half-wish that it might just have decided to tell a little fib on this one occasion. He knew that this wasn't the case, and he also knew that he had absolutely no idea what to do about the boys' chance discovery…

Mum had asked him why he was moping around the place like a wet weekend. She had leapt to the conclusion that he was thinking about Jozza again, and in truth, a small part of his brain was still actively working on a plan to secure her affections. Mum made some tea, then plonked the cups on the kitchen table and went upstairs on some urgent errand. This meant that Nicky was left at the table with Auntie. Now there were two kinds of look that you got from "Howling Legs". One was the caring and serious look, when bad news had to be delivered: the other one was the barely-concealed grin that signalled that the piss was about to be taken on a mighty scale… This was the former, and Nicky wondered what Auntie was about to tell him. She led straight in to the conversation…

'Have you still got your eye on that girl from up the road?'

'Well…maybe a bit Auntie, but I think I'm wasting my time' he answered.

'There's plenty of fish in the sea, Lad' said Auntie, 'You don't want to get too serious at your young age…'

'I wasn't thinking of going out spawning just yet' said Nicky, going with the oceanic metaphor.

'It's a bit late now, even if you did!' said Auntie, with an ironic smile.

'What do you mean, Auntie?' asked the boy with the bemused head.

'Well I saw her yesterday, and she's put on a bit of weight' Auntie said in a matter-of-fact way.

'Her weight doesn't matter' said Nicky, 'She's just a nice, friendly girl'.

'She certainly has been that all right...' said Auntie, almost under her breath. 'Look Love, your Mum and I think it's best if you forget about Jozza and go out with that nice Victoria girl'.

'What is it that you are hinting at not trying to let me know what it is that you are actually meaning?' said Nicky, breaking almost every grammatical rule he could think of in one sentence.

'Think of it like trading in a car...Jozza has gone for an Upgrade.'

Nicky looked blankly at his Aunt... 'From Sports Model – to People Carrier' she said.

'Sorry?' said Nicky.

'Look...She is definitely "Plus One" on the Guest List – okay?' she said, now getting exasperated at the boy's lack of comprehension. There was still no response from her Nephew – so Dear Auntie decided to go for broke...

'For heaven's sake Lad...She's suffering from the Nine-Month Mumps - She'll get given a seat on buses - She's had a temporary extension fitted - She's been playing Knicker Roulette, and lost - She's been proposed and Seconded – and now She's well and truly in The Club...'

'So then, that would mean...?' said Nicky.

'She's havin' what we call a "Grudge Baby" you daft sod!' said Auntie, almost shouting.

'What is a "Grudge Baby" then?' he asked.

'It means that someone else 'as had it in for you!' answered Auntie- shouting properly this time.

What followed should best be described as a pregnant pause...

Confusion and panic had not been confined to the kitchen of a small house in a rural village. Oh my word no...other people had decided to generate their own little parcels of personal angst, due to what was basically, their own curiosity having got the better of them.

Madame Dreadfell had decided to use the Vortex to fulfil one of her own dreams. She had always wondered just what it would have been like to have been a part of the French Revolution. To this end, she had hired a spectacular costume of sapphire blue silk and lace, with the appropriate shoes and fan. The powdered wig was proving to be rather unruly, but she soldiered on in pursuit of her goal...

She had changed out of her normal Academy attire in the Physics ante-room, clutching the antique French hand mirror that was to be her "passport" back to the Period that she wanted to visit. As the portal to her dream lit up with its actinic blue glare, she stepped confidently through the framed rectangle...and into a scene from a nightmare.

She was almost knocked off her feet by a crowd of French Peasants, who had hold of a very well-dressed man, and were propelling him with extreme force toward a rough farm cart in the square. The poor individual was hurled bodily into the back of the cart, where he huddled together with other figures, minus their wigs, and with their lace and gowns in tatters. She stood in shocked disbelief, as she listened to the baying of the crowds that were jeering at the human cargo which had been thrown into the cart. Some were throwing rotten vegetables, and all were screaming vile abuse at the small group, who stood in silence, heads bowed. Madame caught the arm of a passing Peasant, and asked 'What's going on here?' She got a look of disbelief from the grimy man, who stepped back and stared at her regal apparel with a look of utter contempt. 'What is happening to those poor people?' she repeated...Without any warning, the man took another step away from her, and screamed out at the top of his voice:

'REGARDEZ!! - ARISTO!!...'

She suddenly found her shoulders gripped by several hands, and despite her protests, was pushed toward the cart, which had halted in the square. A rather more cultured individual wearing the

246

red, white, and blue sash of the People's Guard approached her. He looked at her, then spat on the ground. 'How fortunate you are Madame! You have saved us the trouble of hunting you down like the filthy Aristo dogs that you are! Your transport awaits (he gestured toward the cart, as another Peasant let down the tailboard). It is a very special day today…The Glorious French Republic has declared this to be "Guillotine Day" for all of you stinking Aristo's. Do not keep us waiting Madame – the people are eager to witness the removal of your head! So let's make haste – come along now, Chop-Chop!'

Madame went into auto-pilot mode, and felled the man with a very creditable right hook. He dropped to the cobbles like a log, and in the ensuing confusion, she turned and made a run for the place where she had emerged. She pulled out her mobile telephone, turned it on, and prayed that the doorway would open up for her. It did – and she dived for safety back through the portal. Professor Strangler was taken by complete surprise as he was knocked over by a flying woman in Renaissance costume, who had come flying out of the Vortex horizontally. Without saying a word, she stood up and dusted herself off, gave him a look which said "Don't you dare say anything Pal…" and felt at her head. Her wig was missing. She walked back to the glowing frame of the Portal as haughtily as she could, and reached through it. When she had retrieved what it was she had dropped, she placed it forcefully back on her head and swept out of the ante-room.

It was a few moments later, when she discovered that what she had placed on her head was in fact a very surprised chicken…

The Latin Supremo and self-made snob Gideon Rundell had fared little better. He had made up his mind to go back and commune with intellects equal to his own, at a point in history where he could converse casually amongst equals. Well, at least, that had been the original plan.

He too had made his stealthy way to the room which housed the mystic Vortex. He zipped open his ridiculously-expensive Harrods holdall, and took out what he knew was what he should be wearing for his visit. Having attired himself to his satisfaction, he stepped forward through the portal. He raised his hand to shield his eyes from the glare of the unexpected sun, and found himself amidst a crowd of Roman Citizens who were all standing and listening to a lone figure standing on a plinth some distance away.

'*Civis salute!!*' he proclaimed loudly, to the nearest man he could find. The man seemed rather startled by the appearance of the unexpected visitor beside him.

'*Unde Venistis?*' said the man.

'*Et Adducam vos in Anglia!*' said Rundell, proudly.

'*Dimito Tace...*' the man answered, looking rather cross.

Rundell decided to wander a little nearer to the Speaker, and get an idea of what he was announcing to the assembled crowd. However, after quite a few angry looks, and more than a few 'Sshhs' from the audience, he gave up. He was passed an amphora of wine by one of the crowd, which he took with a smile of thanks, and helped himself to a large gulp. As the rough wine hit the back of the highly-cultured throat of Rundell, he spewed out the offensive liquid like Old Faithful – completely showering the man who had given it to him. The man took great exception to the actions of the visitor, and took off one of his wooden-soled sandals, with which he began to beat out his displeasure on the skull of Rundell.

There were laughs and general merriment from the crowd of onlookers, as Rundell fled from the attacker – closely followed by his friends, a small dog, and an angry-looking goat. Rundell fled in terror for the door that he had come in, and dived headlong through the portal to escape the unwanted attentions of the Citizens of Rome...

The crowd that had pursued him ground to a halt, and puzzled as to how their quarry had seemingly vanished into thin air. After a minute or two, they shook their heads, and returned to listen to the Speaker on his podium. When there was a short break in the Philosopher's speech, the first man's friend turned and asked '*Qui Erat Phallus in Toga?*'. Thanks to a quite remarkable turn of speed from a modern Teacher of Latin, the two Gentlemen from Ancient

Times would never find out just who "The Dick in the Toga" actually was…

Right then, stuff that for a game of marbles…Thought Nicky, as the facts about Jozza began to truly sink in. He felt quite upset and angry in equal measure, having spent so much of his young life dedicated to the ardent pursuit of someone who had let him down in the worst possible way. Now, there was no mystery. This was no "Whodunit" to be solved after dinner: oh no – he now knew *exactly* who dunnit, and more to the point, what it was that had been dun. His thoughts strayed to that weasel-faced git with the borrowed sports car. Nicky didn't care that he had lied about his actual job of cleaning cars, but he hated him with a vengeance for having the audacity to run his hands over his would-be Girlfriend's upholstery…

Okay. Time for affirmative action. He asked Mum if he could use the telephone… 'As long as you're quick' Mum had said. Auntie had chuckled, and added 'Quicker isn't always better…', before dissolving into gales of laughter. Mum had blushed. Nicky didn't get it.

He called the number that the tall and eager Victoria had insisted that he take. Luckily, it was Victoria herself that answered the phone. He stuttered out an invitation to the cinema, and to his surprise, she agreed enthusiastically – and told him to call for her at seven o'clock. Nice one Nicky, he thought to himself. For once, his anger seemed to have given him the courage to make a positive step in the right direction. He even allowed himself a little smirk as a thought crossed his mind…Jozza would very soon find herself hunting around for a Dummy – only this time, it wouldn't be him!

Nicky pulled his clothing into some sort of respectable order, and rang the doorbell of Victoria's house. Through the obscure glass side panels, he saw a hazy outline approach the door. The door was opened by a wide, knowing grin, which was attached to a Sister of the Younger variety. The girl showed Nicky inside the property, giggling all the time. She seemed to find his very presence hilarious. He was ushered by the tittering teen into the sitting-room. 'I'll (tee-hee) just go and (tee-hee) see if Vicky is (tee-hee) ready yet' she declared, skipping off and up the stairs. Nicky looked around the tastefully-decorated room. One wall was completely taken up with Family photographs.

There was a gasping, heavy-breathing sound from behind him, and Nicky spun around expecting to be confronted by some nightmare creature from hell. He was actually knocked to the floor by an enormous Pyrenean Mountain dog, which pinned him down by the shoulders and began to methodically give him the wash that he should have had before he came out of the house. Luckily, before the huge dog could dissolve his face by means of licking, Victoria appeared at the door… 'Oh Charley! Come on now…that's not how we treat guests!' she laughed. Charley sat down, and raised a massive paw in greeting. Nicky took it gingerly, and shook hands with the friendly furry monster. The girl gave Nicky a big hug, and surprisingly, a rather affectionate kiss, as her younger Sibling tittered behind the door.

'Gosh – your Family are all so…so…well, tall!' said Nicky, looking at the array of photographs on display. Victoria explained that apart from the Tittering Sister, she had two older Brothers who were away at University. They were all a race of Giants. The two Brothers had to bend down in order to fit in to the Family Group shot, and even Giggly Girl was as tall as Nicky's shoulder. As for Victoria herself – well let's put it like this, if she fell over, she would be half way home already.

She smiled at him and slipped on her jacket, 'Come on – we'd better hurry if we're going to make the film on time' she said. Nicky suddenly noticed just how pretty the girl actually was, and felt honoured that she had even agreed to go to the cinema with him at all. She had been delighted when she had seen Uncle Joe's car waiting for them outside (Nicky did have the occasional moment of good planning), and was impressed with their Chauffeured ride into Town. Nicky had just been impressed that Uncle had a) not felt the urge to break wind, and b) managed to keep the car with the wheels pointing

250

downwards. They waved Joe off and went into the cinema, pretending not to hear the squeal of tyres as Joe rounded a car full of Nuns which was impeding his progress…

The film had turned out to be average at best – a modern Vampire tale of squealing College Girls and Hunky Young Studs with rather a lot to say for themselves in the Incisor department. In truth, it had been a bit boring, until Victoria had decided to provide some completely unscripted entertainment, that is…

They had shared an orange drink and some popcorn, and a few kisses. Victoria had then given him a strange and knowing wink, and slowly slid herself down the seat to floor level. In the dark, Nicky wondered just what on earth the girl was doing…He very soon found out.

The next day at the Academy, he had mentioned to his friends that he had taken his new Girlfriend to see the Vampire film. They had asked him all about the Special Effects that were reputed to be so good in the film. Nicky found it extremely hard to describe what they had seen, as he couldn't get the grin off his face.

'I wouldn't bother with any of that Vampire crap…' said Merry.

'No – it's not really my sort of thing either' added Jackson, 'I mean – where's the fun in something that only wants to suck the life out of you?'

'Oh…You'd be surprised!' said Nicky.

Nicky now knew why Victoria wore a badge that said "Head Girl" …

Chapter Thirty:

It will do none of us any good whatsoever to begin to speculate about just how it was, that Uncle Joe got to hear about the discovery of oil beneath the Hallowed Cloisters of St Onans Academy. Suffice to say, that as soon as the merest hint of a potential Business opportunity filtered through to the grey cells of Uncle – he was on it as quickly as a rat up a pipe.

Jedekiah and the Elders had done their best, by HoBi, they really had…but the juggernaut that was Uncle in Cash-generating mode was an unstoppable force of Nature. This human Tsunami was very likely to wash away both your sense of danger, and a tidy slice of your profits if you omitted to read the small-print of the contract *really thoroughly.* Joe did not have a malicious bone in his body, quite the reverse. He was intelligent, generous to a fault, and had concentration second to none. The problem was, that most of Uncle's schemes and inventions contained some tiny flaw that would lead to tears before bedtime. If you signed up with joe to build you a hundred-and-fifty-foot well, it would be done with superb craftsmanship, and an attention to detail that would have impressed Brunel himself. The small problem would manifest itself as you stood back in the company of the smiling Joe, and realised that due to the fact that he had the plans upside-down, you had paid for an exquisite one hundred-and-fifty-foot chimney.

This time though, Joe's enthusiasm had been steered by the Team of Groundling Engineers. He had been gently nudged in the direction of supplying piping and containers for the oil, and things were working out exceedingly well so far. Beneath the Academy, there was now a rapidly-expanding and highly efficient Refining Plant, which was already supplying a whole range of oil-derived products to the Town and local Businesses. Joe was happy, Jedekiah and the Elders were happy, and Obadiehard was up to his elbows in dirt on a daily basis– so he was more than happy. The heating budget for St

Onans had slowly been reduced, as oil production had increased, and now ran at a healthy budget figure of zero…

There had only been one incident as the Refinery had expanded. About half a mile away, and secreted within a thicket of dense trees, was a "vent pipe" where production gasses were burned off. For some unknown reason, the venting pipe had become damaged, and had cracked off at near ground level. Flame had roared out of the un-capped vent, threatening the safety of the local countryside. A Team of Groundling Engineers stood back from the intense heat of the raging column of fire, and wondered just how they were going to extinguish the blaze safely. At that moment, Uncle Joe had come screeching through the wood in his old Land Rover. He had sped straight toward the fire without a moment's thought for his own safety. The Engineers leapt aside, as they saw the face of the man with gritted teeth drive straight up to – and directly over, the tower of flames. The vehicle came to a halt, and by some miracle, as the tyres of the van exploded in the heat, the bottom of the Land Rover's chassis came to rest on the broken vent pipe, shutting off the oxygen, and extinguishing the flames.

The Team of Engineers rushed in to cap off the vent, and a soot-blackened Joe stepped out of the vehicle as the crowd of Workers applauded wildly. Jedekiah dashed over to the smouldering Uncle, unwrapping his head from the wet towels that he had donned for protection against the heat of the fire…

'I say to Thee – Thou art verily a Miracle Worker!' he declared, taking hold of the stunned Joe, and kissing him on both cheeks. 'Thou hast saved us, and the land! May HoBi be Praised!…I tell thee Brother, whatever thou desirest shall be thine, for this act of true bravery and selfless courage…Tell us, what would thou have us give to thee?'

Joe stood and smoked. There was no tobacco involved, he just stood and smoked. He removed his flat cap and beat out a small fire which was still alight on the peak. He looked at the Groundling Elder and replied…

'Well – the first thing that I need is a new set of brakes for that bastard van...'

Founders Day was fast approaching over the horizon. The restored statue of St Onan had been carefully set in place on a tall plinth in the modest Chapel which adjoined the Old Library. The Headmaster seemed to have developed a fixation with the stone depiction of the Academy's Patron Saint, and made daily pilgrimages to it, lifting the cloth which covered it (in the Academy colours, of course) and inspecting the workmanship of Albert Brooks. It was during one of these regular inspections, that he noticed that the cloth was dampened around the area under the chin of the statue. He had immediately summoned his Deputy Dr Chambers, who had in turn summoned Mrs Finucane the Cleaning Supervisor, who had in turn summoned everyone else that she had come into contact with. So now, a gathering of Masters, Staff, and curious Pupils found themselves staring up at the sad stone face of St Onan...

Miles Bannister took off his spectacles and cleaned them on his handkerchief. He replaced them, and peered intently up into the face of the statue. A moment's scrutiny confirmed what he knew that he had already noticed...

'Good Lord!' he exclaimed – 'Look at his face...the statue is crying!'

There was a general movement toward the statue by the assembled crowd. There was no doubt about it...a single tear was running down the cheek of the sculpted Saint.

'It's a Miracle!' shouted the Reverend Felchingham, 'I must call the Bishop!'

'Bugger the Bishop – call the Press!' said Vernon Farmer.

The Rev was insulted by the tone of the Headmaster. There was no need to speak in such a vulgar manner. He had no intention of performing the latter, and certainly not the former...

Farmer suddenly became extremely animated – 'Quick! Grab some little glass bottles and catch those tears in them…we can flog those to the Public at a tenner a time!' he shouted.

'I find that rather insensitive, Headmaster' declared Dr Chambers.

'Bloody right too – make that twenty-five quid each!' said Farmer.

The task of giving notice of the "Miracle" to the Local and National Press was delegated as usual to Dr Chambers. Farmer was already planning just how to extract maximum effect and fame out of the situation, especially since the Academy was soon to be visited by a member of the Royal Household. Yes! This was obviously another sign that awarding him a Knighthood was the correct thing to do – and now it appeared to have been sanctioned by an even Higher Office…His head swum, as he thought of all of the interviews in the Sunday Papers (the "nicer" ones of course, not the ones that featured female expose in the upper-half regions), the television interviews, the guest appearance on Radio Chat Shows, and perhaps even a call to take tea with the Archbishop of Canterbury. Now that his Academy had received a Divine message, as head of the Seat of Learning, he was bound to be asked to give his forthright and morally-superior opinions on *Question Time* for the BBC. My word – he could see it all…

So could Albert Brooks, who leaned over conspiratorially to his fellow ODD agent Mrs Finucane, and whispered… 'I knew that I adn't tightened them bloody washers up quite enough'.

One of the Pupils seemed to be far from happy with all of the attention that the statue was receiving. Jez Christo seemed rather disturbed by the whole affair. 'I can't say that I'm happy with all this veneration of that statue…' he had declared.

'What's wrong with it Jez?, it's only a bit of old marble' asked Nicky.

'It just seems like worshipping False Idols, if you ask me – Dad hates that sort of thing' he said.

'Well now – 'tis loike what they'm doin' in all them Biblical toimes...' stated Trevill, the noted Religious Scholar. 'They'm 'ad that there contest "False Idol", and the people all 'ad to phone in and vote for whichever Idol they wanted to win – an' then they all worshipped it until the next week. Moi Uncle Denzil says it's all in the Bible that Moses went mad at 'em when Ee found out what they'm all up to – and 'ad 'em arrested: moind you - some of 'em got released later on Baal'.

'I always find reading the Bible rather sad...' said Calderman.

'Why's that then?' asked Jackson.

'Well I mean, essentially, there's a decent, honest Chap who is first welcomed, then eventually ignored, shunned, mocked and vilified...' he answered.

'Huh – 'story of my Life...' said Jez Christo.

Their discussion was interrupted by the Scholastic version of the Verruca – Henry Albert Lordsley. The boy had long since decided that it was his duty, and his duty alone, to look down on the other Students who as he saw it, did not have the same Social status as himself. He made little secret of the fact that he considered those boys whose Parents' income fell below a certain level, to be attending St Onans under false pretence. Had his attitude been different toward his fellow Pupils, then he would not have spent all of his time at the Academy to date, walking around with a metaphorical target painted upon the back of his blazer. (He had recently formed yet another "gang" of like-minded individuals, whom he had christened with the title "The Ninjas of the Iron Fist". He had business cards especially printed for his gang. In time-honoured fashion, as soon as the new gang became known, Merry and Weatherill had printed a new set of cards. The originals were located and stolen – to be replaced by the freshly-printed items. Thus: Lordsley's gang now handed out cards with the title "Whingers of the Limp Wrist" on them).

'I hear that you load of Peasants are to be kept well out of the way when the Royal Visitor comes...' Lordsley had sneered. 'I am sure that a Royal has no wish to see your snotty noses and ill-fitting second-hand clothes during his visit'.

William Trevill, Son of the Soil, loyal School friend, staunch Socialist and Defender of the Faith, drew himself up to his full height: 'Roight You – You unwashed cow's arse of an object...whoi don't ye just piss orf through the back of yer wardrobe, and back into "Nurdia", or whatever damn place yer ever arroived 'ere from. Go an' spout yer cobblers to yer Faun mate "Numbnuts", or whatever his name is – and tell the same to that bloody Lion "Asda" while ye're at it!'

A little knowledge can be a dangerous thing. In the hands of Trevill, it could be a deadly weapon.

'Will they really hide us out of the way when the Duke turns up?' asked Merry.

'No Mate...' said Nicky 'but if it makes you feel any better, we could always hide you under a thimble until he's gone home...'

Even though his friends all laughed at the joke, more than a few of them wondered if there might be an element of "selection" about to take place. The friends had survived their early years at St Onans by sticking together and resisting the constant taunts of the wealthier Pupils. Nicky in particular, had always had a feeling that his presence at the Academy was in some way resented, as if admitting the Sons of poorer Parents was somehow an insult to the School and its Traditions. There were times when he wished that he had climbed aboard that glider, when DeVere had made his break for freedom.

It was Mark Davis who had broken the spell of gloom, when he had stated 'I was just thinking...Is there's a Website especially for Masochists?' The rest of the gang looked at their friend in a questioning manner:

'Yeah, I would imagine that there is – why do you want to know?' said Calderman.

'Well I was wondering.... how many "hits" it has had?'

The Headmaster was most insistent: 'We cannot afford to keep a lid on the statue' he had stated. Dr Chambers nodded, and said

'Well quite so, Headmaster – if we keep a lid on it, then won't the Press have some difficulties when they come to film it?...' The Head gave his Deputy the same look that a Grandparent might give to a small Child who absolutely insists in showing you what they have just found up their nose...

Such is the Power of the Press, that the very next morning, the quad was crammed to bursting point with cars, vans, and vehicles of all descriptions belonging to the various agencies of the Media who had descended upon St Onans in order to get film footage of their wondrous Weeping Statue. A hasty deputation had been convened by Vernon Farmer, in celebration of this latest boost to his ego. The assembled throng included Members of the Board of Trustees, the Lady Mayor, the Chair of the Parish Council, Senior members of the local Clergy, and Mrs Wendles – a friend of Mrs Finucane, who had only called in to return a box of heated hair rollers to her.

The scene in the Chapel had been chaotic, with Press crews fighting to get the best pictures of the statue. So far, there were three bloody noses, one soon-to-be black eye, and a trodden-on wig that would never be the same again. The air was alive with the flashes of cameras, making the tableau of the statue upon its plinth look like a very old silent film. The Headmaster fought a way through the assembled snappers, and made room for the guests to line up in front of the weeping effigy.

All eyes were raised up to view the pious expression on the face of the carving. St Onan was depicted with one raised hand holding a loaf of bread aloft to the heavens. His other hand was concealed beneath his flowing robes. The Lady Mayor seemed fascinated by the phenomenon, and turned to Dr Matthews at her side, and whispered... 'What is he holding in his hand?'. Matthews straightened himself, and replied 'Madam – our Venerable Saint is holding in his hand the very Staff of Life...' There was a pause, and then the Mayor nudged Matthews, and asked 'What do you think that he has in his other hand?'

Matthews grinned... 'That is a loaf of bread, Madam...'

The Headmaster had been summoned forward by a Presenter from the BBC who looked as if he might very possibly have been pickled in vinegar many years hence. This gherkinesque individual asked that he be allowed to film an interview with the Headmaster, for the Evening News broadcast. Naturally, the shy and retiring Farmer humbly accepted his request, and duly took up station in front of the statue. One of the Assistants spoke to Dr Matthews – 'Do you think there's any chance of us actually getting a bit more liquid out?' she said.

'No sooner said than done, Dear Lady!' answered Matthews, and produced the hip flask.

It was to be hoped that no "re-takes" would be required, as it was soon a rather wobbly Production Assistant that was holding the cue cards…

As the Presenter asked questions about the Academy in general, and the miraculous stony tear ducts of the statue, Albert Brooks was far beneath the feet of the crowd – down in the vault under the plinth. He reached into his inside pocket, and produced a serious-looking adjustable wrench. Laughing to himself, he crawled over to the corner of the vault and carefully removed one particular stone block. Behind the block was the valve which Albert had installed in order to create the "miracle". It was also the means by which he would get his revenge on that officious prat Farmer, and show him up in front of the Press, for the big-headed self-loving fool that he was. He gripped the valve with the wrench. One and a half turns should do just fine…He waited until he heard the "cistern" which he had installed begin to fill. Timing the gurgling by means of his watch, he then reached over and opened the release valve…

'And thus it is, that we at St Onans Academy feel that we have been given a Sign…One might call it a blessing, and we are honoured to be given the chance to share this blessing with the whole world. If I may make a personal observation, then I mu-'

He didn't get any further with his interview. Beginning as a dribble, then a flow, and then a spurting jet, fluid began to emerge from the statue – from a place much further down its anatomy…From an unseen hole in the front of the Saint's gown, came a spray of water which soaked the Mayor, Cameras and Crew, and all onlookers who were standing East of the statue…

Farmer had watched the whole incident on the Evening News, and wept. His Wife had gone into hysterics, and had taken to her bed with her tablets and a bottle of gin. How he was going to explain this at the next Lodge Meeting he had no idea. The only thing that provided a little drop of consolation was the fact that the ghastly incident had not occurred when the Royal Person had been visiting. My God – if it had, why he might have lived out his days locked in the Tower of London.

The morning papers were no kinder – declaring in bold capitals:

"SAINT BECOMES SINNER AT LOCAL SCHOOL!"

"WEE DON'T BELIEVE IT" said another.

"A MIRACLE? – URINE BIG TROUBLE!" had been the unkindest headline.

The Staff meeting that Farmer had called had been well… rather tense, to say the least. All of the Staff had seen various copies of the morning papers, and most had purchased several copies. As Farmer ranted and fumed, Dr Matthews had sipped from his hip flask and conducted his own review of the deluge of unfortunate news.

'My word!' he declared 'This is a good headline, and no mistake!' he said, flourishing one of the smaller local editions…He chuckled to himself happily.

'Just listen to this everyone – it says "Hey Diddle Diddle" –'

The look on the face of the Headmaster told him that it might be wise not to continue…

Chapter Thirty-One:

And so it came to pass, that Moses did lead his People out of Egypt. Weary and sand-scoured, they laboured through the hot, cruel deserts in search of The Promised Land. When they came to a wide expanse of low cliffs overlooking the water's edge, Moses turned to his Followers and produced a framed photograph of sunrise over the Red Sea. 'Why hast thou brought that photograph with thee all the way through the hot and cruel deserts?' asked a member of the Tribe of Israel. 'I just couldn't bear to be parted with it...' spake Moses.

The Reverend Felchingham warily unrolled the scroll which Crowley had handed to him. He remembered the words of the odd man, 'You must follow the directions upon this parchment implicitly: it shall yet reveal to you all you need to know about yourself in perfect detail. Do not deviate or turn back from this quest – for your true soul shall be made known to you at your journey's end...'

What the so-called "Great Beast" Crowley had omitted to tell the Rev, was that the details which would define his very being were written in ancient Runes...which was a bit of a Great Bugger, to say the least. Thus, before Felchingham could embark on his revelationary quest, he must first embark on a trip to the Ancient Languages Section of the library.

The row had been short, angry, and personal...

Reverend Farmer had produced a list of the Pupils that he considered to be "worthy" of meeting the Royal Visitor. This had been circulated amongst the Staff. What was now circulating around the room was an atmosphere of disbelief, and contempt for a man that openly declared that so-called "Class" should determine the suitability of boys that would meet the Duke. The room was very soon divided, into those members of Staff who were instantly disgusted by the action, those who secretly agreed with it, and those who were determined to say or do nothing – until they saw what the view of the Majority was, and so could come down on the side of reason, without the fear of any threat to their employment prospects...

'Lady and Gentlemen...' said the Headmaster in what he hoped were calming tones...

'That's La*dies*, I think you mean...' said Mr Thwaite, arms crossed in annoyance.

'As you wish...I am just saying, that in order to present the very best view of St Onans, it is paramount that we portray ourselves as turning out Pupils of shall we say, a rather higher level of Social Status and behaviour than, as it were, other Students of the Academy of whom it could be said have singularly failed to achieve those standards...'

Hyde-Jones had turned red in the face... 'So you want to "hand-pick" the boys that you think meet your own criteria? I take it that the idea is to prevent the Duke having to endure the unpleasant experience of coming into contact with The Working Classes?...'

'I merely think that there are a certain number of individuals who are... better suited to displaying the conduct and behaviour which one might come to expect, when meeting a member of the Royal Family' said Farmer.

'Do you have brown eyes, Headmaster?' asked Hyde-Jones, innocently.

'Why on earth do you ask that?' replied Farmer.

'Oh, it's just that I thought that you would have – because you're obviously full of shit...'

Farmer was acutely embarrassed, as a round of spontaneous applause broke out from the Staff. There were cries of "Shame" and "Outrageous", and "I'll have a double" from Dr Matthews.

Newhouse stood up and faced the Headmaster. 'Our job is to Educate – not to Segregate. We set standards and help all of our Students to achieve those goals – irrespective of whatever Class or Social Grouping they may emerge from. To be asked to make divisions between the Pupils is something which quite frankly, I find utterly abhorrent. If I may voice my feelings in the manner of my Latin-speaking Colleague – you may, Headmaster, feel free to osculate my *Gluteus Maximus*...'

Farmer leaned over and sought clarification from Gideon Rundell the Latin Tutor…He turned back to face the Staff looking shame-faced. 'Ah…well, I see. If that is the opinion of you all, then we must produce a short list of boys who we all deem suitable to provide an "escort" for our guest on the day. I shall of course, be guided by your own collective views'.

'I feel that if you do not heed our advice Headmaster, then you may well find yourself with a desk which is covered with letters of Resignation…' said Dr Matthews 'I cannot see that playing out at all well with the Board of Trustees'.

There was a period of silence as the gravity of the situation sunk in for the Head. The door to the Staff lounge suddenly opened, and into the room strode Miss Emilia Piggott, fresh from her brush with temporary incarceration.

'Ah Miss Piggott…' said Farmer, 'That's "Pie-Gott" if you don't mind…' snapped the Secretary. She glared, as Farmer smiled benignly and carried on, 'Would you be so very kind as to assist the Staff to draw up a list of boys who will be showing our Royal Visitor around the Academy?'

Hyde-Jones and Newhouse exchanged the customary "high-five", as the Headmaster swept out of the room, with Dr Julius slithering his way out behind him. Miss Piggott scurried off to type up the requested list, and the Staff filed out of the room with Dr Matthews bringing up the rear, who due to some early liquid refreshment, had developed a list to the right.

'Thanks for backing us up Mate' said Mr Newhouse to Dr Matthews, placing a Brotherly and steadying arm around his shoulders. 'Can't have anyone criticising my Lads!' said Matthews, 'They may not all be the smartest shoes in the shop, but they're all our shoes after all is said and done…' Hyde-Jones gave his colleague a look of approval… 'The boys really do think the world of you, and it's nice to see that you are "down with the kids" Sir' he said. Matthews gave him a tipsy grin: 'Oh indeed yes, my fine fellow! I take a great interest in what the Chaps are up to. They have been playing me some of their new "Rip" music on their tiny portable gramophones!'

'What did you think to it?' laughed Newhouse.

'Oh, it's certainly rather different to *Count Basie* and the Big Band stuff that I normally listen to, but I must say that it has rather grown on me – a little like fungus. I now know all about that Scottish Rapper *McHammer*, as well as those other Chaps like *Fifth Indecent*, *Tidy Tampon*, *Scoopy-Scoopy Dog Doo*, *Ice Pube*, and that rather Poetic person *Emenenaema…*' stated Matthews, rather proudly.

'Just don't start break dancing and spinning on your head during lessons!' said Hyde-Jones.

'At my age, I wouldn't know whether to choose "Hip-Hop" or Hip Replacement!' laughed the History Master. 'I must say though, that I hardly understand a word that they go on about – I mean, I can sort of comprehend the bits about "Hoods" and "Bitches" (Yo, or otherwise…), but why anyone would possibly wish to "Pop a Cap in Yo' Ass" completely baffles me…I mean to say, what a truly appalling way to treat Harris Tweed! And whilst we are on the subject – I was truly disturbed by the inference contained in one particular "ditty" that the Singer was advocating the force-feeding of his Lady Partner…'

Newhouse and Hyde-Jones stared at each other, as they racked their joint brains in an effort to understand just what it was that Matthews was referring to. Their colleague noted their puzzlement, and added – 'You know, that bit where the Young Miscreant declares that what he is seeking to do is to "*Snack His Bitch up*", or something of that ilk'.

Betty Bradley the Catering Supervisor, Head Cook, Academy Chef, and knower of all things in the mystic pudding and pastry departments, was currently (a plain alternative was available for those who didn't like currants…) holding a meeting of her own in the capacious kitchens behind the Dining Hall. She was fussing and fretting over the menu that was to be served in honour of their Royal Guest. Bell-Enderby the Art Master had decided to attend the meeting

264

for the purposes of scrounging a free cake or two, and he now leaned back on the kitchen work surface, where he was determined to spice up the menu with a generous double portion of entendre.

'We'll need to get out our biggest Jugs!' declared Mrs Bradley.

'Not before time, Hnur...Hnur...' added the Art Master.

She gave him a look... 'For the selection of fruit juices and mineral waters, I mean. Doris – what did you think about the meat course?'

'I have got the Main dish sorted out – we'll go for the roast beef and Yorkshire puddings, but I'd really like a bit of something "special" on the side...'

'Wouldn't we all!' said Bell-Enderby, almost choking on his fondant fancy.

Betty tried her very best to ignore the man, his obsessions with the Female chest department a well-known fact. Unfortunately, she surmised, there would be little that she could possibly say, that would not be turned into something vulgar by him. She surmised correctly...

'I'm still a little worried about the desserts though – I had thought about trying something really exotic with those massive pears...'

'Don't forget your big, juicy melons!' tittered Bell-Enderby.

'We've still got all of those moulds in the shape of famous Prime Ministers...' said Doris, now getting annoyed, 'How about if we make a selection of blancmanges for each table?'

'Yes, but I was hoping for something just a tiny bit more sophisticated...I mean, would the Duke be impressed by something big, pink and wobbly plonked in front of him?'

'Fwaaaoorr! – not Half!' exclaimed the Art Master.

'Will you be wanting my special Baps?' asked Doris.

'You bake 'em – I'll sketch 'em!' declared Bell-Enderby, proudly.

'What about the wine?...' asked Doris, being very careful in choosing her words.

'That is a good point Doris' said Betty, herself taking care to avoid the innuendo minefield.

'How do you suppose that the Duke would prefer it?' Doris said, now confident in the knowledge that what she was saying could not possibly be misconstrued.

'How do mean, exactly?' Betty asked.

'Well…would he think it better if I put it into his hand – or do you think he would prefer it if we gave it to him on the table?…'

Bell-Enderby made a sort of 'Yaarrggle!' sound, and had to be escorted from the kitchens by two of the younger Assistants. One of them attempted to prevent him choking by slapping him hard on the back. Betty Bradley would much have preferred to have slapped him hard in the front…

The complex world of Chemistry was taking a few minutes' rest, and Captain Hercules Brayfield was staring out of the window and pondering…He was well aware of the Germanic Ancestry of the Royal Family, but still felt a fierce loyalty to the Crown – even the ones that appear far too regularly in glossy magazines, and only seem to turn up on the Palace balcony in order to sip a free sherry and wave at the Red Arrows. He was also certain that he was about to be rewarded for his lifetime of service to the Academy. What to wear…Evening dress and a wing collar would be rather over-the-top. Much as he felt inclined to do so, the wearing of his suit of armour might be seen as just a little ostentatious. He would settle for his best Cavalry Dress Uniform, and it goes without saying that he would sport his full complement of medals, even the one which, on very close inspection, would be revealed to be his Cycling Proficiency badge – with a ribbon attached. No-one would ever discover that the golden lanyard that he wore had once upon a time seen valiant service as a tie-back for their sitting-room curtains…

The Rev had no time to even think of such small matters. He had deciphered the runes on the scroll after many hours spent hunched over a cheap notepad in the library. He was now on his way to discover his ultimate destiny, with the directions laying on the passenger seat of his car. He had come to the necessary conclusion that written notes were a lot more reliable than any kind of technology – with which Stan would be only too quick to interfere.

The Rev gritted his teeth (although they were not at all slippy) and pointed his vehicle up the A1, and headed Northward. It was many hours before he saw the lights of the Services at Scotch Corner. He pulled in, parked up, and got himself a cup of very strong coffee. As he looked around him at the other passers-through and casual diners, he wondered if any of these fellow travellers were on their own personal quest – their own search for the key to their true destiny. He doubted that the Football Fan with the Newcastle United replica shirt, yet no trousers, was a true seeker of wisdom and truth. As he left the Service Station, he got odd looks from a couple of kids who were playing a violent video game in the entrance area. Ironically, the game which they were playing was titled "Destiny Quest". The Rev smiled to himself, and headed out to his car. He smiled slightly less, when he realised that he had forgotten to visit the lavatory, and had to stagger back into the Café with a rather full bladder. Having lightened his burden sufficiently, he returned to his vehicle and set off…

He drove up the A1M, to the A66 and up past the M62 turning for Manchester and Leeds. Finally, he got onto the M6 and headed for Penrith. Another two stops later (one being somewhat of an emergency behind some bushes – at least that was what he had managed to convince the Motorway Police) he was taking the M74, and then the A9 for the Scottish Highlands. The distance that he had travelled was immense, but that didn't matter to the Rev. His mind was fixed on his mission. He actually felt elation, as he was seemingly able to shut out all thoughts of failure, Stan, and disappointment – and focus all of his concentration on the road ahead of him.

It was a rather tired, yet relieved Rev that eventually arrived in the small town of Stromness. He knew exactly what he must do now – and set about doing it with a spirit of great excitement…Not long now. His ultimate goal lay just a little way across the water, as the scroll had insisted.

The Reverend took the ferry from windy Stromness, to the equally wind-ravaged village of Scrabster. It was here that he sought to confirm the directions which he had been given. After a small amount of money had changed hands, his instructions had proved to be accurate.

The ferry to the Orkney Islands had been the roughest experience that the Rev had ever encountered. He hadn't had the time to be seasick though, because he was gripped with the excitement that the end of his journey was now near.

He consulted the scroll again when he had disembarked from the ferry. Right then…this was it. This was the final leg of the journey that would lead him to everything that he needed to know about himself, and his life.

He took the twisting, winding road of the B9057, driving slowly and carefully in the early morning light, as the wind swept the long grasses to and fro at the side of the road. He had been instructed to head directly for a village called Dounby. From this point, he had been ordered to measure the distance with great accuracy…

'Take ye of Miles Four, and turn ye toward the rising Sun. Ye shall stand beneath the sign which ye shall find there, and thus receive all that thou needest to know of thyself – in all manner, and in all respects…'

That is what the scroll had said. That is what the Reverend Felchingham did.

Measuring the distance as exactly as he could, the Rev drove slowly up the road. There it was! This was really it! He had travelled nearly the length of Britain – but now he had finally arrived. He parked the car on the grass verge. He gathered up the scroll in his eager hands and stepped out and over the road. He was almost too nervous to read the scroll's final words, and his hands shook as he did so.

'Tis in Truth that which thou hast now found – and truly what thou hast become…'

The wind screamed all around him, as the Rev waited for some sort of sign. Would it be a dark, mysterious Messenger? Would it be a blinding flash of light? All he could see was the sign which displayed the name of the Village. Like the man who has just leapt from the plane at thirty thousand feet, only to discover that he has strapped on his Son's School backpack instead of a parachute, the Reverend got the Mother of all sinking feelings.

It was too late now. He had come too far. There was nothing to say...or think...or do. All the Rev could do was to look up at the sign which stated its message above his head...

TWATT

Was there a slight Scots accent to the throaty chuckle which he had just heard...?

Chapter Thirty- Two:

As silently as a smelly one dropped in a lift, the day had crept up and announced itself. In the Town, and in the Villages, the reluctant necks of boys were being checked for tidemarks. White shirts that had been kept in their packets for this specific day, were being taken out and ironed into pristine submission. Unruly mops of hair were being slicked down with hair gel: or in a few of the more extreme cases, beaten flat with camping mallets. Ties were being tied and re-tied several times, in the hope that the Royal Visitor might notice, and appreciate the sight of a "Windsor knot" at least having been attempted. As the various offspring left the house to be collected by the School buses, noses would already have been subject to intense scrutiny for the purpose of detecting clandestine bogies...

Such was the beginning of the day at St Onans Academy, an Educational time-capsule where Boys would be Boys (unless of course they had brought in a note signed in triplicate by an appropriate Parent). Even the group of Ravens which haunted the high gutters of the Old Library roof, had risen early, showered, and now sat preening themselves in readiness for the Royal Visit. Keith, the official "leader" of the gang, turned himself this way and that, glancing over his shoulders at his feathers.

'What I really need is a mirror' he croaked, 'What do I look like from the back?' His fellow Raven Roger eyed him sympathetically. 'We're Ravens, Keith – you look exactly the same as me, believe it or not...'

The Ravens had rehearsed a very competent Barbershop melody, which they planned to perform for their Royal guest. Keith was now fussing about Protocol:

'Now let's try and clarify shall we...Do we swoop, do we flutter, or is it better if we just go for a gentle glide down in front of the Duke?' he asked.

'Does it really matter Keith? I mean: all we are going to do is crap on his car anyway'.

Keith the Raven fixed his fellow Corvid with a steely eye… 'It is comments such as that which have set back the cause of Raven kind for hundreds of years – You, Arthur, will perch at the back, and will not caw until cawed to. Pay attention to what I am saying to you…what the blazes are you eating now? Is that the remains of an apple?"

'Core…' answered the Raven.

Nicky had been given the full inspection. Mum had made certain that his trousers were displaying the required crease, and that his blazer was brushed clean of any stray fibre evidence which might show the Family up if it appeared in any photographs in which her Son appeared. Auntie casually informed him 'It might be an idea to do up your flies'. Nicky shot a glance at the offending region, to find that all was as it should be in the zip department. Auntie giggled to herself, declaring 'Gotcher!'.

Mum kissed her Son, and told him to have a good day. He set off to await the asthmatic bus with his Mother waving him off proudly, and his Aunt making rather rude and hilarious gestures from just behind her. He made the ride to the Academy without incident, and mercifully without contact of the nasally-threatening Mrs Jenkins…

As he walked in through the stone arches of the Academy, Nicky was greeted by an excited Calderman. 'Hey Shep – we've been listed to form part of the Welcome Committee for the Duke!' he said. 'We've all got to go and get our instructions from Vermin and Chambers before He gets here'. Nicky was pleased to hear that he and his friends had not been locked away out of sight as they had feared – and wondered just how big a part Mr Newhouse and Roy Hyde-Jones had played in that decision. He was still a little tired after the previous evening. He had attended the first rehearsal with his new band "Funderthuck". It had gone better than he could ever have hoped for. He hadn't dropped a drumstick once, the kit had stayed put, and no-one else in the band had caught fire or exploded. He had especially enjoyed a song which the band had written which featured a short drum solo – a fast, rocking track which was called *"Baby you can drive my Rolls-Royce, as long as you pay the fee to get the clamp removed first..."* If he did actually get to meet the Duke today, he wondered if it would be appropriate to get a badge put on his drum kit which stated "By Royal Appointment" ...probably not.

William Trevill was in reflective mode. He was making hurried scribblings in a small notebook. 'Do Ee reckon that Oi moight get a few wurds with 'Is Dukeness alone?' he asked. 'Yes, I suppose that you might get a chance' said Calderman. 'What did you want to say to him?' asked Mark Davis, through a shower of salt-and-vinegar crisp crumbs. 'Well Oi thort as how Oi moight enquire as to 'ow come moi Great-Granddad's mine and grazin' land were sort of "borrowed" by the Royal Family – but it seems to 'ave slipped their Majesty's moinds when it came to the small matter of givin' 'em back...'

'I doubt very much if he will have the Title Deeds to the land on him when he comes' said Nicky 'but you never know, it might be worth mentioning it to him over lunch. You could always tell him that your Family need the land back urgently, for the purposes of grazing'.

'We'em don't 'ave any sheep at the moment' said Trevill.

'I was actually thinking of young Davis here...' laughed Nicky.

Davis aimed a light-hearted blow at his friend, but forgot about the crisps which he was holding. The result was that Merry suddenly became the unwilling recipient of a shower of oven-baked crispy dandruff...

Enter Weatherill...Now here was a young man who really knew how to make an entrance. Bets had been made with half of the Academy boys as to exactly what weird or wonderful headgear he would choose to wear today. He approached the group with a wide grin that if it had been any wider, would very possibly have resulted in the top half of his head falling off. All of the boys in the "gang" were quite shocked to witness his uncovered head. What shocked them even more, was the fact that Weatherill had spiked up his hair vertically, and then dyed it in lovely shades of Maroon and Royal Blue – the Academy colours.

'Well done Dick – a supreme effort, if I may say so!' stated a very impressed Calderman. 'Who could possibly fail to be impressed with all of the effort that you have gone to!'

Well someone certainly could fail to be impressed…and here he came right now.

'WEATHERILL!!! – WHAT THE BL- WHAT HAVE YOU- OH MY GOD BOY!! – YOU CAN'T BE SEEN LIKE THAT!!' screamed out Dr Chambers, staring at the boy in disbelief.

'Well yes he can Sir: I would have thought that he will be very *easily* seen, with a hairstyle like that…and in my own opinion, from quite a long way away too!' laughed Merry.

'Look Weatherill – I'm not standing for it! Get that head covered this minute…'

'What do you suggest Sir?' asked Weatherill, casually.

'Get it covered up – and sharpish!' hissed Chambers.

'Do you mean, apart from the spiky bits Sir?' asked Weatherill.

'No I bloody well do not – get some sort of covering…'

'Not quite with you Sir…'

'P-P-PUT A BLOODY HAT ON – AND THAT'S AN ORDER!!' shouted the Deputy mouth of the Deputy Head.

'With pleasure, Dear Doctor…' answered an ecstatically happy Weatherill.

The boys were instructed to make their way to the Staff lounge. This was a rather unworldly experience for them, as the dark rituals which they all imagined to take place within the secrecy of the Masters' inner sanctum were a mystery to them (unless you were summoned there due to some act of recalcitrance, in which case it was perfectly permissible to stand just outside the door and quake in apprehension). The assembled boys fell silent, as a very specific list of "Do's" "Don'ts" and "Don't even think about its" were barked at them by Dr Chambers. They were instructed just how to address their Visitor – but strangely, not where to affix the stamp.

The Royal Person was set to arrive at eleven o'clock prompt. The boys in the "Greeting Party" would gather in the quad at ten-thirty. Before the Duke set foot on St Onans soil, they would have their normal swimming session. Today however, they would instead be introduced to the mind-boggling delights of the fibreglass canoe, or Kayak, or as it was more regularly referred to: 'Aaaaargghh! – help me out! The bloody thing's upside down...'

A similar meeting with the Staff had been held as soon as the boys had been ushered out. The Gentlemen and Ladies of the Faculty all looked just as sheepish as had the Pupils earlier on. As Vernon Farmer the Headmaster looked over them with a Magisterial eye, the Staff shuffled and shifted nervously, all awaiting their own particular menu of threats...

'I scarcely need to remind you all that the reputation of St Onans Academy rests on how our Royal Visitor is treated today' began Farmer, 'For all of our sakes, do not act as if today were just like any other normal day at the Academy, or I fear we may be done for. Think about our future – and remember that it may well rest in your hands...'

'Should I wear my Evening gloves then; do you think?...' asked the voice of Elsie Noakes, through the shocked mouth of Miles Bannister.

'That sort of comment is what I seek to avoid' said Farmer. 'Please remember only to speak if the Duke addresses you, and please, please...do for heaven's sake keep your hands to yourself!'

'Shame!...' called a voice, from the general direction of the Matron.

'Professors Darwin and Strangler – keep the doors to any little "experiments" which you may have on the go firmly locked. I will not tolerate any member of the Royal Entourage being sliced, diced, dissected, electrocuted or accidentally cloned. We have only just finished paying off the Court fine for what happened to the Chairman of the local Chamber of Commerce...'

'Well I did distinctly tell him *not* to put his head in there...' pouted Darwin.

'And as I remember...so did I' added the Matron.

'Yes, well, let's not have any accidents or displays of creativity which are likely to result in our Guests having to leave us, minus their ears. Captain Brayfield – please confine yourself to answering questions on the subject of Chemistry, and do please refrain from feeling that you must give a detailed account of which acids are the best for the purposes of dissolving Foreigners...'

'Mr Thwaite...is that you? You err...Have you had a blue rinse? Well very smart. Now confine yourself to matters Geographical – and do not ask the Duke where his Wife gets her clothes designed, if you please'.

'Rundell, I know that I can rely on you not to let the side down. Good Man' (The Latin Master stepped forward at this point, to receive the "Smug Git of the Year" trophy). 'Madame Dreadfell, I say the same to you – you look stunning, Madam' (there would be a fight over the trophy later...).

'Mr Newhouse...A tee-shirt? Really? On today of all days?'

'It's a "Queen" shirt – probably make Him feel right at home...' said Newhouse.

Had they been detachable, Farmer might well have rolled his eyes.

'Mr Hyde-Jones, you are to head the greeting party. I can rely on you to keep a sharp eye on the boys, can't I?'

'What are you inferring Sir?' said Hyde-Jones, as Newhouse giggled behind him.

'No – err, nothing...I meant, MATTHEWS!...Dr Matthews, what are you doing at the back?'

'Yes Dear Boy...I was merely enquiring if my good friend Darwin here would be kind enough to give me a hand with a couple of bottles of Brandy...'

'Just put them down, Dr Matthews...' said Farmer.

'No can do I'm afraid – I've already drunk them!' answered the smiling History Master.

The rest of the lecture was interrupted by a disturbance out in the quad. Comrade Bill had organised an Anti-Monarchy protest. A small group of boys had assembled just outside the Staff lounge window, and were parading around in a tight circle displaying placards and home-made banners, decrying Rank and Privilege in all its forms. Bill had instructed his fellow Republicans to "dress like Serfs" in order to force home their point. The overall effect had been spoiled by Comrade Colin – who had misunderstood the instruction, and come dressed as a Surfer, complete with waxed board and flip-flops. The Staff noted that one of Bill's Revolutionaries was young Walter, who was unfortunately very politically motivated, but awfully dyslexic. The placard that he was waving furiously said "ACNE!". There was every chance that what it should have read was "ANARCHY!" …

Dr Julius was sent out to disperse the rebellion. The "rally" soon dispersed of its own accord, but not before it dispersed Dr Julius with a sound and thorough battering under the various home-made Weapons of Class Destruction.

Nicky and the boys had reluctantly changed into their swimming costumes. Not one of the boys was interested in the canoe-polo match that Burke and Hair had organised for this morning, as they were all too focussed on the events which would be taking place later. The two teams that Thompson had organised had paddled up and down the small swimming pool, chasing after the elusive ball. Some time had also been taken up with both teams chasing the elusive toupee of Mr Thompson, after it had made a bid for freedom across the turbulent and choppy waters of the deep end. Thompson had retrieved the soggy hairpiece with a look of retribution on his face, and had gone outside to either secure the recaptured wig with stronger tape, or locate some fast-acting adhesive which would hold the skedaddling syrup in place.

It was then that it happened…

The "Blue" team had chased the ball down to the deep end of the pool. Calderman had sent the ball flying in the opposite direction with a deft flick of his paddle, and the canoes all turned and set off in hot pursuit. It may have been Jim Jackson that caught the end of Merry's canoe, or one of the other boys who turned swiftly in the water. Whatever the cause, Merry found himself suddenly waterlogged and sinking extremely rapidly. He tried to slide out of the "skirt" of the canoe, but was unable to do so, as it slipped away and tangled around his legs – as the canoe filled with water and began its decent to the pool bottom. The boy was concentrating hard on getting out of the canoe: so hard in fact, that he forgot all about the need to shout for help. As the ball hit the back of the net in the shallow end for another goal to the "Red" team, the boys all noticed that one of their number was missing…

There was a frantic scramble as the whole group paddled like crazy for the other end of the pool. The end of Merry's canoe was just visible, standing out of the water by only three or four inches. Of the canoe's occupant – there was no sign. In a panic to save their sunken friend, the boys did perhaps the worst thing possible, and got in each other's way – causing a mass collision of hulls as they all attempted to get to their friend at the same time. They could see a mass of bubbles rising from where Merry had sunk, and were terrified that they might be too late to save him.

It was Jez Christo who got over to the spot, and reached down to haul out the choking and frightened Merry. He dragged him up onto the poolside, and began to pump the water out of the limp figure. The boys all stood around the two boys in complete silence, all praying that their friend would take a breath soon. Christo bent Merry forward over his outstretched arm, and delivered a thick blow to his back with the flat of his hand. There was another pause, and then Merry let out a loud gasp, as well as expelling most of the water which he had stolen from the pool during his immersion.

Merry began to cough and splutter, and then sat up and looked at the ashen, worried faces of his friends. His face split into a wide grin, and he said, 'Did I score then – or what?' The crowd of boys burst into hysterical laughter at their friend, out of relief that Merry had escaped a water grave. 'God Almighty Gerry – we all thought you'd drowned!' said Calderman. 'Bugger that' said Merry 'I've just seen a pound coin on the bottom of the pool – I'm having first dibs on it!'. There was more laughter from the gang...

They decided to get dried off. The boys changed back into their uniforms in silence, all still frightened by what they had just witnessed – and what had very nearly happened. Merry and Christo left the changing-room together, and it seemed that yet another unbreakable bond had been forged. Calderman walked to the door of the changing-room, and pushed it closed. He spoke earnestly to the rest of the boys, as they clustered at the exit in front of him:

'Chaps...I think it might be a good idea if we don't tell anyone about what we just saw happen in there. Let's just keep it to ourselves eh? Merry seems to be okay, and we don't want to worry anyone, now do we?'

Mute heads all nodded in agreement. That was it then, the decision had been made. They would not say a word about the fact that Merry had nearly drowned.

They would certainly never tell a word about how they had just seen another of their friends calmly walk across the water and pull him out...

Chapter Thirty-Three:

The first of the sleek, black limousines pulled elegantly into the quad dead on the stroke of eleven o'clock. The first two cars took up stations at either end of the square, and black-suited occupants wearing dark glasses emerged from the rear doors. They spoke into lapel microphones, as a larger and equally mirror-polished Rolls-Royce drew slowly into the quad with barely a sound. A small Royal Standard flew proudly from a little pole at the front, causing the "Figure of Ecstasy" emblem to lean to the side in order to see where she was going. The Security team all turned away from the car and scanned the outer buildings, their hands resting on their chests – with a suggestion that if anyone was to try any funny business, then a) no-one would laugh, and b) what they were likely to pull out of their jackets would make you wish that you hadn't bothered…

As the line of assembled Staff straightened up, and Dr Matthews was politely turned around to face the correct way, His Royal Highness the Duke stepped smiling out of the car. The Reverend Vernon Farmer dashed forward and put out his hand. His progress was halted by the nearest Security guard, who stuck out his foot. Farmer hauled himself up from the concrete, nursing a grazed knee and a very badly-bruised ego.

'Don't move 'till yer told to…' snarled the Security guard.

'Yes…alright Sir…' whimpered Farmer.

His Highness was being warmly greeted by an immaculately-suited Roy Hyde-Jones, resplendent in his English Degree robes. The Duke shook him by the hand, and introduced him to his Lady-in-waiting, the Lady Penelope Fforbes-Grappling. Hyde-Jones kissed the hand of the Lady, causing her to emit a high-pitched laugh. It was an upper-class guffaw that echoed around the quad and sought out all of the shadowed corners. It was a laugh that sounded as if someone were persistently treading upon a medium-sized duck…

H-J passed down the line of Staff members, introducing each Master and Mistress in turn, and explain what subject they specialised in. Farmer followed on at the rear, holding his breath in case of one of his Staff committing some hideous faux-pas. As the Duke approached Dr Matthews, he had stopped breathing altogether. Roy Hyde-Jones introduced Matthews, explaining that he was the longest-serving member of the Academy Faculty, and England's foremost expert on the Old Stone Age period in History. The Duke seemed impressed, and shook the hand of Matthews, asking him 'Have you always been in the Teaching Profession?' The world held its breath, as Dr Matthews smiled and answered 'Oh No Sir...I once had a short spell as a Trapeze Artist'. Farmer put his hand to his forehead in panic... 'I say! – that's jolly interesting...' said the Duke 'May I ask what happened?' 'They let me go...' laughed Matthews. His Highness joined in the laughter, and the duck joined in again...

The Duke raised a quizzical eyebrow as he came to the Matron. She smiled her best devastating smile at the man. 'And may I ask – what is it that you specialise in?' he asked. The Matron leaned forward and whispered something in the ear of His Highness. If the eyebrows of the Duke had raised any higher, then they would have probably ended up around the back of his head. He leaned forward and addressed her again 'I expect that must take an awful lot of practise!' he said. Matron merely smiled demurely.

Next in the line, and still with his earphones in his ears, was Mr Newhouse the Music Master. The Duke stopped in front of him and frowned...Suddenly, his face lit up in recognition, and he grabbed the surprised Master by the shoulders, exclaiming 'Well Bugger me! – it's "Loopy" Newhouse isn't it! Why – I haven't seen you since you and your crew did all that stage work for the Queen and I at the Garden Party Concert a few years ago...well I never – we'll have to have a drink later on: very nice to see you again old chap!' Vernon Farmer had a strange look on his face – which could be described as being identical to the look on the face of the first cow ever to be milked... 'You know our Mr Newhouse, do you Sir?' he said. 'I should think I do!' exclaimed the Duke – 'We had a whale of a time at the Palace when he and his Lads did all the work for the Opera People. The

Queen invited him in for a cup of tea, and he very kindly sorted out our Television and Sound Systems for us. Did some very amusing things with a bowl of fresh fruit and our harpsichord, as I remember. The Ladies-In-Waiting all took quite a shine to him I seem to recall – although from what I heard later, they apparently weren't kept waiting for very long!'…He passed on down the line, and the row of Masters all looked aghast at their grinning colleague.

Roy Hyde-Jones looked back and smiled at his friend: he now understood what "Loopy" had meant, when he casually referred to himself as having "Royal Connections". You didn't need diagrams to imagine what form those connections had obviously taken…

The only slight casualty of the "meet-and-greet" was Betty Bradley. As she went to execute a respectful and low curtsy, the bone panels of her complicated corsetry became interlocked, leaving her crouching like a Grand National jockey on the final straight at Aintree. She was lifted bodily by Darwin and Strangler, and taken off to be dismantled as carefully as possible.

Below the concrete of the quad, Groundling Obadiehard was talking to Uncle Joe, who had turned up below ground in order to supervise the pumping of oil into the barrels which he had secured a deal on.

'Water pressure seems to be dropping, Mr Brother Prentiss…' said Obadiehard.

'No need to call me "Mr Prentiss" Son', Uncle laughed – 'You can call me Joe'.

'I thank thee…Water pressure seems to be dropping Joe Mr Brother Prentiss, can you keep your eye on it?' said Obadiehard. 'If the pressure needle drops into the orange section, thou must turn the little wheel by ten degrees'.

Joe nodded, and walked down the tunnel to keep a watch on the dials.

Nicky and Calderman waited anxiously outside the Old Library. Along with Merry and Kendy, they were to give their Guest a quick tour of the ancient edifice, and point out the window cill upon which

Newton himself had carved his name. Mr Thwaite had done an excellent job of arranging a beautiful vase of flowers on every long table. He stood in a fetching auburn wig and a smart Coco Chanel two-piece suit, at the far end of the hall. Beside him, unfortunately unnoticed by the visitors, stood the spectral figures of an Elizabethan Gentleman, and his trusty equine sidekick. They both stood to invisible attention. The headless horse had even had his tail plaited especially for the occasion.

The Duke paused before an ancient and cracked portrait of a man on a horse, stating 'Now that's what I call elegance...' The Elizabethan Man and his horse were as proud as punch. 'See – I told thee...' said the man 'I said that I would get thee noticed by Royalty!'

'Yeah, thanks Matey...' answered the horse ''praps best not to mention that the bloke in the painting was responsible for killing one of his Wife's ancestors during the Civil War, eh?'

The tour then handed over to Davis, Merry and Jez Christo. They walked their guest slowly through the echoing corridors of the Old Block. As they passed the top of the stairs that led past the Chemistry laboratory, they passed Captain Brayfield, who ripped off a smart salute to the Duke as he shot to attention. When the tour group had passed, Merry had heard a sort of muffled whimper from down the corridor. He walked back to where the Chemistry Master was still standing ramrod-straight at attention. As he neared the tall man, Brayfield issued a strangled whisper...'H-h-have they gone, Boy?' 'Yes Sir' replied Merry 'Gone off up the corridor toward the Metalwork rooms, I think'. Brayfield grimaced, and said 'Do me a favour, will you Lad?' 'Certainly Sir – is there anything wrong?' asked the concerned boy. 'Get me the Matron, and some hot water and a few bandages will you...' Merry was now rather worried about the man, who seemed to be sweating profusely, even in the chill of the corridor. 'Whatever is the matter Sir?' he asked, 'Is it anything that I can help with?' Brayfield winced slightly, and answered 'No Lad, I think not…it seems that when I stood myself to attention, I caught myself with the old Cavalry Sabre – in the "Gentleman's Area", as it were…might just need to visit the old Medical Tent, don'tcherknow…'

Merry dashed off to procure the services of the Matron. As he ran down the corridor, he began to laugh to himself…If indeed it was Captain Brayfield that was to receive the Knighthood – well, he would like to see the look on his face when that sword was brought out!

Beneath the parquet, the concrete, the rubble of the 1930's, and under the compacted soil of the Middle Ages…Uncle Joe was watching the water pressure dial of the oil pumping system like a man possessed…

Professors Strangler and Darwin were sharing a clandestine mug of coffee and a stolen biscuit. Gideon Rundell the Latin Master had fixed a substantial lock to the biscuit tin – with the express purpose of keeping out intruders. For two accomplished Men of Science however, the lock had presented little in the way of a problem. Strangler dunked his expensive cream creation into his mug, and mused… 'Did you see the look that the Duke gave to Matron?'

'Rather difficult to have missed it Dear Fellow!' answered Darwin 'It was the sort of look that a man who has spent two weeks crawling across the Sahara Desert might give to an Olympic-sized swimming pool'.

Strangler gazed absent-mindedly out of the window… 'Have you any ideas as to who might be in line to get the Knighthood?' he said. Darwin joined his colleague at the window, and the pair stared out across the quad, where a column of Staff and boys were following the Duke across the tarmac like a Mother hen leading her chicks across a farmyard. 'I've actually asked Matron what she thinks…' said Darwin 'She says that she has thought about it long and hard…'

'I'm sure she thinks of little else!' said Strangler.

'Is that a friend of hers?' questioned Darwin, frowning as the end of his biscuit fell into his coffee.

'Is who a friend of hers?' asked Strangler, confused.

'That "Little Else" that you mentioned' his colleague answered.

Professor Strangler gave Darwin a pitying look 'Probably Johnathan, very probably...'

Dr Chambers had temporarily detached himself from the group which included the Duke, and was engaged in a rather intense exchange of points of view with the Art Master Bell-Enderby. 'And I am telling you Joshua – there is no way come Hell or High Water, that I am going to allow you to present that painting to His Highness...'

'I have spent a lot of hours on it, I cannot possibly see what objection you might have!' declared an irate Bell-Enderby. Dr Chambers glared at him-

'I can see that you have spent a considerable amount of time on the portrait, that is not the point. I can also quite readily see that the majority of the time which you have spent on it would seem to have been focussed on an area which, I must say, you need not have applied yourself to with quite as much – vigour...'

'I have depicted Her Majesty the Queen as the "Mother of the Nation", and sought to display her caring and Maternal nature toward all of her Subjects...' said Bell-Enderby, defensively. 'I fail to see how the Duke would not be impressed with my depiction of his Wife'.

'You don't see anything at all "indelicate" about how you have painted Her Majesty?' asked Chambers.

'My portrait, although some would say somewhat avant-garde and controversial, will come to be viewed as a Contemporary Modern Classic...I fail to see how the Duke would feel affronted in the slightest by the picture'.

Chambers sighed... 'It is your detailed depiction of the Queen's own personal "Affrontage" that will in all probability, result in you being locked up for High Treason!' he said.

Far beneath the possibly treasonable portrait of our Reigning Monarch, and currently munching on a cheese. Tomato, and pilchard sandwich – Uncle Joe was watching that little dial. Yes, that needle was definitely moving up into the Red...

Above the head of the watcher, if you dug up vertically, tuning slightly left at the old cracked cast-iron drain cover (not that I would suggest that you try that for a moment...) a commotion, fracas, incident, confrontation, or something else beginning with "suspicious intruder" was occurring.

The Reverend Felchingham had driven all night, without the assistance of Roy Orbison or Cindy Lauper might I add, in order to get back to the Academy in time for the Royal Visit. Amongst the celebrated hangers-on would be none other than his Boss, the Bishop. He dared not let the side down by failing to be there when the Church Godfather, the Don of the Diocese, had put in an appearance.

From his vantage point on the highest section of the Academy roof, the CIA-lookalike had spotted the urgent progress of the Rev as he approached the quad. He made an urgent call to "Control" ... 'Unknown vehicle approaching the area at speed – request instructions, over'. There was a crackle of static in his earpiece: 'Halt the car and detain the occupant immediately!' came the response. The man passed the orders on to the men on the ground, who dashed to intercept the Rev as he drove into the Academy.

Still under the bladder-distending influence of several very strong cups of coffee which had ensured that he stayed awake, the Rev had screeched into the quad – to find that his progress was halted by a small fleet of elegant black cars, and five slightly-less elegant Security Staff. As quick as you could say "St Paul's letter to the Ephesians", he had been hauled out of his car and spread-eagled over the bonnet of same. In his caffeine-induced anxiety state, he had made very loud and specific protestations about how he was being treated within the environs of his own Academy. His Protestations went completely unheeded...maybe the Security Guards were Catholics?

Dragged off and into the Headmaster's study, the Rev found himself being interrogated by a bad case of halitosis in an expensive suit. Due to the speed of his sudden arrival, it had been assumed that he might be some sort of Terrorist, with assassination on his agenda. The Rev had insisted that he was merely a very tired Divinity Tutor with a nodding statue of Jesus on his dashboard. This did not seem to convince his captors. He was bent over the study desk, and his wallet was roughly grabbed from his jacket pocket. The Chief Security Guard opened the wallet, and scrutinised the driving license and papers that he found there.

'Control...Black One calling...I have detained the Suspect. Claims to be a Vicar by the name of "Fletchingbum" ...'

'Felchingham!' said the Rev, as his head was forced back down onto the desk top.

"Control" barked back the order – 'Good work Black One...run a full check on him and report back...over'.

The Security Guard gave a smile that had absolutely nothing to do with humour.

'Right then Chummy, or let me see – ah yes, Mr Freakingham...'

'Felchingham!...' corrected the Rev.

'Is it? Well now, you want to learn to write a bit more clearly, then we might be able to read the correct name of the Terrorist Scroat that we have just apprehended' said the man.

'I wish to protest in the strongest possible ter- '

'Oh you do now, do you?' said the Guard, 'Well see here, Mr Reverend Fartingstone, what you need to do is sit quietly like a good little Reverend, or whatever it is that you really are, or I will regrettably be forced to use this...' He reached threateningly into the inside pocket of his black jacket, and pulled out an object which he waved in the Rev's face...

'What – a Tesco Supermarket Loyalty Card?' said the Rev.

The Guard hastily thrust the card back into his pocket, and his hand re-emerged holding a small, black and very dangerous-looking pistol. The Rev doubted that the use of it would earn the owner extra Club points, unless there was a special offer this week on a six-pack of Own-brand body bags...

Back on the roof, the group of Ravens had noted with considerable disgust, that their domain had been invaded by one of the Security Team. True, he had been thoughtful enough to abide by the appropriate dress code, but he presented a most unwelcome intrusion into the Raven's cherished territory. Keith had instructed the Squad to commence a swift "bombing raid" on the interloper. This had been a successful mission, and as a result, the formerly immaculate black jacket of the man now resembled a Newcastle United football shirt.

'Operation "Howay The Lads" completed...' Ronnie the Raven had stated.

'Why Aye Man!' said Keith – 'It looks Cabby!'

'I think the actual word you're looking for is "Canny" Keith...' said Arthur.

They continued to accuse The Rev of plotting an act of violence. He pointed out that he was a well-respected (he wished...) member of the Church of England. What act of Terror would they expect from a C of E Minister? Maybe he would attempt to serve the Duke with a glass of sherry that was warm? Or perhaps endanger his life with a slice of stale sponge cake? He might even have asked the local Churchwomen's Guild to knit him a gun with which to take the Duke hostage...It took the best part of an hour, five telephone calls, half a bag of butter caramels, and a simulated nervous breakdown, to convince the Security Staff to release him. They did so reluctantly, and as he walked off down the pathway toward the quad, he knew that several pairs of eyes were locked onto him. As he reached the end of the path, he heard two things: one was a comment from one of the Guards, who said into his lapel microphone 'It's okay Control, the driver wasn't a Terrorist – he was just a Knob!', and the other was a deep, throaty chuckle, right beside his ear.

Chapter Thirty-Four:

Lunchtime was approaching. What was also likely to appear over the horizon was a heart attack – unless Betty Bradley could be persuaded to calm down. The Dining Hall looked truly impressive, with immaculate white cloths laid over the long wooden tables. Cobwebs from all of the high corners had been removed, and angry spiders evicted under protest.

'Look Betty – do stop fussing…everything is ready, and we've got all the tables set out just the way you wanted them. The Main Course is all ready and waiting, so don't you go getting yourself into a state, or you'll come over all unrequired again…' Doris had said.

Bell-Enderby the Art Master was still smarting from his dressing-down from Dr Chambers about his portrait of the Queen. He had sneaked back to the kitchens in order to wangle a free cup of tea or five, as well as to enjoy the barely-restrained bliss of Betty Bradley's pneumatic assets as they jostled beneath her tabard. Sipping his free tea, he was insisting that Betty pay no attention to criticisms about her choice of dessert to be served to the Duke. She had opted to give the diners (including Royal ones…) a taste of good old traditional School Food. There had been some (The Headmaster, as it happens) who had wanted her to serve up a rather more highbrow menu. Betty had stood her ground – insisting that the Duke would love a change from all that *Four Grass* pate and all of the usual rich stuff that his Family were no doubt given every day. No! what she would give him would be good, honest pudding…Bell-Enderby had applauded her, stating loudly that he had never seen anything at all wrong with her puddings. His support, though laced with end-of-the-pier innuendo, had strengthened her resolve.

'Thank you for your support, Mr Bell-Enderby…I shall ignore the "Knockers". I am certain that His Highness will be impressed when he sinks his teeth into a *Spotted Dick*…'

There was an odd spluttering, gurgling noise from the Art Master. Instead of drinking his tea, it appeared that he was now wearing it...

The tour party had now left the Old Block corridor, and were strolling along the lower floor where Mark Davis and Jez Christo were giving a rather wonderful and well-rehearsed speech to the Guests, concerning the noble figures which were depicted in the Honours Hall portraits. As the group slowed down toward the end of the corridor which led to the Latin classroom, an atmosphere of distinct unease began to be felt. The haughty figure of Vernon Farmer picked up on the fact that there was definitely something missing. He pulled Dr Chambers slightly away from the main body of the Visitors, and hissed to him 'Chambers...am I going mad, or is there something missing?' Dr Chambers looked over the group, then looked again. A third scan of heads confirmed what he dare not even think. Oh good God, there was something missing – and that something just happened to be the Duke...

It is said that History will always repeat itself. This is true – at this very moment, History, in the form of Dr Matthews, was busy repeating itself over the bar of the "Five Crowns" next door. 'Look – I'll go through the order again...that's four pints of Scruttocks Cavalier Bitter, two Vodkas with ice, three Large Red wines, a Port and Drambuie (no lemon...), a Triple Bourbon and cola, a Tequila and orange with a straw, and a double Navy Rum...that's me sorted, now let's see...' Matthews leaned back over the end of the bar, and shouted '....What was it again that you wanted, Duke? – okay...and a double Gin and Tonic'.

Dr Matthews had caught the attention of the Duke, and had suggested that they have a break from the stuffy practise of hearing all about the Academy, and "nip out for a quick snifter" to liven things up. Liven things up they certainly had, and the Duke was now enjoying a hearty and enthusiastic rendition of that Robert Palmer classic *Addicted to Love* on the Karaoke machine, accompanied by a bevy of Local Young Lovelies. He knew all of the words too...

289

After the Duke had won a short darts match, and pocketed the twenty-five pounds in prize money, it had been back to the Karaoke for a few last-minute encores. The small crowd in the bar had gone wild as the Duke and Matthews *Walked 500 Miles*, and sought *The Way to Amarillo* to thunderous applause. The two smiling men rounded the corner of the Honours Hall to find a very concerned group of people frantically searching every available classroom.

Noticing that their Esteemed Guest had not been kidnapped, Vernon Farmer gave a sigh of utter relief. Several of the Security Crew did likewise, now happy that they would not be shot at dawn for allowing their charge to be lost. Farmer oozed his way through the crowd, and announced... 'And now Your Highness, if you would care to accompany the Staff and myself across the quad, I believe that our Head Chef Mrs Bradley has prepared something scintillating for us in the Dining Hall'.

'Don't care if it's Scintillating – just as long as it's bloody edible!' said the Duke, grinning.

As the party made their way across the quad, yet another car pulled up in the centre of the wide space. Behind it was a trailer, out of which was poking the rather battered and bruised remains of a glider. David DeVere, suntanned and smiling, was manhandled out of the front car, and in the general direction of the Boarding House.

'What's going on here?' enquired the Duke, indicating the boy, and the trailer with its sad cargo.

Farmer raced in front of the Duke, hoping to obscure his view 'Just one of our Best Air Cadets Sir...' he lied 'Seems he was blown off course whilst testing our glider, but we're glad that he has been returned safe and sound' he grimaced.

'Is any part of that load of cobblers actually true?' His Highness asked DeVere.

'Not a word of it Sir!' he declared 'I hate the bloody place – that bloke is a complete pillock, and I was trying to escape. I got as far as the South of France, then some of the wires broke, and I couldn't get spare parts. I keep trying to get away, but old Vermin there always has me brought back...'

'Damned bad show...' said the Duke. Farmer nodded in agreement, then scowled at DeVere.

'I know how you feel Son – I hated the sight of my Boarding School too. Still, well done for getting that far! Shame that they caught you, but get yourself ship-shape and join us for lunch'.

Dr Chambers had to stifle a laugh. Farmer was horrified. Damn the man, there was no way that he could give DeVere a good thrashing now. He daren't actually do anything which might threaten his forthcoming Knighthood, even at this late stage. To be honest, once he had got that medallion around his neck, and received the official certificate, he couldn't care less if the wretched boy flew off to Timbuktu (as long as his Father paid what would be a grossly-inflated repairs bill for the damage to the glider).

The boys had all been admitted to the Dining Hall, and as the procession led by the Headmaster entered the building, they erupted into warm applause for their Honoured Guest. The Duke smiled and waved to them, stopping to chat with several of the lads as he made his way up the main body of the hall. He turned around as he heard a commotion back at the entrance doors. The Bishop had just made a hurried re-appearance, in a red-faced and dishevelled state, and was busy elbowing his way in through the ranks of Academy Scholars. During the tour, his attention had been caught by the Matron, who had observed the Cleric holding his neck in pain. She had enquired as to the nature of his medical problem, and had been informed that it was nothing major – he was just in need of something to help with a little stiffness. Matron had smiled, and divulged that she was something of an expert in dealing with stiffness, and that he might perhaps accompany her to her private treatment suite. The Bishop had re-emerged from her rooms feeling much relieved.

As the man had hurried away, Matron had said to herself... 'Well now, so that's what a Bishopric actually looks like...'

The Headmaster swept up the Dining Hall toward the raised dais at the end, whereupon had been set an elegant and suitably Regal dinner seat for the Duke. The members of the Faculty that Farmer had considered worthy enough to join him on the "Top Table" (i.e. those who could be trusted not to speak with their mouth full, break wind, or eat peas with their knife) all stood to attention behind the altar-like expanse of white linen, awaiting their Guest to join them. They waited patiently, then they waited some more – this time with just a touch of annoyance. Farmer stared down the long hall. The Duke was standing about half way down the room in front of the left hand bench seating. Even above the clamour of the Student diners, he could very plainly hear the Duke, as he said to the surprised boys 'Come on then you Chaps – budge up a bit! Let' make room for an Ex-Naval Man eh!'

Farmer strode down the length of the hall until he reached the Duke...

'Sir – Perhaps you would care to take your seat on the Top Table?' he enquired, shooting angry glances at the boys either side of him.

'Ye Gods no Man!' said the Duke 'Always ate my rations with the Ranks – and I always will. We're all Chaps together eh, aren't we Lads!' he said, laughing and elbowing the boy next to him. 'All serve on the same Ship – we don't have time for any of that bloody snobbery, it gets in the way of a good feed!'

'But – but...' stammered the Headmaster.

'But nothing, Vernon – now stop buggering around, and go and fetch me a spare knife and fork, there's a good chap!'

The Duke shared the laughter of the boys around him – all amazed that Herr Farmer had been brought down to size in his own kingdom. Farmer grinned a painful grin, and gestured at a nearby Prefect to fetch their Guest some emergency cutlery. The Duke was now seated amongst the boys quite happily, and was engaged in animated conversation with a group of them. The Head stamped back to the Top Table, tripping on the edge of the dais as he did so, and tipping a vase of flowers into the lap of Gideon Rundell, who swore loudly.

'What was that, Rundell?' demanded the Head…

'I said "Flocks", Headmaster – these flowers look like Flocks' Rundell hurriedly replied, retrieving an escaped flower from his shirt pocket.

The Head froze him with another glare. He stood in front of his own seat, which had a very obvious empty one beside it, and tapped the side of his wine glass to call for silence. The hubbub of conversation subsided, and Farmer announced… 'In honour of His Royal Highness the Duke, we shall now say Grace, and sing the Academy Anthem'. Madame Dreadfell said the Grace, which was rather confusing, as midway through she decided to slip into French. The Anthem however, was sung heartily in English. Even if it had been sung in Ancient Greek by members of the Chorus from the English National Opera – it would still have been crap. Jonef Kendy thought that he would show his allegiance to his Academy by standing on the bench seat, and placing his right hand on one of his hearts. Mark Davis took the opportunity to honour their Guest with a twenty-one-bun salute…

Roy Hyde-Jones had arranged with young Weatherill that he act as "Wine Waiter" at lunch. The boy was summoned over to the Masters' table, and given instructions to serve wine to the Duke. He shot off into the kitchens, reappearing with a large bottle of fine vintage, and an even larger grin. Weatherill had been instructed to cover his Academy-coloured spiked hair, and had required little encouragement to put on a hat. He walked calmly and smartly down to where the Duke was sitting. He leaned slightly over the shoulder of their Guest, and enquired 'Would you care to partake of a little wine Sir?'

The Duke proffered his glass, which Weatherill expertly filled without spillage. When the Duke looked up at his "waiter" – he exploded with laughter…

'Now that – is what I call a bloody nice hat!' said the Duke, in between chortles 'You know – I think I may have seen one just like that somewhere else...'

Weatherill bowed graciously, then straightened up and beamed. He had been told to wear a hat. A hat he was wearing, as per instructions. What had caused the Duke so much amusement was the fact that Weatherill was wearing a perfect replica of the Imperial State Crown...

Nicky found himself three seats away from the Duke, and lucky Calderman was right on the left of the man. He listened with amazement at the conversation that was taking place between his Mate and the Duke.

'So excuse me Sir, but without wishing to cause any offence...Should we address you as "Your Royal Highness", or "Your Highness", or is "Sir" acceptable?' asked Calderman.

Between mouthfuls of roast beef, the Duke answered 'For goodness sake just call me "George" – that's what they christened me!'

Nicky was amazed, especially when "George" called down the table – 'Hoi there Davis, pass that gravy down here, you greedy bugger!'

No "airs and graces", no "stuck up" attitude, no time for Farmer and his Cronies on the "Top Table", and willing to muck in with the lads like a regular Student?...Yes, this bloke could certainly consider himself one of their gang. Nicky also noticed that his friend Calderman didn't seem the least bit overawed by the fact that he was sitting having lunch with a member of the Royal Family. He was laughing and joking with the Duke as if it was something that he did every other Sunday. There was just the possibility that the Duke was enjoying being "normal" for a few hours, without the usual bowing and crawling that no doubt took place all around him wherever he visited.

As the Duke and the boys enjoyed themselves in the Dining Hall, a worried man in a tunnel below ground was not having such a good time. Uncle Joe was getting more than a little concerned about the water pressure for the oil pumping operation. That needle was starting to judder its way into the Red section of the dial. Obadiehard had gone off for his lunch. Joe tried to remember what the Groundling Engineer had said to him…Ah yes, now he remembered: if the needle climbed into the Red area he said – then Joe should go to the valve junction, and turn the little wheel up to Ten…Joe was certain that was what he had said.

Well…almost certain.

Chapter Thirty-Five:

The Duke had been really happy with Betty Bradley's *Spotted Dick*. He had enjoyed the pudding so much, that he had asked for a second helping – with extra custard. He had made a point of visiting the kitchen and shaking the excited Cook by the hand. She had almost fainted with joy, especially when he had agreed to have a photograph taken with her and Doris.

Next stop for the Duke was to plant a sapling on the lawn outside the Headmaster's study. This was the moment that Vernon Farmer had been waiting for – where he would get the chance to be photographed with a member of the Royal Household. The next photograph that he was looking forward to, would be the one which showed him receiving his Knighthood. That would be the one that he would send copies of to all of his Freemason friends, thus cementing his position as Most Important Person in the Lodge. He could see it all…village fete opening and Golf Club memberships beckoned. His Wife would become a Lady (if she would ever stop doing that particular thing with her nose), and the smelly dog would be groomed – like it or not. Their rusting old car was going to go too – it was Bentleys all the way from now on. The future was Quail's eggs and posh biscuits, and in future, they would insist on having their Friday night fish and chips *delivered…*

So onto the well-manicured lawn walked the Duke, the Staff, various Pupils, members of the local Press and Media, the Bishop, and of course Albert Brooks the Groundskeeper, who was the man who was responsible for digging the hole into which the ceremonial sapling would be plunged. The Duke, Farmer, Chambers and Brooks stood in the centre of the circle, which surrounded the perimeter of the lawn like participants in some strange Ancient Druid ritual – but with cameras and mobile telephones. The two men that were attired in robes glanced at each other: neither of them wishing to risk asking the question 'where were you earlier? 'of the other, because both responses would prove to be equally embarrassing.

With great solemnity, the sapling apple tree was lowered into the hole by Albert Brooks. The Groundskeeper partly filled in the area around the tree, and then stood back, leaning on his shovel in time-honoured fashion. Farmer clicked his fingers impatiently at his Deputy Dr Chambers, who handed him a brand new and gleaming spade. With great ceremony, Farmer handed the spade to the Duke, and said 'And now Sir, if you would be so good as to complete the planting of the tree...' The Duke took the spade from the Head's hands, and stepped forward. He pushed up the sleeves of his immaculately-tailored suit slightly, and set about the task of putting the remaining soil back into the waiting hole. Just as he was about to pat the ground flat, horror of horrors – there came the jaunty ringing of a mobile telephone...

Farmer shot angry glances all around the assembled crowd, seeking the perpetrator of the hideous and unwarranted interruption. The Staff looked at each other, then back at the Head, with a sort of "well don't bother looking over here – it wasn't me...' expression. The Duke straightened up, passed the spade to a nearby Aide, and began to fish in his pocket... 'Damn and blast it to bloody hell!' he said, 'Sorry about this Chaps – It's me, I'm afraid!'. He pulled out his mobile phone and looked at the screen. A rather embarrassed look came onto his face, as he said 'Sorry – I'd better take this call, it's The Wife!'. As the crowd stood in silence, the Duke had his short conversation with Her Majesty. None of the assembled audience were near enough to actually hear what was being said, but were aware that the Duke's contributions seemed to be limited to a variety of "Yes Dears", "No Dears", "Just as soon as I can Dears", plus one "Well tell him not to pick at it Dear – I'll have a look at it when I get home". He surprised all of the people gathered around him by ending the conversation with 'Love You too – see you later, Sausage!'.

The silence that followed was a little longer this time...It was broken by the Duke replacing the phone into his pocket, and stating 'Now then...where were we?' The Aide with the spade returned the implement to the Duke, who completed his allotted task in the manner of a professional Gardener – (not one of those from the television show which sneak round and transform your perfectly normal back garden into a gravel pit with fountains, whilst you are out at the shops). The Duke drew himself up to his full Regal height, and declared:

'I am happy to plant his small tree today, in the knowledge and hope that it may blossom and grow into a thing of true beauty, to be admired by Generations of Academy Students for years to come. As a famous ex-Pupil of yours drew on the falling fruit of such a tree to provide him with a theory that changed the understanding of Science, I hope that future Generations may formulate yet more amazing Scientific Theories, whilst sitting in its kindly shade. I hope that all of you Masters will never forget, that the humble seed which we plant today – may yet grow into the mightiest tree in the forest, if it is cared for and nurtured...

It is an honour for me to be asked to come here today, on the Anniversary of your Ancient Founder, and take part in such an important ceremony. I hope that the planting of this tree will be a reminder of the bond that is now created between yourselves, and -'

'Granny Smith?' said Dr Matthews, in a rather-too-loud voice.

'– The Royal Family!' said the Duke, laughing at the ad-lib from the History Department.

He waved a mock-admonishing finger at Dr Matthews, who gave a polite bow in return. There was warm and very genuine applause from the crowd as the ceremony ended. The gleaming new spade fell to the ground as the Aide joined in with the clapping. It was the Bishop who bent down to retrieve the fallen tool. As he did so, the laws of comedic certainty decided to kick in – and he broke wind with considerable force and volume.

'Kamikaze...' said Mr Newhouse.

'Sorry?' asked Hyde-Jones.

("Divine Wind") translated Newhouse.

Hyde-Jones nudged his friend, 'Dunno about the "Kami" bit Loopy – but I would say that old Bish definitely needs the "Khazi"!'

As the Bishop was forced to endure looks of disgust and utter contempt, the crowd heard an obviously amused voice call out 'And there Endeth the Lesson!'

The voice belonged to the Duke...

*(It is perhaps worth mentioning at this point, that is was some considerable time later, that the brass plaque commemorating the planting of the tree by His Royal Highness was delivered and installed by highly-skilled local Craftsmen. It might also be interesting to note that the engraving on that plaque was later found to refer to the Headmaster as "The Reverend Vermin Farter". The bill for the engraving apparently remains unpaid...)

With a face that was as angry as he could ever remember, and as purple as a pair of Matron's naughtiest undergarments, Farmer led the party back down the curling high-walled path, and down toward the Assembly Hall. It was here that the Headmaster would present the Duke with an Heraldic shield bearing the coat of arms of St Onans, and a framed parchment which bestowed upon the Duke the Freedom of the town of Granchester (to be honest, there was more than a handful of people present that thought that not only should the Duke be given the town for free – but that he was more than welcome to take it away with him. They would even gift-wrap it for him if he wanted).

Vernon Farmer was almost vibrating with excitement, as he knew that the Royal Visitor would be shortly making a speech in front of the whole Academy – a speech in which HE would be named as the recipient of a justly-deserved Knighthood. As the Staff and their Guest filed up onto the stage, the boys of the Academy cheered wildly. The Masters took up their positions in a curved line of seats at the rear of the stage. At the front was the long table which only normally saw action when there was prize-giving going on. Behind the table were chairs for the Head, his Deputy, the Mayor, and of course, a red velvet-upholstered on for their Very Special Guest.

Farmer raised his hands and called for quiet in the hall. He thanked the Duke for honouring the Academy with his presence today – pronouncing the word "Honour" with a little more emphasis than was strictly necessary. He also thanked the Lady Mayor for her attendance, and then announced that the presentation of the Academy shield was to be made by the Mathematics Tutor, Mr Miles Bannister. Miles rose from his seat, clutching the ceremonial shield. He strode manfully to the centre of the stage, and half-turned so that he could address both the audience, and the Duke. The speech that he had spent hours preparing and rehearsing had been delivered with skill and clarity – right up to the point when Mrs Elsie Noakes and her friend from the Spirit World had decided to take part...

'And so it is, with great pleasure Sir, that I pre-'

'OOooohhh! I say! Isn't he handsome! He's so much better looking when you see him in person...'

'Oooh, I know...' chirped up Mrs Wormall, her ghostly bingo-buddy 'It's just a shame that he didn't come dressed in his Naval Uniform – you know, I do love a man in uniform!!!'

'And he's a lot taller than he looks on the television too!' said Elsie...

'Oooh, Elsie...' said Mrs Wormall, in a worried voice.

'What's the matter Dearie?' Elsie asked.

'We forgot to curtsy!'

The Duke took the shield from the hands of Miles Bannister. He gave the Mathematics Tutor a look of utter bafflement. Bannister merely gave him a rather pained smile, and shrugged his shoulders. 'Thank you Mr Bannister...' said the Duke, adding 'And you too, Ladies, I think'.

Farmer hurried around the table, pushing Miles Bannister toward the stage exit as he did so. He then asked the Duke if he would be so kind as to hand out some AWARDS to Students who had achieved particular HONOURS in the year so far. The Duke readily agreed, probably because this had all been pre-arranged. However, he was fast becoming aware that there were some things which were likely to occur within this Academy, that defied any amount of arranging. Or Logic. Or bloody common sense, come to that.

Thompson the Sports Master helped the Duke hand out the prizes for outstanding Sporting Achievement. As the Duke shook hands with the boys who received their trophies, the unpredictable and eccentric toupee of Thompson began to spin on his head alarmingly. The man shot up his hand to halt its revolutions, hoping that the Duke had not noticed. He had. The Duke actually thought that it was quite a good trick – especially as you couldn't see any of the wires…

Holding both of his hands on his head in terror and frustration, far beneath the stage, was Uncle Joe. The needle on the dial was now bouncing against the very top end of the Red zone on the display. In panic – he grabbed the wheel that he had been shown, and turned it full on until it would not move any further. Right…if that didn't do it, well…it just better had, that's all.

The Language Tutors Madame Dreadfell and Gideon Rundell had taken the stage, and were about to hand out awards for linguistic prowess, when one of the buttons on the over-stressed blouse of Madame decided to part company with its stitching. It had flown across the stage and struck Rundell in the eye. Now the Duke didn't remember most of the Latin that he had been taught at school – but he remembered just enough to know that what he had just heard the Latin Tutor utter was a jolly naughty word indeed.

It was now the turn of the Science Masters Darwin and Strangler to make the awards to high-achieving students. Darwin's rather informal approach toward the Duke had made the Security Team rather nervous. They now formed into a cluster at the side of the stage, utterly failing in their attempts to look unobtrusive. The boys looked on, and assumed that the men were about to burst onto the stage and give them a few songs from the film *The Blues Brothers*. Darwin handed the award to Strangler, who handed it to the Duke. Just as the Royal Visitor extended his hand toward the boy who was receiving the award, there was a thump, and an ominous rumbling from behind the curtain on the other side of the stage. As the crowd watched, a large, translucent pale blue sphere emerged from behind

301

the curtain and rolled across the stage. The Security Team all saw it – and instantly reached into their jackets. Without warning, the ball accelerated toward them, leaving them no time to react, or to move out of the way for that matter. The black-suited men were thrown into the air like well-dressed skittles, as the ball cannoned into them, before bouncing down the steps and out of the rear hall doors. The boys burst into spontaneous applause, assuming that the whole thing had been a stunt set up for their Guest. The Lady Mayor had fainted, and two of the Security Team actually took a bow...

Farmer was almost in tears. If there was one day on which he had hoped that things wouldn't stray into the realms of madness, then this was it. But it wasn't, and it didn't look as if there was any chance in hell that it would be.

For the sake of safety and sanity (not that there was any likelihood of either), Farmer decided to cut short the rest of the prize-giving, and hand over to the Duke for what he knew, would be (for him at least) a life-changing moment. He announced His Highness again, and led the applause. The Duke walked from his chair at the back of the table, to the central position on the stage where the lectern had been sited. As he did so, he could not help but notice the "sculpture" that someone had affixed to the front of the lectern. To go into detail about the "addition" would be wholly unnecessary, but suffice to say that the projection was comprised of three main pieces, rather large, quite purple, and very visibly Male...

Farmer had followed the eye of their Royal Guest, and noted in horror what the Duke had just spotted. Grabbing the Mortar Board from the head of Dr Chambers, the Headmaster made a wild swing of his arm in the direction of the offensive article. The rows of heads followed the Master's hat as it arced across the stage – landing on the protruding end of the sculpture.

'OLE!!!' shouted Mr Newhouse, as the boys all clapped again.

Chapter Thirty-Six:

There are numerous skills that one is compelled to learn when one is a member of the Royal Family. It may be assumed however: that amongst this catalogue of Etiquette, will not be the ability to completely ignore a papier-mache phallus that is stuck to the front of a lectern, the tip of which is currently wearing a Mortar-Board Schoolmaster's hat.

If indeed, the Duke was "ad-libbing" …then clearly, The Boy done well.

At the back of the hall, boys were packed in tightly. None of them wanted to miss the speech by the Duke, and more to the point, he was rumoured to be about to announce who it was that was to receive the Knighthood – and they had all placed a bet on their "Favourite". Also clutching home-made betting slips, and crammed in at the back amongst the boys, were Mrs Finucane the Cleaning Supervisor, Albert Brooks, and the Groundling Elder Jedekiah, who was a staunch supporter of Royalty.

When the hall fell silent, the cultured tones of the Duke rang out around the room. His speech to the boys was far from stuffy, and it drew generous applause from the audience on several occasions. He spoke about the great History of St Onans, and how it had achieved its status through the hardworking endeavours of its Students. He spoke of what the Academy had already achieved, and imagined what it might possibly achieve in the coming years. He noted that lack of money or opportunity should be no barrier to achievement – the only barriers to success being those imposed by the boys themselves. He spoke of Duty. He spoke of Honour. He impressed upon the boys the need to speak up for those who are denied a voice in Society.

He told the boys – 'Should we ever, as educated members of the Human Race, find ourselves thrust onto the burning embers of ignorance…then we must pull ourselves off without delay!'

The Duke earned a standing ovation for that comment. (On hearing this, Mr Newhouse was obviously overcome with emotion, and had to wipe his eyes with his handkerchief)

When the clamour of appreciation had subsided, the Duke leaned forward onto the lectern. He withdrew a sheet of paper from his breast pocket and placed it on the polished oak. He glanced around the hall, taking in the face of every boy and Staff member that was present...

'In accordance with the various Duties which I am called upon to undertake, some are immensely more pleasurable than others...' he said. 'I am extremely pleased – no, delighted, to say that today is one of those more convivial occasions. I would like to thank each and every one of you, for the very warm welcome which I have received, and for the kind gifts that you have seen fit to bestow on me. I hope that I may be able to return that hospitality...and today, the day on which we celebrate your Academy's Founders – perhaps I can!...'

This is it! Thought Farmer...here it comes. He could feel his palms beginning to sweat at the thought of the announcement that the Duke was about to make.

'It might be assumed that the busy day-to-day lives of the People that work to keep this great Country running, are in the main overlooked by My Family and I. I assure you – nothing could be further from the truth! The Queen and I take a constant interest in those people who by their daily efforts, "keep the wheels turning", as it were.

From time to time, it is brought to our attention, that certain individuals in a position of Leadership, seek to use their position in order to make the lives of their fellows better on so many levels. Selflessness of this nature cannot, and will not, go unnoticed or unrewarded'.

(Any second...thought Farmer...)

'One particular individual has been consistently brought to Our attention, due to their diligence, caring for others, organisational excellence, and drive to improve the lives of all with whom they come into contact. Such persons are unfortunately rare in today's Society. You are therefore, extremely fortunate to have such an individual within this very Academy'

(Applause…)

'This person has shown Leadership above and beyond that which any of us might come to expect. They have respect, and their advice is eagerly sought, and generously given without question. Well, Ladies and Gentlemen…It is my humble and sincere pleasure to announce that a member of this Academy has been chosen to receive a Knighthood – in honour of their ceaseless service to both the Academy, and the Community at large…'

(Wild Applause…)

Farmer brushed down his gown and straightened his tie, in readiness…

'I am delighted to tell you, that this honour will be presented (Farmer set off toward the Duke) - to Your very own Mr Jedekiah Cartwright…'

Farmer stopped in mid-stride, and tripped over his own feet, landing on the floor just behind the Duke. 'YOU BLOODY WHAT??' he shouted. He hurriedly sprang to his feet, and rushed over to the lectern, snatching the piece of paper from the hand of the Duke…

'No – No – there's got to be a mistake!' he squeaked, as he hastily scanned down the words of the Duke's announcement speech. The Duke snatched the paper back, as Security Team hands grabbed Farmer and dragged him off the stage, where still screaming out his protestations, he was firmly ejected through the rear exit doors.

'Took that rather well – don't you think?' said Mr Newhouse to Hyde-Jones, who was busy trying to stifle his hysterics with a folded handkerchief.

Jedekiah was almost knocked to the floor, under the weight of slaps on the back that he was receiving from the boys. There was not a single Student within the Academy, that did not have the utmost respect and admiration for "Uncle Jed", as he was widely known. Albert Brooks gave the highly-embarrassed Elder a big hug, and Mrs

Finucane planted a very wet kiss on his cheek. Praise was not something that Jedekiah ever sought, and he found it rather uncomfortable to suddenly be receiving the plaudits of the crowd.

'Feckin' good on yer! – Ye deserves it, Jeddles!' she laughed, kissing him again.

The Duke diplomatically ignored the wailing beyond the rear doors, and carried on with the last part of his speech.

'And if it were already not a day of shall we say, surprises – I have another very happy piece of information to impart to you all. There are individuals in this world who arise in the morning, carry out their daily chores, and then retire for the night in the knowledge of another day well spent. These people ask no recompense, other than to see a job done well. They may labour away anonymously for years, never being noticed or acknowledged. It is my pleasure today: to mention by name such a person who has worked tirelessly and without complaint within this Academy for many years. They too, have extended their ethos of hard work and service out into the Community – where they are loved and respected just as much as they are within these Ancient walls.

It is truly an honour to announce that a similar award, that of "Dame of the British Empire", is to be quite rightly awarded to one whose continuous contribution has been, well, simply outstanding. It is my pleasure to recognise this Lady's lifetime of hard work and dedication..'

The Female Staff suddenly became very alert... "Dame"? that meant a Woman! (unless it was Thwaite – no, it couldn't be). Wow!...who could it be? Madame Dreadfell stood up very swiftly, standing proud and erect. Matron leapt to her feet, dropping her pens, and as she bent over to pick them up, dozens of the boys also found themselves to be standing proud and erect.

The Duke smiled enigmatically, and declared proudly 'The Award of the Title of "Dame" is to be awarded to one who has been an Unsung Hero of St Onans for far too long…The Honour will be presented to Mrs Clodagh Fionnaula Concepta Immaculata Finucane...'

The roar that went up from the boys was truly deafening...

As the cheers rang out, mixed with cries of 'We love You – Mrs F!' Albert Brooks cried a genuine tear of pride for his fellow ODD Agent. As the boys threw ties, shoes, handkerchiefs, and Lordsley into the air, he hugged his friend in congratulation.

'Well – say something then!' he urged the shocked Mrs F.

'Well...well...err...ahh...Feck Me!'

Hyde-Jones turned to Mr Newhouse, and asked 'Did he say her name was "Clodagh"?'

''S'right...' said Newhouse 'Her actual first Christian name was "Chiarmyn". I once asked her about that - it came from what her Father had said when he found out that her Mother was expecting another child...'

Chapter Thirty-Seven:

Now there's a pretty turn up for the four-leafed clover of Good Luck and no mistake! Such were the words (minus the odd "Feck" here and there...) of Dame Finucane, as she tried to come to terms with the fact that she was now a Titled Lady. Suddenly, she looked downcast and rather glum...

'What's the matter, Mrs F?' asked Brooks 'How can you look so miserable when you've just had such brilliant news?'

'I suppose they'll make me give up me feckin' job now – what with bein' a Lady with a Title. I had only just got that feckin' eejit Farmer to pay for a new mop for the Day Rooms, and he was thinkin' about layin' out the dough for a new floor polisher too...' she sighed.

'Pull yourself together, Agent J-Cloth!' said Brooks, 'Now that you've got a Title – well, think about it...you can pull rank on that Gobshite Farmer any time you want! – an' he won't dare answer back either!'

At the back of the Assembly Hall, a queue of boys was already forming, to have their picture taken with Jedekiah and Dame Finucane. Never one to miss out on an opportunity, Weatherill was charging £3 a time for a photo - £10 if you wanted it framed, and £15 if you required it framed and delivered to the classroom of your choice. As the eager lads posed and hugged the newly-honoured couple, Newhouse, Hyde-Jones, Matthews, Darwin, Bannister and Strangler all joined the queue at the back.

Beneath their feet – quite some way beneath, things were not quite as jolly...When the pressure dial on the water pumping system had exploded, sending bits of metal whirring down the tunnel like an angry partridge, Uncle Joe had decided that discretion was indeed, the better part of valour. An even better part of valour – was not being blown from here to Hereford by a pumping system that was causing all of the feed pipes to throb alarmingly. In panic, he consulted the schematic diagram that hung on the wall opposite the main pumping valves. He made his mind up that the central node was the most important, and so when he opened the main pump doors – that was the one that he went for, opening the valve fully.

Joe wished that he had gone to Night School and trained to be a proper Engineer. Everyone else would shortly wish that he had brought his Reading Glasses, because what he thought was the diagram of the branched pumping system which cooled the oil pump operations, was in fact a map of the London Underground Network. Turning St Pancras on full was not going to be very helpful…

Dr Chambers and the Staff were now out in the quad, as the Duke said his goodbyes to the Academy. He walked down the line of Masters, and shook them all by the hand. He took the entire crowd by surprise when he "high-fived" Mr Newhouse the Music Master. No-one was really surprised as Dr Matthews passed the Duke a glass of Champagne, which he raised in salute all around the watching crowd – and then downed in one gulp.

When Uncle Joe explained what he had done to try and relieve the pressure in the pumping system, Obadiehard had given an even bigger gulp – and then shouted for anyone and everyone in the immediate vicinity to evacuate the area…

'What did I do, exactly?' Joe enquired innocently.

'Well, Joe Brother Mr Prentiss…Dost Thee remember that pipework that I told thee didst lead to the statue – the one that our friend Albert was working on?'

'Sounds familiar…' said Joe.

'Well unfortunately, thou seems to have diverted the "shut-off" supply valve, and sent all of the water which was supposed to be cooling the pumps, back down the system until it can find a way out'.

'So will it find a way out on its own then?' asked Uncle.

'We shall surely find out about it pretty soon. Canst thou imagine trying to force two thousand gallons of water through a pipe made to take fifty gallons maximum?'

'Yeah I can – I once had a week in a caravan in Yarmouth, and the toilet wasn't working' said Joe.

'The pressure will build up mightily in the pipes under the statue…Thou hadst better hope that Albert had the sense to put in a cut-off valve – or…'

'Or what?' Joe dared himself to ask.

'Or St Onans shall be the first Academy to put a statue of their Patron Saint into orbit…'

*(oh – by the way…have a guess who forgot to put a cut-off valve in?)

Not present at the "Waving-off" ceremony for the Duke, was Vernon Farmer. He had been forcibly restrained and gagged by the Security Team who had ejected him from the hall following his outburst. They had reluctantly released him, and he had sped back to his study. He sat fuming behind a desk littered with Legal Casebooks. The Reptilian Dr Julius sat in the leather armchair, himself completely surrounded by books – some open, some carelessly tossed away into corners.

'Well keep bloody well looking – there's got to be something in one of these damned moth-eaten things!' screamed Farmer.

Dr Julius did not answer. He lowered his snake-like visage, and carried on the hunt as instructed. Farmer was incandescent with rage that he had been passed over for a Knighthood – and so now he and Julius were poring over old books of Court proceedings, to see if they could find any means by which an appeal might be lodged.

After the golden promise of the day of sweet fruit that Vernon Farmer had expected, it was a cold knife to his soul to see things going so sour. He thought that it would be difficult to imagine just how things could possibly have been any worse.

Imagination can be a wonderful thing…

The Security Team did one final visual "sweep" of the quad and its surroundings. All seemed to be clear, with no threat being perceived anywhere in the vicinity. As the Duke bade them all a final farewell, Dr Matthews raised his voice above the crowd:

'Three Hearty Cheers for His Royal Highness the Duke…HIP - HIP!'

310

'HOORAY!'

'HIP - HIP!'

'HOORAY!'

'HIP - FLASK!'

'HOO – EH?'

The Duke ducked inside the Rolls-Royce, which set off with two Security Guards standing on the running board on either side of the car. They juddered to a sudden halt, as a group of Morris Dancers skipped into the quad, and began circling the vehicle with bladders on sticks a-waving, and little bells a-tinkling.

'Sorry we're late!' called Brian, the full-time Greengrocer, and part-time Leader of the Troupe.

'We're sorry you turned up at all!' shouted Mr Newhouse.

Within the safe confines of the car, the Duke nodded discreetly to the Security men. They slowly detached themselves from the vehicle. In a thoroughly well-rehearsed routine, they then proceeded to detach the Morris Men from consciousness. Having finished their street cleaning, the Men re-mounted the car, and it began to resume its majestic glide out of the quad.

There comes a point when the physical properties of copper tubing can no longer resist the expansion forces that are being exerted upon them. There is very probably a clever and complicated term for this phenomenon, probably something like "lateral co-efficient of thermal adhesion and applied thingummy-doodah". In terms of Uncle Joe, it was pronounced:

'The F***ing thing's goin' to blow – leg it!'

And lo Brethren…leg it they most certainly did.

Mrs Ida Middlebury was a kind soul, who on occasions would assist her friend Mrs Finucane to clean some of the more problematical areas of the Academy. At present, she was on her hands and slightly arthritic knees, polishing the brass plaque on the floor in front of the restored statue of St Onan. She had felt what she assumed was the beginnings of an earth tremor a few minutes ago, and now it was thumping and vibrating the floor beneath her like a huge and incredibly angry mole. She was not particularly surprised when the vibrations tipped over her new tin of brass polish. She had been rather more surprised, when the statue above her had burst from its plinth with a roar, and taken off vertically through the roof of the small chapel…

In fact, she had been so surprised, that she would have to throw this pair away…

Outside the Academy gates, there was a large crowd of well-wishers and general sightseers who all wanted to catch a glimpse of the Duke. The car slowed as it approached the huge stone arches, and out on the main road, Police outriders prepared to mount an escort for His Highness.

The Duke glanced out of the car window, waved at a few people in the crowd, and declared 'It looks like rain Jeremy – do you think?'

The statue of St Onan completed its graceful parabola above the chapel, and returned to earth with a muted whistle as it fell. The Security Guards were flung off the sides of the Rolls-Royce, as a life-size statue smashed down onto the bonnet of the car, flattening the front of it entirely, and wedging the tiny Royal Standard up the nose of St Onan.

Apart from the initial screams of the watching crowd, there was little or no sound after the explosive impact…The Duke stepped calmly out of the back of the car, put his hands in his pockets, and surveyed the severely crimped Roller. He waved away the Security Agents that ran to see if he was flat or not.

'Well that's a bit of a bugger…Do you think it will "tap out" at the garage, Jeremy?'

Jeremy sat staring ahead of him, where he was now enjoying unhindered views of the bum of St Onan. He seemed to be in some sort of trance. He was also sitting in some sort of puddle. (Unexpected flying Saints can apparently have that effect on you…)

Poor Jeremy was unloaded from the wrecked Rolls-Royce, and was placed in the car behind – still folded up in his driving position. Plastic sheeting had already been placed on the seat, as there was no point having to have two sets of expensive leather car seats professionally cleaned if it could be avoided.

Mark Davis had dashed over to the gates. He was very disappointed when he arrived there. What he found was a battered Rolls...and not the buttered rolls which he had been expecting.

From within the stuffy confines of the Headmaster's study, came the sound of a would-be Knight, who was weeping into a musty Legal Encyclopaedia.

Chapter Thirty- Eight:

There are very few certainties in Life. It would be fair to say that there is only a small number of things that you can *absolutely* count on – unless of course, you are lucky enough to be given an abacus for Christmas.

Here is one definite certitude, assurance, dead cert and gold-tipped sure thing…

If Reverend Vernon Farmer was suffering, then you can put your money on the fact that there will be plenty of other people that are going to suffer an equal measure of torment…He had never thought of himself as a particularly vindictive man, but since plenty of other people did, that was proof enough to him that his quest for revenge should begin – right now. In times of mental turmoil, he always found that a quick tiptoe through the accounts of St Onans would always provide him with an idea for exacting punishment upon The Great Unwashed. There was no finer way of taking revenge, than via the complicated and punitive world of Finance. They had all laughed at his humiliation, and he now wished that he could choke the life out of those who were mocking him…What better way to do it, than by a severe tightening of the Purse Strings!

(Master Percy Strings of Form 5b, Eldest Son of a freelance lettuce-grinder, was at this point, blissfully unaware of the Headmaster's intentions…)

Now that the Royal Visit had been and gone, the boys felt more than a little deflated. Merry had bemoaned the fact that everyday life at St Onans would now have to return to normal. Nicky had asked him precisely what Dictionary he had used, when he researched the word "normal", and Calderman had enquired if the poor boy had recently suffered a blow to the head – and if not, then would he like one?

'It's like when Mum and Dad took us on holiday to the seaside' Merry moaned to his friends.

'What – you're freezing cold, bored, and covered in sand?' asked Jackson.

'No you idiot – I mean that I feel just like one of those poor little crabs that we used to see in the rock pools…' answered Merry.

'Explain please?' said Calderman.

'Well…they spend their whole lives having to walk sideways' said Merry in a sad voice.

'And…?'

'And – they've got sod all to look forward to…'

Mark Davis put down the bar of chocolate that he was busy demolishing, and said 'As I see it Chaps: life is what we make it. If we look for boredom and dissatisfaction in life, then we can't really complain if that is the only thing that we find. We should seek opportunity and Happiness – and if we can't see any, then we should make our own! My personal philosophy on life is the "The proof of the Pudding is in the Eating" … so there!'

'You are the proof of having eaten a great deal of puddings…' laughed Calderman.

Davis frowned: 'Look Calders – every time I make any sort of statement, whatever it is that I say, you always seem to come back with a comment that is hilarious and very witty – what's your secret?'

'Straight Men…' said Calderman.

When the group had finished laughing, Nicky said 'Well I can tell you one thing that I am not looking forward to, and that is the "Mock Exams" at the end of Term. When we've done those – that means that the next exams that we take will be our "Finals". Just the thought of an examination of any sort terrifies me!'

'Unless of course, it's Matron doing the examination…' said Jackson.

'It's alright for you Brain-boxes who can remember facts and figures that you haven't even learned yet – but I still don't know what I am going to do when I leave the Academy!' Nicky said.

Calderman laughed, and punched his friend lightly on the shoulder… 'Well I wouldn't be too worried if I were you Mate –

everyone knows that you're going to be a great big rich Rock Star…Look, truth is, that we'll all probably be coming to you looking for a job. I've read the reviews in the local papers Shep – you and that band "Funderthuck" are really going places'.

'Sleaford…' said Nicky.

'What?' asked Calderman.

'We've got a gig at the Crown and Strap next Saturday…But that's not "going places" is it, I mean…you never hear of anyone saying "that band is really going place", now do you'

'You have to start small' insisted Calderman.

'But just supposing I stay small – what happens then?' Nicky asked.

'Dunno – ask Merry' said Calderman.

The friends tried not to laugh as Merry launched a one-man attack on Calderman. As he tried to keep Merry from doing him any personal damage, Nicky's friend said: 'All I'm saying is – you should bloody well go for it, if you've got the chance. It won't be any use looking back when you're old and saying, "What If", now will it?'.

He was absolutely correct. Nicky didn't want to get old, have to look back, and say "What If". For one thing – trying to say that when you had lost your dentures would be impossible…

This was all due to the problems that when you really drilled down to it (sorry), were caused by oil. We all know about the problems which Mankind is causing to the Planet by the constantly poking holes into its surface, and the climatic changes created by Humanity's seemingly insatiable dependence upon Fossil Fuels.

The problems for Uncle Joe had begun when the Groundlings had made their chance discovery of a vast reservoir of crude oil under the soil. Overnight (or at least just as soon as he could persuade Jedekiah to sign a contract) Joe had seemingly become an Oil Magnate. The real problem with this, was the fact that Joe was apt to prove beyond any reasonable doubt, that what he really was, could better be described as a Misfortune Magnet. The very recent occasion where his actions had almost put a statue of St Onan into orbit, had led to the implementation of some very strict rules as regards what he should (and most importantly, should *not*), be involved with.

Obadiehard and the Groundling Engineering Team had placed a ban on Uncle tampering, touching, or otherwise twiddling with any part of the complex machinery involved in the oil extraction process. Joe considered this decision to be very harsh – as in his own opinion, he was an Engineering Expert. Other people (usually those on the receiving end of Uncle's "expertise") saw the situation somewhat differently. Yes – he was indeed an Expert... "Ex" meaning "something that has been", and "Spurt" meaning "A drip under pressure" ...

Joe had accepted the new rules with good grace. However, he felt very much that the situation was identical to the one which had occurred on his Wedding Night. About to retire for the night to their wedding bed - his new Bride had placed her hands on her hips, and instructed Joe that "Until you know exactly what each piece of equipment is, and you know just how to operate it correctly to ensure satisfaction – you can keep your hands off it!"

Nicky's problems stemmed from a different type of oil – Teenage Turmoil.

To an outside observer, everything in the boy's life was going extremely well. He was doing well at school, he had a new band, and he had a new Girlfriend (even if her somewhat urgent and thinly-disguised desires were a cause for abject terror). What was the problem? There were kids at the Academy who would willingly queue up in torrential rain for the chance to have what Nicky had got at this point in time. The problem for Nicky, seemed to be one of balance. His school work took up a lot of time – if he wanted to achieve the good results that he needed. The new band took up more time with rehearsals, and then gigs, and then more time when Crusty the Vocalist had to be taken back to the venue to apologise...Victoria was a completely different matter. The problem with the girl was to try and convince her that there was not sufficient time to actually do what she had in mind. It had worked so far, but Nicky knew that it was only a matter of said time, before the lustful girl cornered him. Their relationship so far seemed to be based on her desire to be a Photographer. She was all too willing to turn off the lights – and see what develops…

He was also acutely aware that money was tight at home. Mum didn't mention it, and Auntie was always trying to supplement it, but he knew that unpaid and overdue bills were causing a lot of sleepless nights in the house. Nicky knew that he ought to go out and get a "Saturday Job", or some after-school employment of some kind, which would bring in a little cash and help him to make a contribution to the home finances. If he did that though – then his music career would suffer, his school work might suffer, and he was damned sure that if he didn't pay Victoria enough attention – then she would make him suffer. He had been offered a small job in the village "Save-U-More" supermarket, but had turned it down politely. Nicky knew that Jozza worked there after school during the week, and he just couldn't stand the thought of having to face her. He was happy with the idea of filling shelves, but the constant reminder that someone else had been filling Jozza was too much to deal with…

In the spacious yet Spartan meeting room beneath the Academy, Jedekiah, still bemused by his completely unexpected ennoblement, was talking to some of the Masters from "above ground". When the serendipitous discovery of oil had catapulted the Groundlings into the cash-saturated world of high finance, Jedekiah had insisted that only sufficient funds would be retained by them, that allowed them all to fulfil their daily needs. Profits were to be diverted into a vast range of local projects which would benefit the needy. There was already a hell of a lot of profit, but then as Jedekiah had pointed out – there was a great deal of unfortunate people out in the world who through no fault of their own, needed their assistance.

The oil business taking place beneath ground level, was probably one of the best-kept, yet most widely-known secrets at St

318

Onans. After yet more vicious rumours of cuts to the Staff budgets by Farmer had leaked out, some of the Masters took a vote to approach the kindly Elder in a bid to secure extra funding for their own Departments.

Matron had been the first to seek an audience with Jedekiah, and other Masters had tagged along with her, in order to possibly reap the benefits of her considerable Charm...

'So all that I am asking for Jedekiah – sorry, that should be "Sir" Jedekiah...is a small sum of money which would enable me to expand my tiny business, and reach out to the Public on a wider basis...' said Matron.

'I bet I can guess what it is that you actually want to reach for!...' smirked Darwin.

Matron silenced him with a scowl.

'I am a Woman whose needs are simple...' she declared.

'You are a Woman whose needs are *Sinful*...' corrected Strangler.

Determined to press on in the face of heckling, Matron said 'I merely require a small amount of funding, with which to give my business a little more substance'.

'The substance in question, being leather...' whispered Darwin, a little too loudly.

Matron rounded on the man angrily: 'Now look here Johnathan – I do my very best to provide a service which is of great benefit to all of my Clients. I always try to ensure that not one of the people who visit my treatment rooms, ever leaves without feeling completely satisfied! And I would also point out, that in respect to the fees which I charge – well, I insist on exercising a great degree of restraint...'

'Yup – Manacles, mostly...' giggled Darwin.

Jedekiah held up a Fatherly hand... 'Please Gentlemen...' he said calmly 'Do pray allow me to hear what the Good Lady has to say...'

'Okay – but until she turns up, you might as well listen to Matron' said Darwin.

The Matron sighed. She knew that Jedekiah was just and fair, and more to the point, totally unaware of her "Specialist" services outside Academy hours. She was in point of fact, an astute, and very focussed Businesswoman. She also brought a whole new meaning to the phrase "Naked Ambition". She decided that the only way of securing the funding that she needed was to throw herself into the proverbial Lion's Den…

'I realise that you may consider certain aspects of my behaviour to be undesirable, and that other people at St Onans think that what I do is questionable – but I can assure you Sir, I have absolutely nothing to hide…My Life is an open book!' she stated.

'Madam, from what thy Colleagues have informed me, thy Life is an Open *Blouse*…' answered Jedekiah, straight-faced.

There were muffled guffaws from the other Masters.

Jedekiah smiled at the Matron… 'I am aware that some of thy methods may be considered, somewhat unconventional, but I am sure that thou hast thy heart in the right place. We shall discuss this in private, and I am sure that we can thrash something out…'

'At about twenty-five quid for the full hour…' whispered Darwin.

Dr Matthews had sat at the back quietly, and sipped his triple gin-and-tonic with the experienced (if a little bleary) eye of one who had already secured funding for an enterprise of his own design. He had sneaked in early, and had a conversation with "Sir Jed" which had centred around the need to expand the underground bar known as "The Vault" to include its own bespoke distillery. Somehow, Matthews had managed to persuade Jedekiah (a strict tee-totaller) that the profit from such an enterprise could be employed to help those people in Society who were afflicted by the curse of Drink Problems. Matthews had always admitted that he himself had a problem with drink…

Two hands, but only one mouth…

Chapter Thirty- Nine:

The recently-spurned Headmaster, The Reverend Vernon Farmer, with his robes askew, and spectacles oddly-angled upon his ashen face, had woken up. In fact, he had not been to bed, and had spent the entire night poring over various documents which now littered his desk top, and most of the floor of his study. He shook his head in order to dispel the muzzy feeling that had overtaken his brain. Removing a novelty quill pen from his ear, he attempted to focus on his task again. Right…There were *two* occasions during the year that Honours were handed out. Of course! There were the awards pertaining to the Birthday of Her Majesty, and then Ta-Daa! there was the New Year's Honours List. He may have been overlooked for the former, as he was after all, a more "recent addition" to the Academy – but there was no way that he intended to be excluded from the latter.

He had become friends with "The Right People", he had made sure that the Academy had featured prominently in the Press and Media, and he had greased all of the appropriate palms that he could think of. There was no need to panic- his Freemason friends would see him alright; he was sure of it. How could they possibly ignore him – he had made certain that his cap and apron were the cleanest and whitest in the whole Lodge, and he even made sure that he put the seat down when he had finished…

As far as he saw things, the way to recognition and glory lay in making St Onans the place of education with the best reputation in the land. Bugger Harrow or Eton! Those Schools were the "Household Names" – just how did they maintain their reputations? St Onans was just as worthy…and yet was viewed by the world at large as Harrow*ing* and Moth-Eaten. His eye fell sleepily upon the open pages of a magazine that no doubt Miss Piggott had left in his study. Yes!…That was it! All of the Best Colleges appeared on the television, on that programme *University Challenge*. There was a new quiz programme for Schools called *Brainbox Battle* ...He would see to it that the application forms went out today.

In the meantime, there were Academy fees to be looked at. The richer Parents would be only too happy to pay more for their offspring's education, providing it was pointed out to them that in future, being educated at St Onans would be Exclusive (although he would be billing them separately for the capital "E"). It was time to close the ancient oak doors to those Students who were only here because they got financial assistance to do so. If the boys of the future turned out to be thicker than a treacle and concrete sandwich – then so be it: at least their Parents would be able to afford pinstripe trousers and wing-collars.

He crossed the room to the tall cupboard in which he kept his spare gowns and regrettably unused canes. He took down the Lordly robes which he had hoped to be wearing sooner, rather than later. As he once again put on the hideously-expensive robes, lovingly caressed the deep maroon velvet and fur trimmings. They suddenly felt odd and uncomfortable about his narrow shoulders – but his resolve was set.

No-one witnessed Vernon, however determined, squirming in his ermine...

Nicky felt that he had to have a long chat with Mum and Auntie, about him making some sort of contribution toward the running of the house. He had felt for a long time that it was unfair to keep expecting his Mother and her Sister to keep paying for his stage clothing and new drum sticks. He managed to talk Uncle Joe into letting him do some paperwork, and a little light Safety Inspection work, for the oil producing concern beneath St Onans. When he had explained to "Sir Jed" about his need for time off to study, and to rehearse with the band, the Elder had been very accommodating. So now he had a part-time job which was well paid, and where conditions were clean, warm and safe. It was also a very good place to hide himself away from the extremely persistent attentions of Victoria – especially for some reason, during the period of full moon.

Uncle Joe often hung around in the tunnels too. This may have been due to his pride in the oil operation. It might also have had something to do with his need to hide at the moment. A small "side-line" that Joe had branched out into, had been to produce and distribute his latest brand of footwear – aimed primarily at the Sicilian market. It was rumoured that Certain Gentlemen from Certain Well-known Italian Families were rather anxious to make his acquaintance. His "Cosy-Nostra" brand of Carpet Slippers had not gone down too well...

Mum was pleased that her Son was able to bring in a bit of extra cash, but perhaps even prouder that he had been mature enough to have made the decision himself. She herself was rather worried that the boy was getting to the point where he would have to make big decisions about his future. They had spoken quite often about Nicky's desire to go to College to study Art. Certainly, his drawing and painting skills were more than good enough to get him there, but what of this "Band" thing? Mum admired her Son's drumming abilities, but she had the usual Motherly concern that her offspring was focussing so much of his time and effort into a project which might not lead anywhere. "Howling Legs" had expressed a different opinion – saying 'F*** it! Let the Lad have a go: he can always go back to College later if it doesn't work out...as one of those "Manure Students", as they call them'.

'Do you mean "Mature" Students?' said Mum.

'Not necessarily...' said Auntie 'As I understand it, that is the term for people who end up going back to College – because they were shite...'

This deep discussion on the merits of the English Further Education system was interrupted by the ringing of the telephone. Auntie answered the call. There was quite a few "I sees", and an "Oh – really". When Auntie replaced the receiver, Mum enquired as to who had called.

'It's Her Ladyship again – Sheila' said Auntie. Mum raised her eyes skywards.

'That was the local Ex-Racing Greyhound Adoption Society, wanting to know if we would be willing to give a character reference for Cousin Sheila. They said that she had been down to their kennels, and enquired about adopting an animal that they have retired from racing at the Dog Track'.

'Well I think that's a very nice, Christian, and caring thing to do!' said Mum.

'Oh I agree – it would be, if it were anyone other than Cousin Sheila...'

'Why do you say that?' asked Mum.

'Because Sheila is a bloody Weirdo...' answered Auntie.

'Oh no - adopting a retired Greyhound is nice...' insisted Mum 'We'll have to help her buy a new dog basket, and a smart collar and lead for it – and we could even get her one of those sporty little coats that you often see them wearing when they're out for a walk...'

'Can't see the point of that...' said Auntie.

'Why?' asked Mum.

'Sheila has adopted the mechanical Hare...'

Cousin Sheila called back in person later that night. She suggested that she pick up Mum and Auntie, and treat them to a day out at the local Wax Museum, where they could visit the newly-installed "Chamber of Horrors". Auntie had told Cousin Sheila that it would be a bad idea to go there - as she had heard that they were stock-taking...

With pre-exam nerves getting the better of him, Nicky thought that it was a good time to seek advice about his future, from one reliable and knowledgeable source that he knew that he could rely upon. He wrote a polite enquiry note on a sheet of Mum's best writing paper, and approached the Desk. As he did so, he distinctly heard the low and menacing growl which came from his ex-Satchel Briefcase, which was a constant hazard to the fingers of the unwary. He placed the folded letter into the drawer, closed it respectfully, and whilst the mysterious forces within went about the business of formulating a response, went and got himself a drink.

His day-dreaming in the kitchen (under the ever-watchful eye of Dave the Chicken, who was also engaged in the task of helping Auntie to select her Lottery numbers for this week) was interspersed with bouts of panic. Had he swatted and revised enough to get him through the exams which were looming? Just how good was his memory? And if it was in fact quite good after all – then why couldn't he remember that?

Nicky returned to the living-room, where he sauntered casually up to the Desk and opened the special little drawer. There was a pale blue piece of folded notepaper inside. He reached into the drawer and withdrew the note. Well...not really very helpful at all Mr Desk, I'm sorry to have to say, he thought. The reply said:

'Be Always prepared for The Unexpected Surprise...'

He picked up a pen, and scribbled 'Such as What?' on the back of the note, and opened the drawer to put the note back in. When he pulled the drawer open, he shouted out in shock, as a rather angry-looking Weasel leapt up out of the drawer, over his shoulder, and made its escape through the back kitchen door. As he looked cautiously into the drawer from where the creature had emerged, he saw another small slip of paper inside.

This one read *'Told You ...'*

He decided that he would be well advised to heed the wise words of the Desk, and get in some much-needed study before it was time to go to bed. Soon after he had made that decision, the telephone rang twice. No-one found out who had called. No-one answered it, because there was nobody in the house who spoke Bell...

Bells of a different kind (please note the seamless link there...thank you) were ringing for Detective Mike Posta, in the

Police Headquarters. These however, were Alarm Bells, not the kind that warned of a fire, flood, or other imminent disaster, but the spine-chilling clangings of a sudden moment of realisation...

Since the "Abduction" of his beloved motor vehicle, a Master from St Onans Academy had made a bloody nuisance of himself by turning up at the Police HQ, and demanding to see the Officer who was in charge of the theft case. Dr Julius had begun to attend the Station on a daily basis, and demanding to know why the Police had not found his vehicle, why CID and Uniformed squads had found not a single clue, and why Interpol and the SAS had not been immediately brought in to assist. As the soluble aspirins fizzed around in his glass, Mike Posta knew that he now had two pains to deal with – one in his head, and another more persistent one, in his arse.

Reluctantly, he had the odd man shown through by a Uniformed Desk Sergeant into one of the smaller interview rooms.

Dr Julius sat down, or rather seemed to slither down into position on the plastic chair. Posta noted that the eccentric man seemed to be terrified of sitting opposite the CCTV camera, and instead, folded himself defensively into the other corner of the room. Try as he might, Mike Posta just could not get comfortable in the same room as this man. In his job, he had often faced down armed robbers, violent burglars, and on one occasion a psychotic murderer who was convinced that he was in fact two separate Assassins from the Court of Vlad the Impaler – both called Kevin. But this bloke, well, he gave him the creeps.

He listened again as Julius raved on about how he paid his taxes, and how any half-competent Police Force would have located his car last Tuesday well before three o'clock, and how he would reveal all the details of the Police stupidity to his Brother – who had been at a famous London Hospital for many years...(Yes, thought Posta, probably in a store-room somewhere, in a jar of formaldehyde...) When the point came that Posta could stand no more, and Julius seemed to have run out of threats against the Police, he showed the man the door as kindly as he felt able to, and saw him escorted thankfully away from the premises – for the time being, no doubt. He called the Sergeant over, and said 'Pat – do me a big favour will you? I need a full vehicle re-check on the National PNC Computer, and you might like to run a full detail check on Chummy for me while you're at it…I'll get the teas in'.

The Sergeant grinned, and went off to run the checks. Of the vehicle, there were no "hits" or further details to be found. It was what was uncovered about the man himself that had proved to be the most disturbing…

The end-of-term exams had arrived, passed, and left without leaving any forwarding address. Nicky and the boys had done as well as they were likely to, given that they didn't really place much importance on exams that only really interested the Academy. During the exam period, there had been one strange incident though. Nicky and his friends had heard about it, but had not unfortunately had the honour of being present at the scene of the fracas….

It had happened during a Biology examination for the Sixth Form. The boys were sitting in silent rows in one of the larger Old Block classrooms. Professors Strangler and Darwin had been appointed as Adjudicators, and were instructed to ensure that there was no talking, cribbing, horseplay, or copying answers which might be written on a fake false limb. As the boys scribbled away in frenzy, the Masters were at the front desk, talking very quietly.

'No further sightings of our "spherical friend" then?' asked Darwin.

'Nope – all quiet on the globular front, it would seem…' Strangler answered.

'Don't know why they chose to use this room again' said Darwin, 'I mean, we usually hold the exams in room 19 for the Lower Sixth?'

'Seems like old Matthews is using it as a store room for something or other – so we've been shuffled into here. Still, I don't mind…it's a nice bright room, but I must admit, the sun shining off that bloody mirror ball on the ceiling is beginning to give me a migraine…' said Strangler, shading his eyes.

'Why is there a mirror ball in here anyway?' asked Darwin 'I mean to say, it's a room of learning – not a bloody Disco. Can't we get something and cover it? It might be putting the boys off, and we don't want any excuses for having to abandon the exam'

Strangler walked quietly down the aisle between the desks. He stood and stared up at the ball covered in mirror facets which hung from the ceiling. He walked to the back of the room as silently as he could, and picked up a spare chair. Bringing the chair back into the centre of the room, he carefully stepped up onto the seat. He regarded the ball closely – did it just move? He could swear that there was a movement on the surface of the object, almost as if he were watching it breathe. He stretched up a hand to touch its gleaming surface.

And that is when the devastation occurred…

Chapter Forty:

When the exams had been marked, and before the Masters had started to get bored with reading the same answers time after time, and had begun playing Marshmallow ping-pong with a confiscated bag of goodies – it had been noticed that the boy Jez Christo had come up with an absolute scorcher...

The Mathematics question had been a complex one which involved some rather intricate and convoluted calculations on Probability. The question had centred on the mathematical chance of random events. Christo had pondered over how best to answer this...For instance, what was the probability of *that* particular car driving past *that* particular tree, on *that* particular day when the bad storm had caused the tree to fall on it.? And which event had been the "random act"? Was it the tree falling? Or maybe the act of driving the car past it at that particular moment? If the car had been delayed, would the tree have waited? Perhaps it would have sent a coded tree-signal up the line to its older and less-sturdy friend, to ensure that a new Nissan got the roof-rack full of Elm that it was due...

The answer, however constructed, was anything but finite.

Christo got around the problem in superb style. He postulated that since the exam was subject to so many variables (i.e. time, room number, seating arrangement, climate conditions, moisture content of paper etc.), it was impossible for him to know if he would be likely to pass the exam on this particular day. Another Student sitting in the same seat, but taking an exam in a different subject, on a different day, might therefore be more likely to pass that exam than He. Without being able to predict or study the actual percentages of exams passed over all subjects for that room, and that seat, then only the time and date could be seen as fixed. It may well be, he argued, that he was not intended to pass that exam on that day. The variable factors may have forced him to fail. Let us just suppose that an identical Student who has undertaken an identical amount of study sits the exam. The odds should be precisely the same, if we factor in all of the aforementioned "variables". Thus - if Christo were to take the exam and pass it – then the two factors of pass and fail would cancel each other out. The resulting probability would therefore be exactly the same as if he had not taken the exam at all.

That is why he left his paper blank...

Miles Bannister had no choice but to award him full marks.

The last day of the Term was now waving at the boys from over the top of that bit of crumbled brickwork which the Builders swore had been repaired ages ago. There was some animated discussion amongst the boys as to who would be doing what in the break, and who would like to be doing what to whom – given half a chance, and perhaps a decent run-up.

The ever-cheerful and engaging Kendy had some very definite plans. Part of the boy's instantly likeable Alien make-up comprised an innate ability to commune with all forms of Nature. He was able to enjoy the close company of a variety of Wildlife, who seemed to regard Kendy as both a friend, and usually, as a perch. His adoptive Guardians thought that his abilities were remarkable. They were slightly less impressed when they returned from various shopping trips to find the boy sitting on the living-room sofa, surrounded and covered by Starlings, Sparrows, Robins, Field Mice, and a cute but regrettably rather incontinent Owl. If St Francis of Assisi had ever worn jeans and trainers, then here was the perfect copy.

There were a large group of Badgers at the bottom of the overgrown garden, all rather sett in their ways. Kendy had of course befriended them. And there was your problem...the Badgers were not at the bottom of the garden, they could be found on a regular basis, sprawled out on the living-room carpet. The one that had taken up residence in the downstairs loo had to be chased out with a mop. Kendy's main pastime during the Term Break, would be to try and persuade the Wildlife to go back out into the Wild...

Jim Jackson was being taken to New York by his Parents. His Elder Brother lived and worked there. Perhaps he would get Jackson a part-time job as another sky-scraper whilst he was there.

Merry had gleefully accepted an offer from Trevill to go down to his Parents' home in deepest Dorset. It wouldn't surprise Nicky or any of his friends, to hear that a strange and hairy little Piskie had been sighted in the area…

Calderman was always something of an enigma. He had the ability to surprise by making unexpected revelations. He had told the Gang that he was going to spend the holiday on his Father's yacht. (Nicky knew that the boat could not have been a very large one – because Calderman had stated that his Dad kept it moored in a basin).

Mark Davis had given very little away…Davis was well-known for "having his fingers in many different pies" – or at least, having his fingers wrapped *around* many different pies.

And what of David DeVere? The serial Escapologist had said nothing of his plans. He had received a severe lecture (and punishment) when he had been hauled back to the Academy after his latest "vacation". The more Eagle-eyed amongst you might have noticed that when the Duke had left St Onans after his visit, one of the Royal Security Team in the black suits and dark glasses seemed to be significantly shorter than the others…

Nicky himself decided to stop worrying about where his young life was headed, and just get on with living it. As he took stock of his achievements, he actually realised that he had done quite well. He had lost, and then won, a Girlfriend: he had been asked to join a great Rock band (and had survived a gig at the local Youth Club – a feat in itself): he was making a contribution to the House like a real Man: he had learned to Waltz and Tango (albeit both at the same time…): he had not done too badly in his exams (he hoped), and had actually shaken hands with Royalty! He had received countless words of Wisdom from the Desk (and even acted on some of them), and it had been a long time since he had been savaged by the Briefcase/Satchel.

Great! He could finally calm down a little…The lovely and lofty Victoria was away with her own Family, and doing "Horsey Things" somewhere out in the Countryside. He could stop having to constantly look over his shoulder, in case of lusty attacks. His only worry was that the girl might appear from the fields on horseback like a Texas Ranger, in which case he might well end up being lassoed, hog-tied, and dragged off behind her mount – to be dealt with later. In all honesty – he doubted if he would be that lucky…

Uncle joe had managed to get through the Spring Term without getting killed – or getting anyone else killed, for that matter. Mum and Auntie were…well, they were just Mum and Auntie really, and that was all that Nicky could, or would, ever want from them.

He had even managed to avoid Cousin Sheila. Nicky thought that it was a complete injustice that so far, the Authorities had too. Still…you couldn't keep a Good Woman down. Perhaps in future, you ought to try Mace, or a Taser, or a Police Dog, or a Police Dog with a Taser and Mace – (just to make sure…)

Oh – and a sharp stick.

Chapter Forty- One:

There was loud laughter coming from the Games Field. Just outside the large hut that served as the lair of Albert Brooks the Groundskeeper, and the secret HQ of the organisation known only as the ODD, there was a wide puddle. It was over this puddle that Brooks had just placed his waterproof Combat jacket, so that the newly "Damed" Mrs Finucane could step across it.

'There ye go Milady! – all safe and sound!' declared Brooks.

Mrs Finucane blushed slightly, and said ' 'Tis a Silly Fecker Ye are...let's get inside and crack open the Good Stuff!'

Omitting to give the "secret knock", and choosing instead to open the inner shed door with the Secret Screwdriver, Albert ushered his Lady visitor inside. Once they had settled into the ragged chairs and Brooks had poured them both a very generous measure of Ireland's Finest, he slunk off tittering, to the cupboard at the end or the wooden room. He returned with a plate which was full of little round chocolates – all stacked neatly into the shape of a pyramid.

'Ooh – with these chocolates, Mr Brooks, Ye are spoiling Us!' said Mrs F.

'So 'ow do it feel then – bein' a Lady of Status?' asked Brooks.

''Tis a bit weird...Oi don't know what to make of it yet' she answered.

'Well I tell Ye what Ye does – tha' makes the bloody most of it. Ye deserve all of the Honours and more – and I raise a toast to Ye...for daring to strike a blow for the Working Classes against the Tyranny and Oppression of...well... Them bunch of Bastards!'

'I'll tell Ye one thing' said Dame Finucane.

'What's that?' laughed Albert.

'Now Oi 'am a Real Lady – Moi lazy Sod of an 'Usband can be makin' his own bloody sandwiches for work!' she laughed. 'And another thing...'

'Yes... Milady?' asked Albert.

'Milady would like ye to fill her Feckin' glass up!'

Plans had been laid at the end-of-term sherry gathering in the Staff lounge. One of the plans was that they should cease serving the cheap sherry, which according to the educated palate of Dr Matthews was 'Quite honestly – piss'. The other plan was to hold an end-of-term party. Hyde-Jones had attempted to make a break for the door at the mention of this, but was thwarted by the Party Planner Mr Newhouse, who turned with a grin and shook the key to the door at him. Roy Hyde-Jones and the other Masters knew what was coming. The legendary parties of Mr "Loopy" Newhouse didn't have "Guests" – they had "Survivors".

Detective Mike Posta sat at his desk and drummed his fingers on the table in front of him. Opposite him was sitting his Duty Sergeant. Both men had very disturbed looks on their faces. 'And you're sure about this, are you Pat?' asked Posta, almost hoping that the response would be negative…

'Unfortunately Yes Sir, I am sure' he replied.

'What – nothing at all?' said Posta.

'Well the Interpol Boys are still going over the files, but some of them go way back – as you can imagine. It could take a while, as the paperwork for 1944 is a bit sketchy, to say the least. We've e-mailed the photo over to the Russians, and they've confirmed that it's him. We're still trying to find out which Country he was last registered in as a Citizen, but the bastard seems to have had more faces than a box full of pennies!' said the Sergeant.

Mike Posta spent a few moments in contemplation. Finally, he seemed to reach a decision:

'Right Pat…' he said 'Before we have to throw this one upstairs for the Big Boys to play with, I'd better pay another visit to the Funny Farm, and try and see if I can prise any more information out of Chummy'.

From the Police Headquarters, it was only a short drive to the imposing front arches of the Academy. Posta parked the car in the quad. Outside the Old Block was standing a huge black horse, decked out in Medieval finery, and casually pulling hay from a feedbag which was tied to the drain pipe. Okay – just a normal day at St Onans then.

He walked purposefully up the narrow winding path toward the Headmaster's study. How was he going to do this? What he wanted, was for that Snob Farmer to spill the beans on his "Assistant". Beans or no beans – he was sure that whenever he was able to get to the truth, it would smell just as bad.

Although on Duty, he rang the bell out of professional courtesy. He heard the bell jangle inside the corridor, and a moment later, Miss Emilia Piggott (don't say it Woman – or I swear, I'll give you such a slap…) let him in. He knocked at the Headmaster's door. There was no answer after repeated knockings, and so Posta let himself in, closing the door soundlessly behind him. He walked over to the Head's desk, and noted the papers which covered the highly-polished green leather top. My word – someone really had been a busy boy. Posta scanned the various papers with his trained eye, soon deciding that using them both might be a better option.

There were letters, and there were copious lists, as well as pieces of paper that had been used to scribble down random ideas. Posta chuckled to himself…he was rather glad that he didn't have a Son that was expected to attend St Onans. The rise in Academy fees that Farmer was planning was exorbitant, to say the least. There were also papers headed "Financial Target Ceiling", and a rather more disturbing one titled "Means Testing – Cancellation of Bursary and Scholarship Funding". My God – was he proposing to exclude boys whose Parents couldn't pay the appropriate full fees? If the Press ever got wind of this, then there would be riots, and he didn't fancy having to do all of the overtime required for Crowd Control. As he read on, Posta became aware of voices in the corridor, two voices in fact. It sounded like Farmer was coming back to his study with someone in tow. He suddenly felt awkward to be in the Headmaster's rooms without the usual Chaperone. He could well imagine that Farmer might be just the type to put in an official complaint to his Superiors, that a detective had gone into his study and read his personal and private documents without having a Warrant. Nothing to worry about there, because all that he had done was to – Ahh.

As Farmer and his Assistant entered the room, Posta had already taken the appropriate action. He had swiftly opened the window, and dived through Commando-style onto the lawn.

The Head blustered into the room, almost shouting the very one-sided conversation which he was having with Dr Julius. Dr Julius had made the unwise step of disagreeing with Farmer over certain matters, and with the kettle of his anger still boiling over, the Head was in no mood to listen to a measured debate of any description.

'I am not asking for your opinion Julius – I am giving you a very clear statement on how matters are going to be…' he growled. 'I will raise the level of the fees. The better-off Parents will stump up the cash in order to maintain the high standard of education for their Brats – and those that cannot…well, I am afraid that I shall be forced to let them fall at the wayside'.

Dr Julius nodded in assent.

'It is not as if I am planning to be the sole beneficiary of these changes – absolutely not! The whole Academy will benefit by keeping out those boys likely to lower the standards to which we should aspire. We want to turn out the next generation of Professors and Politicians – not Lackeys and Layabouts…By the exclusion of the "Riff-Raff" we shall see the profile of St Onans rise ever higher, and you Julius, shall rise with it if you keep your mouth shut, and follow orders…'

'I have alwaysss followed orderssss…' answered Julius, quietly.

'And another order for you then – stop going on about your damned car! I am sick of hearing you bleating about it. It is gone, stolen, nicked, purloined, taken, half-inched. That's all you need to know. When my plans come to fruition – why, you shall have a new car, one for every day of the week if you wish! In the meantime, it will benefit you to remember why you are here, and that the constant involvement of the Police may just lead to your undoing. And in the name of all that is Holy – do NOT leave your old copies of "*Die Spiegel*" in my waste-paper basket for all to see. Now go and get me a cup of tea and some aspirin, I feel a headache coming on…'

The Head settled himself down to address the paperwork on his desk. He was pleased with what he had managed to plan so far. He would let these next two terms play out, and then he would turn the screws on the new intake of boys.

He received the cup of tea and tablets from Julius. He swallowed the painkillers, then waved the grovelling Assistant out of his study with a motion of his free hand. Farmer turned back to the papers. The wind seemed to be getting up outside, and he could see that a breeze was moving the curtains slightly. He would have to get that lazy Yorkshire Oaf Brooks to seal up those windows properly. The Head pinched the bridge of his nose – still so much to do before he could even consider calling it a night. Those memos to the Parents informing them of the new uniform and increases in the fees should really go out first thing tomorrow. Also, he needed to speak to the Board of Trustees. Now then: should he get the Dictaphone? No, he would do it himself.

The Academy was silent, as silent as an Amusement Arcade during an unexpected power cut. Farmer had heard Miss Piggott leave hours ago, but then considering her dainty walk and lightness of foot, so had people who lived in Kidderminster. The only sounds in the study were the rustlings of papers, and the echoing tick-tock of the wall clock, as its oscillating pendulum scythed away the remaining seconds of the day. There was the slightest movement of the curtains by the window. Farmer glanced up from his work: had that idiot Julius left a window open again? He stood up awkwardly, having sat in one position for far too long, and limped over to the window. No – the window was shut firmly. He yanked the curtain shut again, and turned…

'Good Evening, Vernon...' said the figure of Gerald Goodwill, who was sitting in his chair.

'But you – you're – shouldn't you be...' stammered Farmer.

'Why Yes...I should be, but as you may plainly observe – I am not...' drawled Goodwill.

'I'm calling the Police!' shouted Farmer, his voice sharp with panic.

Goodwill smiled, opened the desk drawer, and withdrew an old but still very lethal Service Revolver. 'We shall discuss the matter of the Boys in Blue shortly' he said, levelly, 'But I must firstly inform you that any call that you attempt to make, will be an extremely short one – after which you will find that it is *you*, and not the number, which is ex-directory...'

Farmer stared in disbelief at the Former Head. Goodwill stared back, and said 'Oh do please ask...you know you want to'.

'What do you want?' asked Farmer.

'There – Good Boy!' said Goodwill. 'Now do take a seat, and Kindly Uncle Gerald will explain exactly what the nice Mr Farmer is going to do. Please refrain from attempting anything "Heroic", if you wouldn't mind – I have spent quite a period of time incarcerated with naughty boys who have taught me some deadly, swift, and above all *silent* techniques for ensuring that inconveniences are dealt with. Failing that, I may well blow your wedding tackle out through the back of your head – I do so love to have choices in life...'

Farmer sat down. He had no choice. There was no-one to call, no "panic button" that he could press, and no Secretary to hold in front of him to absorb a bullet. Goodwill was rifling through the desk drawer, whilst keeping the pistol steadily pointing at the Head...of the Head. Eventually, he found what he was searching for:

'Ah... "Snout", thank goodness for Confiscation' he said. Goodwill lit a cigarette, and brought his legs up onto the desk. As he blew clouds of satisfying smoke into the air, he spoke again...

'Let me tell you a little heart-warming Bedtime Story. Once upon a time, there was a dreadful little boy, who grew up to be a

338

dreadful little man. This absolute Bad Egg was in the German Army during the Second World War, and soon decided that what he really wanted to be, was an even worse little man – and so he joined what we know as the SS Guard. The name of the little boy was Hans Schlitt. Now this boy Hans hated having to fight the horrid British Army, because he was so frightened. In fact, Schlitt would often Schlitt himself with fear!...

What little Hans liked best was being a coward and a bully, and he got to be very good at it. One day though, a man had told him that the horrid British had won the War – and poor little Hans wouldn't be allowed to bully people any more. They were going to take him to a great big Court Room, where he would have to admit that he had been so very naughty. Hans didn't want to go there, and so he ran away with some friends to a lovely land called Uruguay.

He changed his name to Henry Bollich, and sold anti-Christian beverages from the paniers of a tricycle. He then moved to Bolivia, where he masqueraded as an Entertainer – in a musical troupe known as "Edgar LaPinch and the Bendi Boys". When he had to move again, well blow me down! – he changed his name again, to "Kurt Fondle", Stage Magician. He also spent some time in Patagonia – under the alias of "Rapier Jane McDuff".

My goodness! What a lot of names little Hans has had...Let me tell you some...

Simon 'Squeaker' Stephens, Brenda Dribble, Denis McQuandry, Romeo M'Nestroni, Kitty Danzig, 'Pinky' Forskyne, Ed Ceterra...

When he was nearly hunted down, he hid in a University in Calcutta, sleeping every night in a library, under a bust of Julius Caesar. Can you guess what he decided to call himself next, Children? See – it is not only your Pupils who do their Homework...

I don't know how you came across this slimy little piece of shite, Farmer: but unless you do *precisely* what I tell you, then I shall have no hesitation in informing the Authorities that you have been harbouring a wanted Nazi War Criminal for many years....'

'But…but…they'll put me in jail!' squeaked Farmer.

'Oh dear – do you think they might? How tiresome. But wait a moment Vernon! Oddly enough, I know where there is a nice, clean, empty cell, just waiting for a Tenant' said Goodwill, 'It appears that the former Resident has unexpectedly gone away…' he laughed.

Goodwill dropped the end of his cigarette onto the carpet, and ground it out with his foot.

'Do carry on with your plans by all means. I shall be watching. You will not know where I am, but trust me, I shall observe you closely. I shall require you to ensure that all profits are paid to myself. If there is anything left over after I have taken my "cut", and if I am feeling particularly generous – why then! I may even allow you a little pocket money of your own..'

There was a knock at the door. Just for a split-second, Farmer thought that Goodwill had pulled the trigger. It was Albert Brooks, smelling strongly of Irish Whisky…

'They've all buggered off now – am I alright to lock up?' he asked.

'Yes Albert' said Farmer… 'I think…I think I may be finished here'.

When the Headmaster turned around, the chair was empty…

Chapter Forty- Two:

So that was it then…the end of another Term at St Onans.

For some it had been a good Term. Other terms had been used by those that thought it not quite as good.

Mr Thwaite sat on his own on a stool in the bar known as "The Vaults". Sir Jedekiah shook him a cocktail, and poured it out into a tall glass frosted with sugar. Thwaite sipped the drink, and as Jedekiah listened sympathetically, told him 'You know, I have always dreamed of becoming a Dame…'

Keith the Raven hunched dejectedly over the end of the gutter, and gazed out over the empty quad. Now that Term was ended, he didn't really know what to do with himself. His fellow Raven Buddies edged along the gutter to join him. One of them extended a silken black wing, which he placed around the shoulder of their Leader.

'What's the matter Boss?' asked Arthur.

'Oh, nothing much, I was just thinking to myself about how much I shall miss those little buggers' said Keith.

'But you always told us that they can't be trusted…' said Arnold with the unruly feathers.

'Yeah I know…but I had so many dreams…I mean, we were going to fly over in formation, an' crap on 'em – like we rehearsed' sniffed Keith, 'What are we supposed to do now?'

Arthur the Raven nudged his Leader and said…

'Cheer up Boss – the kids at Central College don't break up for another week…'

Vernon Farmer sat motionless. He had not moved for well over an hour.

Always be very, very careful if you have decided that what you really want to do is to shake that tree.

You never know exactly what may fall out of it...

****

Coming Soon!...

"Summer Term – The Darling Buds of Mayhem"

Grab that bucket and spade Kids!

It's a glorious Summer at St Onans. Maybe...

Tune in to Academy TV, then meet some extremely un-Roman Romans and Hereward the almost-awake. Try a Time-Travelling holiday through "The Vortex" (luggage extra...)

Nicky suffers more teenage angst – and the Rev suffers a severe attack of Stan...

A fellow student performs miracles, and a riot is in progress at a local hotel.

M19 Agents have a secret weapon – Mrs Stokes, and evil Dr Julius is unmasked.

The Groundlings arise (nearly), as ex-Head Goodwill turns the screw.

With the annual cricket match being invaded by Genghis Khan and his lads, drunken dressage being performed at a local horse show, possibly the world's slowest police chase, a roof-top protest to resolve, and an alien life-form to sober up; it's looking like just another term for the inhabitants of St Onans Academy.

Take another ride on the riotous rollercoaster of weird and wonderful goings-on...

All this – and some serious Rock and Roll!

Don't drop your ice-cream...

Also available by Nicholas Barrett:

Michaelmas Term (or- Why is that boy naked?)
ISBN 9781784651640

Advent Term (or- Snowmen don't wear Thermals)
ISBN 9781546307969

47375464R00199

Printed in Poland
by Amazon Fulfillment
Poland Sp. z o.o., Wrocław